MAIN COURSE ENGLISH

EXCHANGES

Students' Book
Part A

Judy Garton-Sprenger   Philip Prowse

Project Adviser
T. C. Jupp

HEINEMANN EDUCATIONAL BOOKS
LONDON

Contents

Unit	Communicative aims	Key Structures
1 Personal information Lessons 1–5 page 1	Personal details: written and spoken Describing and comparing education Talking about wishes and intentions Talking about personal experience and skills *Writing*: letters of enquiry *Reading*: Personal details – scanning for information *Spoken communication*: an interview	Present simple tense: revision Present perfect tense: recent past, with *just*, indefinite past, unfinished past with *since* and *for* *Want, would like, hope, intend, be going* + *to* + infinitive *Like, enjoy, prefer* + gerund *Can, be able to* Direct and indirect question formation *Because* (reason), *in order to* (purpose), *but* (contrast), *so* (result)
2 Money and possessions Lessons 6–10 page 15	Talking about spending money Comparing costs and making plans Discussing alternatives Comparing the past and present *Writing*: letters of enquiry report writing *Reading*: Questionnaire – for intensive reading *Spoken communication*: instructions	Conditional sentences: cause and effect, Type 1, Type 2 Comparison of adjectives Comparisons with *as much as, the same as* *Too* + adjective, *not* + adjective + *enough* *Used to* for state or habit in the past Time clauses with *until* Pronoun: *it* Indefinite and possessive pronouns
3 Opinions and arguments Lessons 11–15 page 29	Discussing and comparing different customs Explaining what you mean and what you understand Reacting to behaviour, opinions and advice Stating and explaining your opinions *Writing*: letters of enquiry and personal letters *Reading*: Story – for reaction and discussion *Spoken communication*: finding out someone's opinions and trying to remember something	Passive voice: present simple, past simple and present perfect tenses Reported requests and commands (with *ask* and *tell*) Obligation with *ought to, should* Clauses with *but, whereas* (contrast) Constructions for expressing agreement Adjectives formed from participles Sentence connectors: *first of all, secondly*, etc.
4 Work Lessons 16–20 page 43	Discussing a job: advantages and disadvantages Describing the qualifications and qualities needed for a job Describing a day's work Comparing pay Talking about learning and using foreign languages *Writing*: letters of application application form personal narrative *Reading*: Advice for job-seekers – for information and deduction *Spoken communication*: making an appointment and describing a process	Present perfect continuous tense Future: *will* Obligation and necessity with *must, have (got) to, need to* Conditional sentences without *if* Gerund as subject, and after prepositions Defining relative clauses (contact) Adverbials of sequence

| 5 News!
Lessons 21–25
page 57 | Reporting public events
Reporting a sequence of events
Discussing possible explanations
Discussing future possibilities

Writing: narratives
future plans
Reading: Mystery story – for deduction
Spoken communication: explaining what has gone wrong | Reported statements and questions
Future: *will*
Past perfect tense
Past continuous tense
Constructions for expressing probability and certainty
Statements introduced by *it*
Possibility with *may (have)*, *could*
Adverbials and prepositions of place and time |

Test
Songs
Listening passages
List of irregular verbs
Acknowledgements

Key to symbols

 Oral work

 Written work

 Reading

 Listening

 Do-it-yourself English: Individualised activities

 Games, puzzles and crosswords

 Songs

 Important points to note

Unit 1
LESSON 1

Personal details: written and spoken

STEVE

```
Full name:      Stephen Andrew Wilson
Address:        58 Vicarage Avenue, Oxford
Telephone:      -
Age:            21
Marital status: Single
Nationality:    British
Education:      Primary school in Leeds;
                secondary school in Oxford:
                7 'O' Levels, 3 'A' Levels
                (English, Spanish, History);
                University of Sussex: B.A. in
                Social Anthropology.
Occupation:     Teacher.
```

JENNY

```
Full name:      Jennifer Anne Langley
Address:        105 Clarendon Gardens, London W9
Telephone:      229 0192
Age:            23
Marital status: Single
Nationality:    British
Education:      Primary and secondary school in
                Norwich: 6 'O' Levels, 2 'A'
                Levels; Hornsey College of
                Art: B.A. in Art and Design.
Occupation:     Assistant in the design
                department of the National
                Portrait Gallery.
```

What do you do?

I've just left university and I'm teaching at the moment. But I prefer being a student and I want to travel. I don't like being in the same place for too long.

I've been at the National Portrait Gallery since I left college two years ago. I really enjoy working there, but I'd like to specialise. I'm very interested in Aztec art.

Do you know Steve well?

We've known each other for years. We play in a band together. He's great — always cheerful and full of ideas. But he's broken up with his girlfriend, so he's a bit depressed at the moment.

What's Jenny like?

Well, I've known her for about a year now. She's lovely and we get on very well. We like doing the same things most of the time — going to the cinema, going for long walks in the country, and swimming. We even go to evening classes in Spanish together! But she's very independent too, and that's important.

Unit 1

 **Study**

MEXICO

STUDY ABROAD: MEXICO

The National Autonomous University of Mexico offers three scholarships for study or research at the university.
Conditions: Candidates must
1. be British and resident in the U.K.
2. be graduates or have a similar qualification
3. have a knowledge of Spanish
For information and application forms please write to:

 **Questions**

1. Jenny says, 'I really enjoy working there.'
   What does she mean by 'there'?
2. Steve's friend says, '. . . so he's a bit depressed at the moment.'
   Why is Steve a bit depressed?
3. Jenny's boyfriend says, '. . . and that's important.'
   What does 'that' mean?
4. Who can apply for a scholarship to Mexico? Give reasons for your choice.
   (a) Steve   (c) Both Steve and Jenny
   (b) Jenny   (d) Neither Steve nor Jenny

SCHOLARSHIP APPLICATION FORM (to be typed or written in black ink)

1. Country or Institution offering scholarship: *National Autonomous University of Mexico*
2. Family name (block capitals): *WILSON.*
3. Other names:
4. a) Date of birth: *2nd June*
   b) Male/Female:
   c) Married/Single:
   d) Nationality:
5. Address (block capitals):   Tel no.
6. Occupation:
7. Subject of study or research: *Mexican society*
8. Knowledge of foreign languages (fluent/good/slight): *Spanish (fluent), Portuguese and French (good)*
9. Schools and university attended and examinations passed:
10. Interests: *Folk music, travel, football.*
    Signature: Date:

 Complete

Both Steve and Jenny have decided to apply for a scholarship to Mexico. Complete Steve's application form. Then copy out the application form and complete it for Jenny. Her birthday is on September 12th.

  Ask each other and complete

Ask another student the following questions and complete the form.
What's your name?
What languages do you speak?
What do you like doing in your spare time?
Where do you come from?
What do you do?

Example:
Spoken: What do you like doing in your spare time?
I enjoy playing and listening to folk music very much. I also like travelling and playing football.
Written: Interests: Folk music, travel, football.

PERSONAL DETAILS
Full name:
Nationality:
Occupation:
Interests:
Knowledge of foreign languages:

English for the classroom
Excuse me, how do you say *ingenjör* in English?   Engineer
طبيب   Doctor
funcionário   Official

Language Study Exercises 1.1 1.2 1.3 1.4 1.5 1.9 1.10

LESSON 2

Describing and comparing education

EDUCATION IN ENGLAND AND WALES

Different areas of Britain have different systems of primary and secondary education. This simplified diagram shows the most usual system.

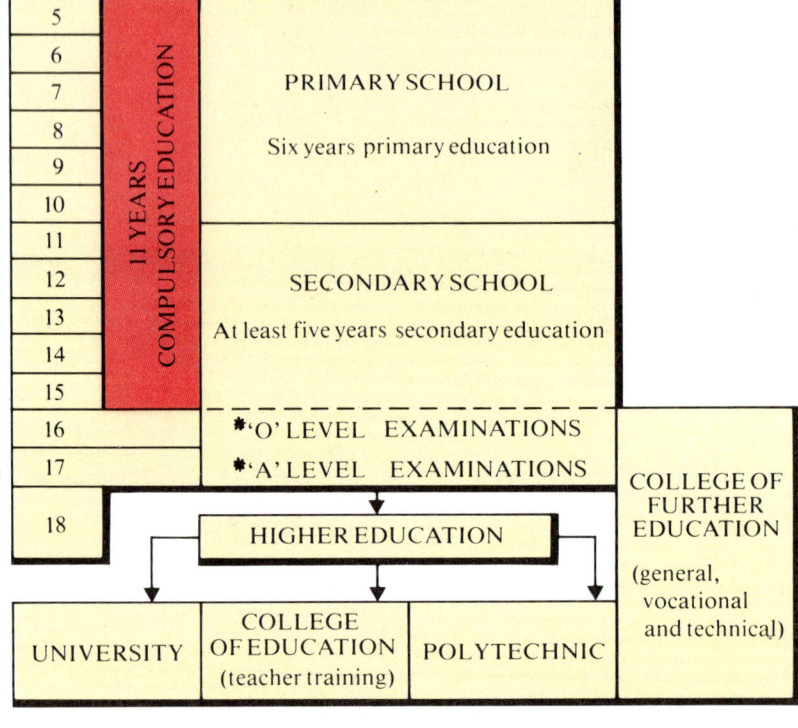

 * 'O' = Ordinary
* 'A' = Advanced

EDUCATION IN MEXICO

Jenny bought a book about Mexico. Here is an extract from the book.

> Compulsory education begins at the age of six. But many parents send their children to nursery schools for two or three years before they start primary school. Children usually leave primary school at twelve after six years compulsory education. At the age of twelve, secondary education starts. Pupils go either to general secondary schools or to vocational schools. The vocational schools prepare pupils for work. After three years secondary education, pupils receive the Secondary School Certificate. Higher secondary education also lasts for three years. At this level there are three kinds of schools: Preparatory, Teacher Training and Technical. The preparatory schools prepare pupils for university. On completing higher secondary education, students receive the *bachillerato* or a professional certificate. Higher education begins at eighteen and students go to university, teacher training college or technical institutions.

Complete

Read the description of education in Mexico and complete the diagram.

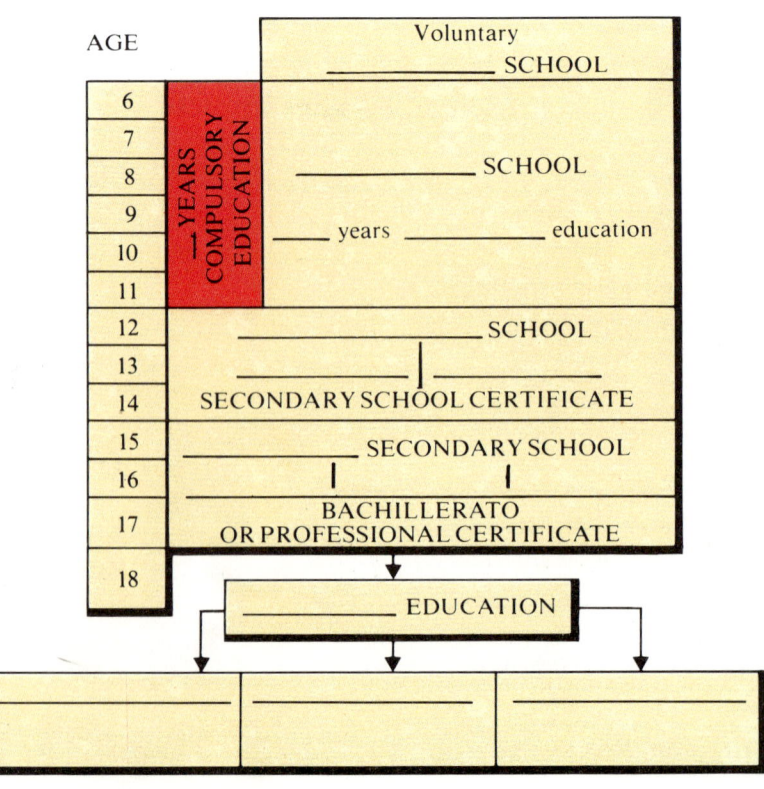

Unit 1

 Draw a diagram

Study the diagrams of the British and Mexican educational systems.
Draw a similar diagram of the educational system in your country.

Ask each other

Ask questions about the British and Mexican educational systems.
How many years of compulsory education are there in .... ?
When do pupils start .... school in .... ?
How long does .... education last in .... ?
When does higher education start in .... ?
At what age do pupils take the .... examination in .... ?

 Write notes

Make notes comparing the educational systems in Britain, Mexico and in your country.

	England and Wales	Mexico	Your country
Nursery education	Not compulsory. 2 or 3 years.		
Primary school	Compulsory. Starts at age 5 and lasts for 6 years.		
Secondary school	Starts at age 11. Compulsory for 5 years.		

Write sentences

Make up sentences comparing the educational systems in Britain and in your own country.
Examples:
Different: Compulsory education in Britain starts at five *but* in Mexico it starts at six.
Same: Primary school lasts for six years in *both* countries.

 Discuss

Here is the timetable of a fifteen-year-old student at secondary school in Britain.

Is it similar to a school timetable in your country?
What differences are there?
Does school start and finish at the same time?
What are/were your favourite, and least favourite, school subjects?

| SCHOOL TIMETABLE |
Times	9.00-9.30	9.30-10.40	10.40-10.45	10.45-11.55	11.55-13.00	13.00-13.10	13.10-14.20	14.20-15.30
MON	REGISTRATION	HISTORY	BREAK	FRENCH	LUNCH	REGISTRATION	SOCIAL STUDIES	MATHS
TUES	REGISTRATION	GEOGRAPHY	BREAK	PHYSICAL EDUCATION	LUNCH	REGISTRATION	BIOLOGY	ENGLISH
WED	REGISTRATION	PHYSICS	BREAK	HISTORY	LUNCH	REGISTRATION	MATHS	ENGLISH
THUR	REGISTRATION	FRENCH	BREAK	GEOGRAPHY	LUNCH	REGISTRATION	PHYSICS	SOCIAL STUDIES
FRI	REGISTRATION	MATHS	BREAK	ENGLISH	LUNCH	REGISTRATION	BIOLOGY	RELIGIOUS EDUCATION

 English for the classroom

Excuse me, what is 'maths' short for?
Mathematics.
How do you spell it?
M-A-T-H-E-M-A-T-I-C-S

Language Study Exercises 1.8   1.15   1.18   1.21   1.22

LESSON 3

Talking about wishes and intentions

Steve and Jenny were both invited to an interview for a scholarship. They met in the waiting room.

STEVE: What do you want to do in Mexico?
JENNY: I'd like to study Aztec art.
STEVE: That sounds interesting. Have you ever been there?
JENNY: Yes, I have. I spent a week in Mexico City a couple of years ago. But if I get a scholarship I intend to see as much of the country as possible. What about you? Why do you want to go to Mexico?
STEVE: Well, I did Anthropology at university. I'm a teacher at the moment, but I'm bored. I'm going to give up teaching – I want a change.
JENNY: Oh, I see. Do you live in London?
STEVE: No, I live in Oxford. How about you?
JENNY: I live in London. I work at the National Portrait Gallery.
STEVE: Really? How long . . .
SECRETARY: Mr Wilson? Would you come in now, please?
JENNY: Good luck!
STEVE: Thanks. I'll need it.

MR HYDE: I see from your application form that you want to study Mexican society. What exactly do you mean?
STEVE: I want to study the growth of the oil industry. And I hope to find out how the oil industry has affected village life in Mexico.
MR HYDE: Oh, I see. And how good is your Spanish?

(*Five minutes later*)

MR HYDE: That's very interesting Mr Wilson. Finally, can you tell us why you want to go to Mexico, rather than to another country?
STEVE: Ah . . . well . . . because Mexico has such a big new oil industry.
MR MENDOZA: New? Mexico has had an oil industry for many, many years . . .
STEVE: I'm sorry. I meant . . .
MR HYDE: I think that's all Mr Wilson. Thank you very much.

Questions

1. Steve says, 'How about you?' What question is he asking Jenny?
2. Steve says, 'Really? How long . . .' What question was he going to ask?
3. Mr Hyde says, 'I think that's all.' What does he mean?
4. Do you think that Steve will get a scholarship?

Unit 1

  Study and complete

Look at the details about Jenny on page 1 and at her conversation with Steve on page 5. Read Steve's interview again. Now complete Jenny's part of the interview.

MR HYDE: Good morning, Miss Langley. My name's Hyde and these are my colleagues, Miss Baker and Mr Mendoza.
JENNY: ....
MR HYDE: Can you tell us exactly why you want a scholarship?
JENNY: ....
MR HYDE: And how good is your Spanish?
JENNY: ....
MR HYDE: I see. Is your boyfriend also applying for a scholarship?
JENNY: ....
MR HYDE: Can you tell us something about your present job?
JENNY: ....

(*Five minutes later*)

MR HYDE: Now are there any questions you want to ask?
JENNY: ....
MR HYDE: The scholarship starts in January. Anything else?
JENNY: ....
MR HYDE: Well, thank you very much Miss Langley. I think that's all.

 Study

Wishes
STEVE: What do *you want to* do in Mexico?
JENNY: *I'd like to* study Aztec art.
STEVE: *I hope to* find out how the oil industry has affected village life.

Intentions
JENNY: *I intend to* see as much of the country as possible.
STEVE: *I'm going to* give up teaching.

 Ask each other: wishes and intentions

Examples:
Do you intend to study English next year?
Are you going to take any exams in English?
Do you hope to travel abroad? Where do you want to go? What would you like to do?

 Survey

Ask five other students why they are studying a foreign language.
Example: Why are you learning Spanish?
Write down their answers.

Because I want to study in Mexico.

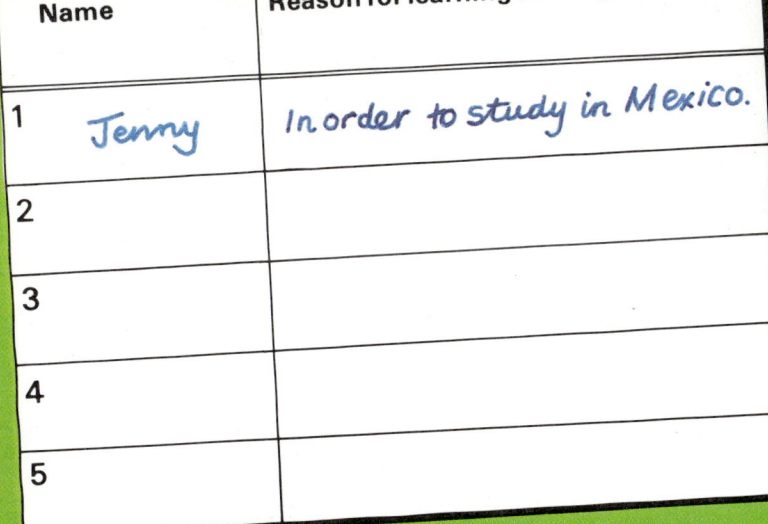

Name	Reason for learning a foreign language
1 Jenny	In order to study in Mexico.
2	
3	
4	
5	

Then write a short summary of the results of the survey.
Example:
Three students are learning English in order to go to university.
Two students are learning English in order to get better jobs.
And two students say they are learning English because they enjoy it.

Language Study Exercises 1.6 1.7 1.13 1.14 1.19 1.20

LESSON 4

Talking about personal experience and skills

Jenny got a scholarship, but Steve did not. Then Steve saw this advertisement in the newspaper.

STEVE: Well, I really want to know what the Oxford Community Project is.
PAM: It's quite simple. We arrange lots of activities for young people in the area. Mostly in the evenings and at weekends – sports, music, drama and so on.
STEVE: That's very interesting.
PAM: We work closely with local schools and youth clubs. If you are interested, why don't you come in for an interview? How about tomorrow at 2.30?

Steve went for an interview the next day.

PAM: Have you ever worked on anything like this before?
STEVE: No, I haven't. But I'd like to work with young people.
PAM: We're looking for people who can teach lots of different activities. Are you good at sport?
STEVE: Fairly good. I play football at weekends and go swimming regularly.
PAM: Are you able to get on with different kinds of people?
STEVE: I think so. My students at the school come from lots of different countries.
PAM: Can you play any musical instruments?
STEVE: Yes, I play the guitar and the piano – mostly folk music and rock.
PAM: Oh, good. Well, thanks very much. Now are there any questions you would like to ask?
STEVE: Yes, there's one thing. How much . . . ?

 Ask and answer

Make up questions about the conversation between Steve and Pam. Ask another student your questions.

Examples:

WHO (questions about *people*)
Who interviews Steve?
WHEN (questions about *time*)
When does the Project arrange activities?
WHY (questions about *reasons*)
Why is Steve calling about the advertisement?
WHERE (questions about *place*)
Where do Steve's students come from?
WHICH (questions about *alternatives*)
Which instruments can Steve play?

  Questions

1. Steve says, 'That's very interesting.' 'That' refers to
   (a) young people in the area
   (b) evenings and weekends
   (c) the Oxford Community Project
   (d) sports, music and drama
2. Pam says, 'Have you ever worked on anything like this before?' What does she mean by 'anything like this'?
3. Steve says, 'I think so.' What does he think?
4. Steve says, 'Yes, there's one thing. How much . . . ?' Can you finish Steve's question?

Unit 1

 Listening

Steve also telephoned about these two advertisements.
1. Listen to the telephone conversations and fill in these forms.
2. Can Steve apply for these jobs? If he can't apply answer:
   No, because he hasn't got/can't . . .

JOB: SALARY; QUALIFICATIONS OR SKILLS REQUIRED; 1. 2. 3.	JOB: SALARY; QUALIFICATIONS OR SKILLS REQUIRED; 1. 2. 3.

 Mime

Play this game in pairs or in teams. Think of a skill or activity, then mime it. The other students try to guess what the mime is.

 Study

Role Play

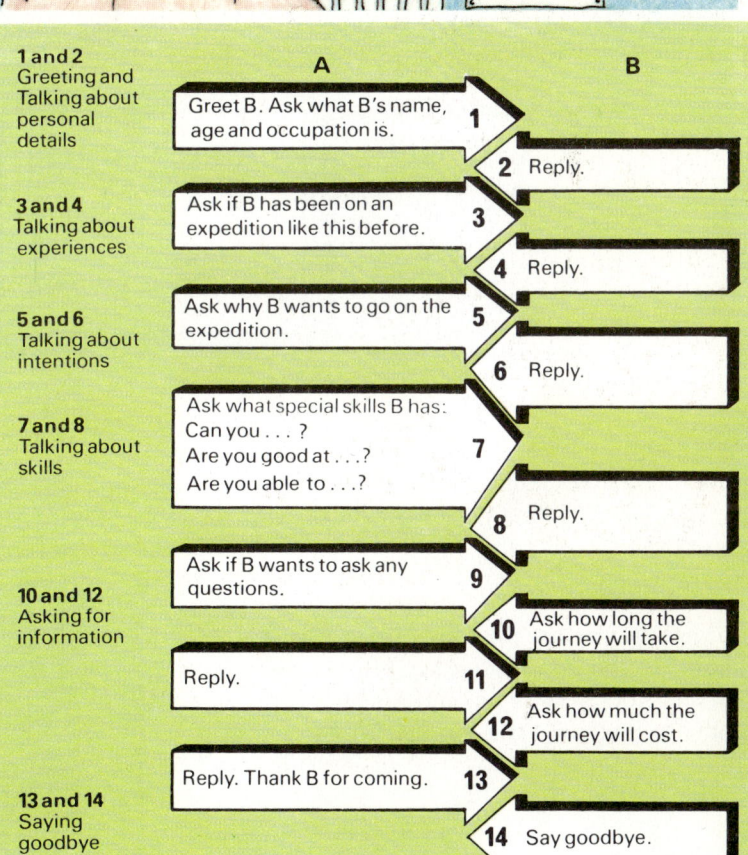

ROUND THE WORLD EXPEDITION BY TRUCK AND BOAT NEEDS TWO MORE MEMBERS.

TEL. 01-434 1191

A is the leader of a group of young people who are going to go around the world by truck and boat. The journey will take six months and cost each member about £1500. Members need to be able to cook, swim, drive, repair engines and speak two foreign languages.
B wants to join the group.

Language Study Exercises 1.11 1.12 1.16 1.17

LESSON 5

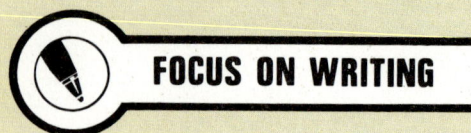
FOCUS ON WRITING

Letters of enquiry
This is part of the letter Jenny wrote about the scholarship.

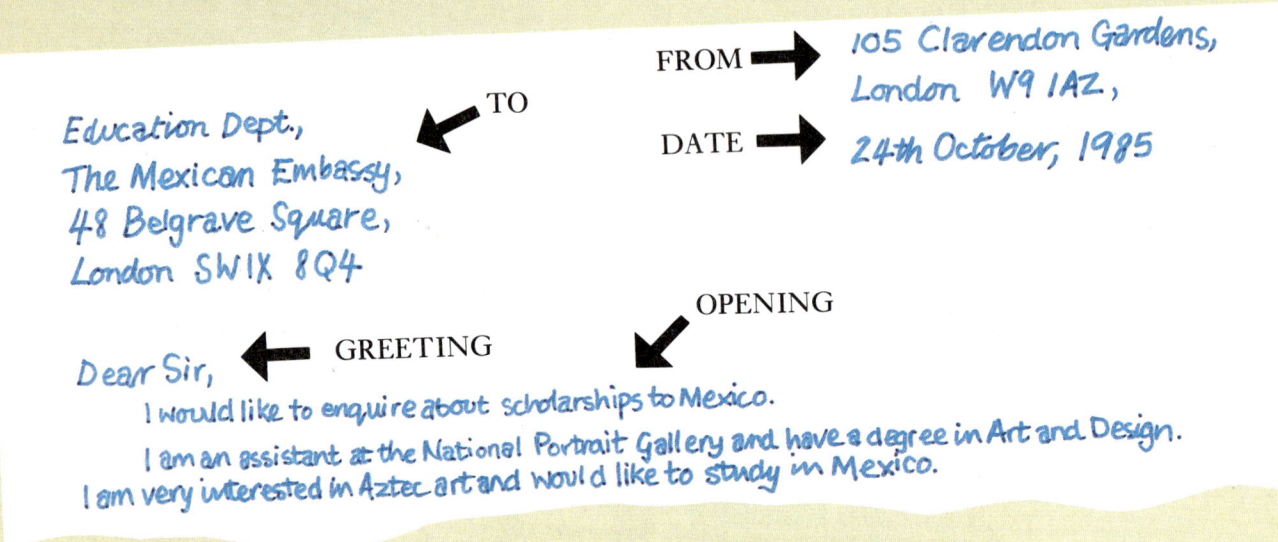

1. *Opening:* Jenny begins the letter by saying exactly *what* she is writing about.
Write the *Opening* of replies to these advertisements. Use your own name and address.

EXPLANATION

2. *Explanation:* Jenny continues the letter by explaining *why* she is writing and giving personal details.
Write the *Opening* and *Explanation* of a letter of enquiry in reply to this advertisement.

In the *Opening* say *what* you are writing about. In the *Explanation* say (a) *who* you are, (b) *why* you are writing, and (c) *when* you can come to England for a summer course.

9

Unit 1

FOCUS ON READING

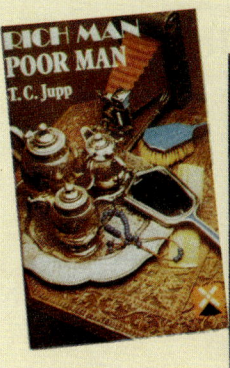

Reading English books
Here are some examples of books in English which you can read now. Read a new book with every unit of this book. The *Focus on Writing* section at the end of Unit 2 shows you how to write reports on the books.

Reading: Scanning for information
Often we do not read every word in a passage or in a book. We quickly look at the passage (scan) for the information we want. There are some new and difficult words in the passages below. But you do not need to understand these words. You can answer the questions by scanning.

Before reading
Look at reading passages 2 and 3. What are they? Do they come from advertisements, personal letters, election leaflets or official forms?

Reading purpose
Read each question and then find the answer in passage 1, 2 or 3.

1. How many countries voted on 7 June 1979?
2. What is the name of the Labour candidate?
3. What is Mrs Catherwood's first name?
4. For how long did Alex Gordon live in Glasgow?
5. Who studied at Cambridge University?
6. What was the name of the TV programme the Catherwood family were in?
7. What does Alex Gordon do?

Discuss
Which candidate do you prefer?

1
On Thursday 7 June 1979 you will have your chance to make history.
You will be able to vote, in the world's first international election, for the Common Market's European Parliament. So 7 June is special because this election will take place in nine different countries, at the same time, for the same purpose. For the first time, the ordinary people of Europe will be having a direct say in how the Common Market is run.

2
ALEX GORDON: Born 1929. Lived in Glasgow until 1963. Married with two daughters, aged 14 and 10, and has lived at Kettering since 1964. A teacher since 1960, and now a technical college lecturer, and formerly employed in electrical power engineering. Holds BSc pure science, MSc in computing, Certificate in Economic and Social Studies, and Post Graduate Certificate in Education. Active Labour Party member since 1950. Labour Group Leader on Kettering Borough Council. Member of Association of Clerical, Technical, and Supervisory Staffs, and the National Association for Teachers in Further and Higher Education. Also member of the Co-operative Party.

Alex **GORDON**
LABOUR AND EUROPE

Euro-candidate for Northants

3
CONSERVATIVE ✗

FRED CATHERWOOD

Sir Fred Catherwood is married, with three children, Christopher and Bethan, who are at University and Jonathan, who is taking 'A' levels. With his wife Elizabeth and the family he has lived for fifteen years at Balsham, near Cambridge where he studied as an undergraduate and rowed for the University reserve crew. He also served for four years on the University Appointments Board. He qualified as a Chartered Accountant. He has been Chief Executive successively of Richard Costain, British Aluminium and John Laing. He was Chairman of the British Institute of Management. Fred Catherwood's public service has included five years as Director-General of the National Economic Development Council and he has just completed four years as Chairman of the British Overseas Trade Board where he concentrated on the promotion of British exports to Europe. He was knighted in 1971. He broadcasts regularly on radio and television and, on a lighter note he and Elizabeth, Christopher and Bethan once got to the quarter final of the television quiz 'Ask the Family'.

Euro-candidate for Cambridgeshire and Wellingborough

English Language Scholarship

Do this activity in groups of six students. Three students are in Group A and three in Group B. Group A are the scholarship candidates and their instructions are below. Group B are the interviewers and their instructions are at the bottom of the page.

Group A: the candidates
COVER THE BOTTOM HALF OF THE PAGE.
YOU MUST NOT LOOK AT B'S INSTRUCTIONS.

1. Read the scholarship advertisement.
2. Discuss the advertisement and the application form with the other candidates.
3. Complete the application form for yourself.
4. When the interviewers are ready, you will have your interview.
   Give them your application form.
5. You can ask questions at the end of the interview.
   Ask if you will get pocket money *or* when the scholarship will start.
6. At the end, the interviewers will say who has got the scholarship.
   Ask the interviewers about their choice.

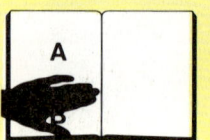

THE WORLDWIDE STUDENTS CENTRE
Sea Walk
Bournemouth
England

The Centre offers a scholarship of three months (or one term) to a student of English. The scholarship will cover the return fare to England, registration, tuition, accommodation and food. The successful candidate will study at The Worldwide Students Centre in Bournemouth for a least three hours a day.

ENGLISH LANGUAGE SCHOLARSHIP   Application form

Name _____ (Mr/Mrs/Miss)
Date of birth _____
Address _____
Education _____
_____
Occupation _____
How long have you been learning English? _____
Hobbies and Interests _____
_____
Write 100 words stating your reasons for wanting a scholarship

---

Group B: the interviewers
COVER THE TOP HALF OF THE PAGE.
YOU MUST NOT LOOK AT A'S INSTRUCTIONS.

1. Read the scholarship advertisement and the application form.
2. Choose the chairman.
3. Decide what questions you will ask. Each interviewer will ask two or three questions. Make a list of your questions. Look back at Steve's interview for examples.
4. When you are ready, the chairman asks the first candidate to come in.
5. The chairman introduces the other interviewers and asks the candidate to sit down. The chairman asks the candidate for his/her application form.
6. The interviewers read the application form.
7. The interviewers ask questions.
8. The chairman asks the candidate if he/she has any questions.
9. The chairman thanks the candidate.
10. When you have interviewed all the candidates, decide who will get the scholarship.
11. Then the chairman tells the candidates who has won the English Language Scholarship.

Information
Pocket money is not included in the scholarship.
The scholarship can start on 1st January, 1st April or 1st October.

LANGUAGE STUDY

Lessons 1–5

STRUCTURE

1.1 Study

> **PRESENT PERFECT TENSE**
> **RECENT PAST**
>
> The present perfect tense can describe a *completed* action in the recent past. The result can be seen.
> Examples: He's *broken up* with his girlfriend, so he's a bit depressed.
> Steve *has applied* for a scholarship.
> *Just* shows that the action happened a short time ago.
> Example: I've *just left* university.

1.2 Make sentences

Example: What's the matter with Steve? he/break up/with his girlfriend
He's broken up with his girlfriend.

1. Why are you phoning the police? there/be/an accident
2. Why isn't Steve at work? he/give up/his job
3. Jenny doesn't look very well. she/have/flu
4. You're back late! we/go/to a party
5. Where's your homework? I/forget/it

1.3 Drill

Example: Steve left university three months ago.
Steve has just left university.

1. The bank closed a few minutes ago.
2. Steve and his girlfriend broke up last month.
3. Jenny's car broke down this morning.
4. The President returned to Washington yesterday.
5. Steve arrived for the interview a moment ago.

1.4 Study

> **PRESENT PERFECT TENSE**
> **UNFINISHED PAST**
>
> The present perfect tense is often used with *since* and *for* to express the unfinished past.
> *since* refers to a point in time.
> Example:
> PAST ⇧ I've been at the National Portrait Gallery NOW
> since I left college.
>
> *for* refers to a period of time.
>
> PAST We've known each other NOW
> for years.

1.5 Make sentences

Example: Steve and I have known each other   (years)
(1968)

Steve and I have known each other for years.
Steve and I have known each other since 1968.

Unit 1

1. Steve has been a teacher (July) (three months)
2. Jenny has been interested in Aztec art (a long time) (she left college)
3. Steve has lived in Oxford (he started secondary school) (ten years)
4. Jenny has known her boyfriend (last summer) (about a year)
5. Steve has been depressed (a few weeks) (last month)

1.6 Study

> **PAST SIMPLE AND PRESENT PERFECT TENSES**
>
> The present perfect tense can refer to the indefinite past.
> The past simple tense refers to a point in past time.
> Examples:
>
> PAST -----------?----------- NOW
> Have you ever been there?
> Yes, I have.
>
> PAST ↓ NOW
> I spent a week in Mexico City a couple of years ago.

1.7 Ask and answer

Gloop has come to our planet in a UFO. He is visiting the USA for the first time. He's in Los Angeles on the last day of his visit. Ask him questions. Look at the examples on page 13.

Week 1
Sun. Arr. New York
Wed. Niagara Falls
Thur. Disney World
Fri. New Orleans
Sun. Grand Canyon

Week 2
Mon. Las Vegas
Wed. Los Angeles
Sat. Dep. Los Angeles

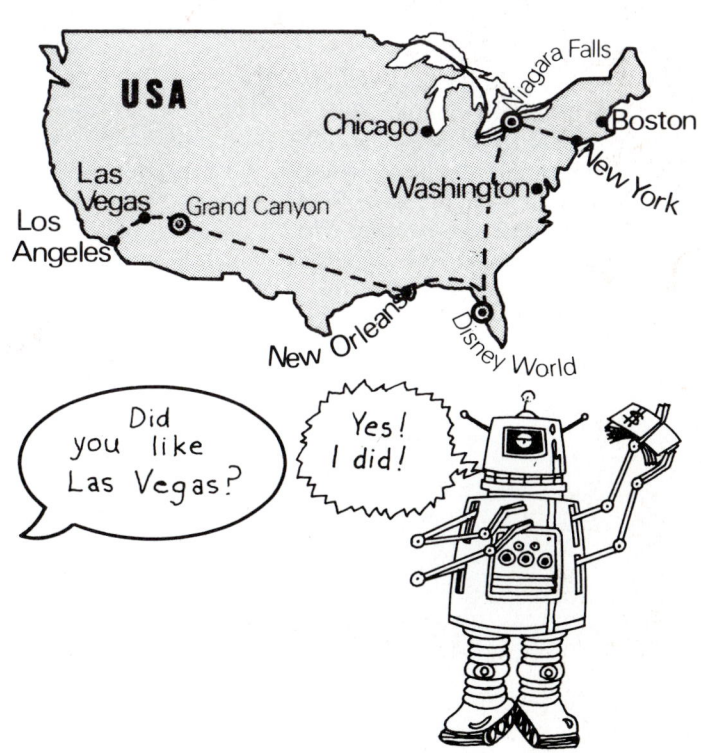

Examples:

S1: Have you been to Washington?
Have you been to New Orleans?
When did you go there?
How long did you stay there?

S2: No, I haven't.
Yes, I have.
A week ago.
For two days.

1.8 Study

> REVISION
> PRESENT SIMPLE TENSE
> STATEMENTS
>
> POSITIVE NEGATIVE   QUESTIONS
> I, you, we, they work/don't work   Do/Don't I, you, we, they work...?
> he, she, it works/doesn't work   Does/Doesn't he, she, it work...?

1.9 Study

> LIKE + NOUN or GERUND v. WOULD LIKE + NOUN or INFINITIVE
>
> *Examples:*
> Steve likes folk music.
> I like playing football.   (Stating an attitude)
>
> Steve would like a new guitar.
> I'd like to play football on Saturday.   (Stating a wish)

1.10 Make statements

Examples: You often go dancing. Why?
I like dancing.

You're at a party and you want to dance. What do you say?
I'd like to dance.

1. You often drink tea. Why?
2. You want a cup of tea. What do you say?
3. You're in a restaurant and order a steak. What do you say?
4. You regularly eat steak. Why?
5. You often go swimming. Why?
6. You want to go swimming. What do you say?
7. You want to listen to some music. What do you say?
8. You often listen to music. Why?
9. You go out every evening. Why?
10. You're sitting at home and you're bored. What do you say?

1.11 Study

> GERUND ('-ing' form)
> The gerund is used in the following ways:
>
> AFTER VERBS
> *Examples:* I *prefer being* a student.
> I really *enjoy working* there.
>
> AFTER PREPOSITIONS
> *Examples:* The Japanese are good *at making* cameras.
> How *about coming* to see us?
>
> AFTER PHRASAL VERBS
> *Example:* I'm going to *give up teaching*.

1.12 Complete

Example: Jenny likes ... in London. (live)
Jenny likes living in London.

1. It's difficult to give up ... (smoke)
2. Steve doesn't enjoy ... very much. (teach)
3. Would you mind ... a message? (take)
4. I'm interested in ... for the job. (apply)
5. What about ... for lunch? (meet)
6. Some people hate ... (fly)
7. Jenny is very good at ... (swim)
8. Steve liked ... a student. (be)
9. Do you prefer ... in the town to ... in the country? (live)
10. Jenny loves ... to the cinema. (go)

EXPRESSING REASON: WHY and BECAUSE

1.13 Make sentences

Example: Why is Jenny learning Spanish? (want/study in Mexico)
Because she wants to study in Mexico.

1. Why is Steve waiting outside the phone-box? (want/make a call)
2. Why are those people waiting on the corner? (hope/see the film star)
3. Why are the men working late? (intend/finish the job)
4. Why is Jenny running? (want/catch the bus)
5. Why is Steve saving his money? (be going/buy a car)
6. Why are the team training so hard? (intend/win the match)
7. Why is Steve learning to drive? (would like/get a better job)
8. Why is Jenny queueing? (want/buy a ticket)

EXPRESSING PURPOSE: IN ORDER TO

1.14 Drill

Example: Why is Jenny learning Spanish? Because she wants to study in Mexico.
In order to study in Mexico.

Now do the same with the answers to exercise **1.13**.

EXPRESSING RESULT: SO

1.15 Match the sentences and join them with *so*

Example: I had toothache. I went to the dentist.
I had toothache so I went to the dentist.

I had toothache.	I answered the advertisement.
I wanted to borrow a book.	I phoned the station.
I lost my passport.	I went to the library.
I didn't know the time of the train.	I looked it up in the dictionary.
I broke my leg.	I went to the dentist.
I was looking for a job.	I went to hospital.
I saw the accident.	I telephoned the police.
I didn't understand the word.	I called an ambulance.

1.16 Study

> INDIRECT QUESTIONS
>
> The word order in indirect questions is the same as in statements.
>
> *Examples:* Can you tell us exactly why *you want a scholarship?*
> I really want to know what *the Oxford Community Project is.*

Unit 1

Compare: Why *do you want a scholarship?*
What *is the Oxford Community Project?*

1.17 Drill

Example: What's your name?
Can you tell me what your name is?

Where do you come from?
What languages do you speak?
Why are you learning English?
When do you want to start the course?
How long do you intend to stay?

Drill

Example: How old is he?
I want to know how old he is.

Where does he live?
What does he do for a living?
How long have you known him?
When did you last see him?
Why did he take the money?

VOCABULARY

EDUCATION

1.18 Complete

1. Engineering is a ... subject.
2. In England, ... education starts at 11.
3. Steve went to the ... of Sussex.
4. Biology and physics are science ...
5. 'O level' and 'A level' are both ...
6. In most countries, nursery education is ...
7. In England, ... education starts at 5.
8. Primary education is ... in Mexico.
9. Some children go to ... school before they go to primary school.

*Look at the word down the centre. What is this puzzle about?

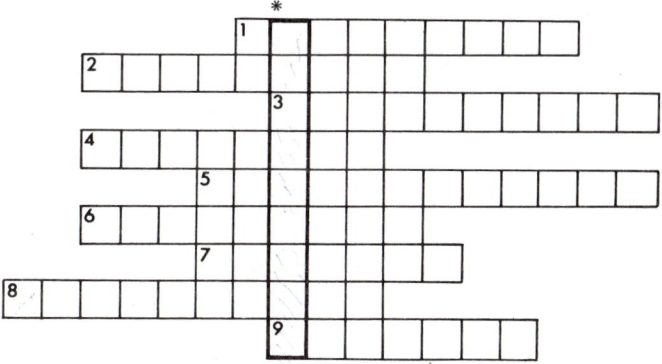

WHAT DO YOU SAY?

 1.19 Listen and choose the most suitable response

1. (a) How do you do.
   (b) I'm a nurse.
   (c) I'm looking for my keys.
   (d) I'm going to call the police.

2. (a) Football, fast cars, and girls.
   (b) He'll have soup and steak, please.
   (c) He's not feeling very well.
   (d) He's a very interesting person.

3. (a) How do you do.
   (b) Fine thanks, how are you?
   (c) I'll explain – it's really quite easy.
   (d) I'm feeling much better today, doctor.

INTONATION AND STRESS

1.20 Respond to the statements below with surprise, by repeating the words in italics

Example: The director's office is *on the third floor.*
(You think it's on the second floor.)
On the third floor?

1. The coach leaves at *half past eleven.* (You think it leaves at half past ten.)
2. Take *the second turning* on the left. (You think it's the third turning.)
3. It's *a blue car* with some parcels on the back seat. (You think it's a green car.)
4. First *turn on the radio*, then take off the back and look inside. (You think you must turn off the radio.)
5. *Primary education* starts at eleven and lasts for six years. (You think it's secondary education.)

SENTENCE LINKING

1.21 Complete

Put in *and* or *but*.

A famous film-star was born in 1926 and died in 1962. Her family was poor, but she became rich and famous. She worked in Hollywood and made nearly thirty films, including *Gentlemen Prefer Blondes* and *Some Like it Hot*. She could buy anything she wanted, but she was very unhappy. Her real name was Norma Jean Baker, but everyone knows her as Marilyn Monroe.

Put in *so* or *but*.

A man wanted to build a swimming pool, ... he was very lazy ... he decided to buy a hole. The holes weren't expensive ... he bought the biggest one in the shop. He started driving home with the hole on the back of his truck, ... on the way, the hole fell off. He turned back to look for it, ... it was getting dark ... it was difficult to see anything. Unfortunately, the hole was in the middle of the road, ... he fell into it!

1.22 Write a paragraph

Read Steve's description of his education in Lesson 2. Study the use of *and*, *but*, and *so* in the paragraph.
Write a paragraph describing your education (primary/secondary/higher). If you are still at school or university, say what you would like to do. If you have left school, say what jobs you have had.

Unit 2 Lesson 6

Talking about spending money

Daily Globe
Another great Globe Exclusive

SPEND SPEND SPEND

'Now we're going to spend and spend and spend,' said Liz, wife of the millionaire milkman, Fred Mills.
'Yesterday I couldn't afford new shoes. Today I can buy anything I like.'

WORLD RECORD
Dark-haired Liz, a £35-a-week cleaning woman, was with her husband when he received his million-pound cheque. This was a world record for a football pools win.
'We can do what we want now,' said Liz. 'No-one can tell us what to do. That's the most important thing.'

TOO OLD
Fred and Liz started spending at once. OUT went the family's black and white TV. 'Too old,' said Fred. IN came a brand-new colour TV. OUT went Liz's old winter coat. 'Not smart enough,' said Fred. IN came a fabulous fur coat.

COME BACK
35-year-old Liz bought presents for her friends and family. Among the items she bought were a gold watch and a thousand-pound diamond ring.
'If you've got a million pounds, you don't have to count the pennies,' said Liz. 'Come back tomorrow, Liz,' said a happy shop owner.

ADVICE
Liz's mother, 57-year-old Mabel Jones, was delighted at the news. But she had a piece of advice for her daughter.
'If I were Liz,' said Mrs Jones, 'I'd give some of the money to charity.'

 Ask and answer

Make up questions about Liz and Fred. Ask another student your questions.

Examples:
WHAT   What are Liz and Fred going to do?
HOW MUCH   How much did Fred win?
WHY   Why did Fred buy a new T.V.?
HOW OLD   How old is Liz?
WHO   Who gave Liz some advice?
CAN   Can Liz buy anything she likes?
DID   Did Liz buy a new dress or a new watch?

  Questions

1. What personal details (age, occupation, etc.) can you find out about Liz Mills?
2. Liz says, 'That's the most important thing.'
   What does she mean by 'that'?
   (a) that the cheque was a world record
   (b) that she and Fred can do what they want
   (c) that she and Fred are rich
   (d) that she and Fred can buy lots of things
3. Why was the shop owner happy?
4. Mabel Jones 'was delighted at the news'. What was 'the news'?

Unit 2

  Study and complete

choose the IDEAL KITCHEN AND WIN £500

FAMILY MAGAZINE COMPETITION

What is the most important machine in today's kitchen? Put these machines in order of importance. Then give reasons for your choice. You could win £500 to spend on kitchen equipment.

A	Dishwasher	£224.75
B	Electric kettle	£16.95
C	Electric tin-opener	£13.99
D	Food mixer	£75.95
E	Freezer	£169.95
F	Refrigerator	£148.90
G	Toaster	£16.75
H	Tumble dryer	£139.95
I	Vacuum cleaner	£62.25
J	Washing-machine	£221.00

My order of importance

A ☐   F ☐
B ☐   G ☐
C ☐   H ☐
D ☐   I ☐
E ☐   J ☐

Mr/Mrs/Miss _____
Age _____
Address _____
_____ Postcode _____
I think a/an _____ is the most important item because

Ask each other

1. What do you think are the most and least important items? Why?
2. What is your order of importance?
3. What was the total cost of your first four items?
4. What equipment do you have in your kitchen at home?
5. What equipment would you like to have?

 Make a list and discuss

What would you do if you were Liz?

If I were Liz, I'd give some of the money to charity.

Make a list of the things you would do and the things you would buy in order of importance. Then discuss your list with another student.

Example: First of all I'd get some new clothes. Then I'd have a holiday. Then I'd buy a new house and I'd put the rest of the money in the bank.

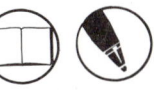 **Study and complete**

Fred and Liz Mills have just bought a lot of kitchen equipment.

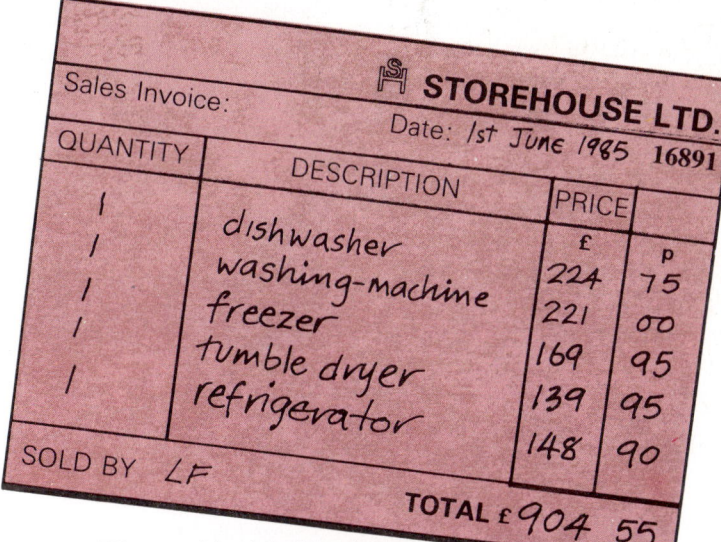

They paid with this cheque.

You have just spent £210.35 at Storehouse. Write a cheque to pay the bill.

Language Study Exercises   2.1   2.2   2.3   2.8   2.14   2.16   2.17   2.19

LESSON 7

Comparing costs and making plans

Fred Mills was a milkman until he won the pools. Liz worked as a cleaning woman in a factory. But, suddenly, they were rich.
At first, everything was wonderful. Both Fred and Liz stopped working. They bought new furniture for their house and two big American cars. They spent a lot of money on clothes and parties. Everything they had was bigger, better and more expensive than before.
However, Fred soon started to worry.
'If we carry on spending like this,' he said, 'soon there'll be no money left.'
'Don't be silly,' replied Liz. 'We'll never be able to spend it all.'
But Fred decided to write down how much they spent on different things.

Here is Fred and Liz's weekly budget. It shows how they spent their money in a typical week. For comparison, there are also budgets for a single student and a married couple with children.

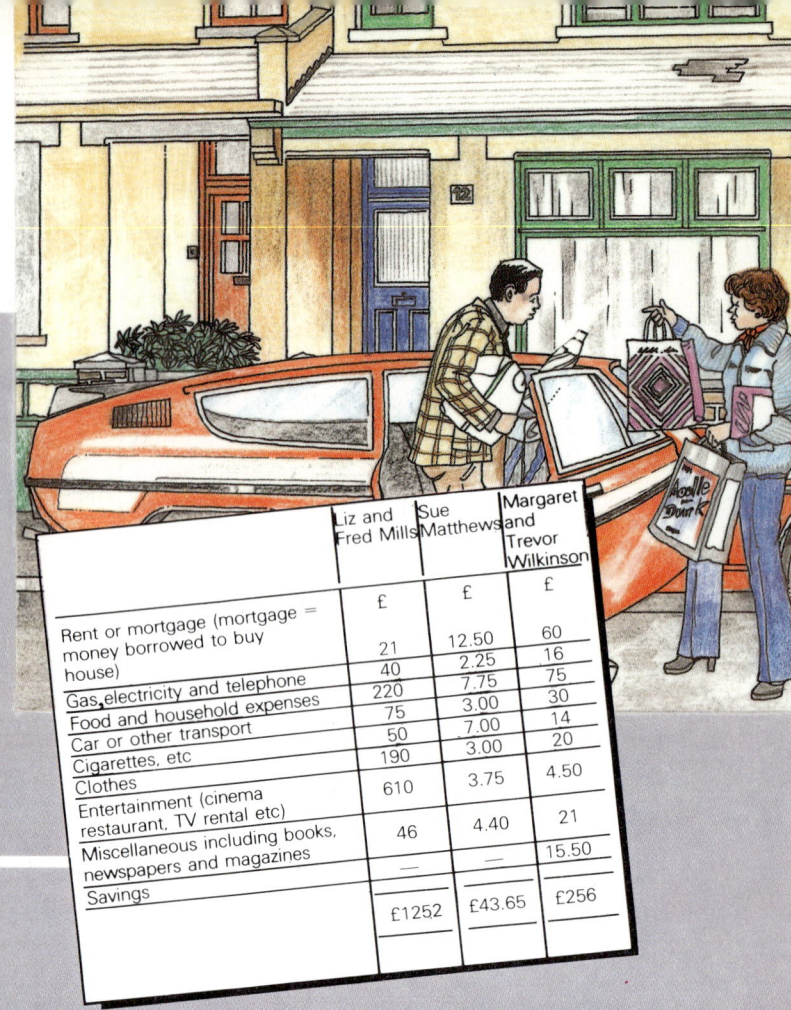

	Liz and Fred Mills	Sue Matthews	Margaret and Trevor Wilkinson
	£	£	£
Rent or mortgage (mortgage = money borrowed to buy house)	21	12.50	60
Gas, electricity and telephone	40	2.25	16
Food and household expenses	220	7.75	75
Car or other transport	75	3.00	30
Cigarettes, etc	50	7.00	14
Clothes	190	3.00	20
Entertainment (cinema, restaurant, TV rental etc)	610	3.75	4.50
Miscellaneous including books, newspapers and magazines	46	4.40	21
Savings	—	—	15.50
	£1252	£43.65	£256

Sue Matthews is a medical student at Newcastle University. She shares a house with four other students. Every summer she works for fourteen weeks. For the rest of the year she lives on her student grant. Her grant is £1660, so for 38 weeks her weekly income is £43.65.

Margaret and Trevor Wilkinson live in London. They have three children. Trevor works in an office and Margaret is a shop assistant. Their weekly income is £256.

 Ask and answer

Make up questions about the three weekly budgets. Ask another student your questions.

Examples:
WHO   Who spends most/least on ....?
HOW MUCH   How much does Sue spend on ....?
WHAT   What do the Wilkinsons spend most/least on?
WHICH   Which family spends most/least on ....?
DOES/DO   Do the Mills spend £50 a week on food?

  Questions

1. 'At first, everything was wonderful,' means that later things
   (a) got better
   (b) got worse
   (c) stayed the same
   (d) got much better

2. Fred says, 'Soon there'll be no money left.' Is he right? For how many years can Liz and Fred spend £835 a week before the million pounds is gone?

Unit 2

 Tell each other

Look at the family budgets on page 17 and compare them.
Examples:
The Wilkinsons spend *about the same as* Sue Matthews on entertainment.
The Mills spend *about ten times as much as* the Wilkinsons on clothes.
The Mills spend £610 on entertainment out of £1252. That's *about a half.*
Sue Matthews spends £4.40 a week on books out of £43.65. That's *about a tenth.*

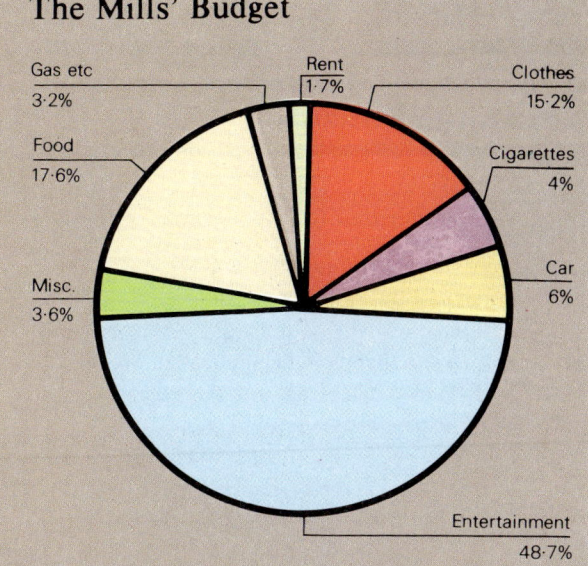

The Mills' Budget

 Write out your budget

Write out your weekly budget. Compare your budget with those in this Lesson and with another student's in your class.

 Discuss

Imagine that you have won the Ideal Kitchen competition in Lesson 6. You can choose kitchen equipment from the list on the form, up to a total cost of £500. Work with another student.
Example:
If we choose the washing-machine and tumbler dryer, we won't have enough money for the dishwasher.

If we carry on spending like this, soon there'll be no money left.

 Role Play

Suppliers 1: Office Master
2: Bureau Contracts
3: Modern Office Design

Work with another student. A big company is opening a new office. The company needs to buy office equipment: 200 square metres of carpet, a photocopier, 4 desks and 15,000 sheets of typing paper.
You and another student are buyers for the company.

Remember:
* You want to open the office as soon as possible.
* You want to spend as little money as possible.
* However, you do not want to buy bad quality equipment. You want the office to look good.

You have contacted three suppliers. Look at the suppliers' estimates and decide which equipment to order from which supplier.

Example:
A: If we order the desks from Office Master we'll have to wait twelve weeks.
B: Let's get the desks from Bureau Contracts then.
A: But they're more expensive. They cost nearly twice as much as Office Master desks.

Item	Supplier	Price	Quality	Delivery
Photocopier	1	£4500	Excellent	6 weeks
	2	£3000	Very Good	6 weeks
	3	£500	Poor	Now
Desk	1	£318	Good	12 weeks
	2	£500	Excellent	Now
	3	£198	Good	10 weeks
Carpet (per square metre)	1	£9.00	Good	6 weeks
	2	£12.00	Very Good	Now
	3	£8.50	Good	12 weeks
Typing Paper (500 sheets)	1	£3.50	Excellent	Now
	2	£3.20	Excellent	Now
	3	£3.40	Excellent	Now

Language Study Exercises 2.4 2.5 2.6 2.11 2.15

LESSON 8

Discussing alternatives

Liz and Fred decided to buy a house.

LIZ: Listen! This is what we want – luxurious, modern, eight-bedroom house in beautiful country area . . .

FRED: I'm not so sure. If we moved from here, we'd lose all our friends.

LIZ: Don't be silly. They'd come and see us. Anyway we'd soon make new friends. There's a double garage and it's got a swimming pool. We could have parties by the pool.

FRED: That's nice. But don't you think the house is too big? Eight bedrooms? We don't need more than three.

LIZ: It's got oil central heating, too.

FRED: That's a pity. Gas is much cheaper.

LIZ: Never mind. We can afford anything now!

FRED: I don't want a big house.

LIZ: Well, I do.

FRED: All we need is a three-bedroom house in the town with a garden. There must be lots like that.

LIZ: No, there aren't.

FRED: Well, what other houses are there in the paper?

 Ask and answer

Make up questions about Liz and Fred's conversation. Ask another student your questions.

Examples: HOW MANY ... bedrooms?
HOW BIG ... garage?
HAS IT GOT ... oil or gas?
WHAT ... would Fred like?

  Questions

1. Why doesn't Fred want to move?
2. Liz says, 'They'd come and see us.' Who are 'they'?
3. Fred says, 'We don't need more than three.' Does he mean (a) friends? (b) houses? (c) bedrooms? (d) cars?
4. Fred says, 'That's a pity.' What does he mean by 'that'? Why is it a pity?

 Listening

Listen to Liz's description of the houses advertised in the newspaper. Write down the house details in this table.

	Example	1	2	3	4
Kind of house?	Detached				
No. of bedrooms?	8				
Age?	Modern				
Garden?	Yes				
Garage?	Double				
Area?	Country				
Heating?	Oil				
Other important details?	Swimming pool				
Price?	£165,000				

detached

semi-detached

cottage

terraced

Unit 2

 Discuss

Discuss the advantages and disadvantages of the four houses Liz described. Remember that Fred and Liz have different ideas about houses. What would they say?

Example: The eight-bedroom house,

Advantages	
Modern	'It would be easy to clean.'
In a beautiful area	'It would be nice to live there.'
Double garage	'We could put both cars in the garage.'
Swimming pool	'We could go swimming every day.'
Attractive garden	'It would be lovely to have a garden.'

Disadvantages	
Eight bedrooms	'It's too big.'
In the country	'We'd lose all our friends.'
Oil central heating	'Gas is much cheaper.'

 Tell each other

What is your ideal house? Say what kind of house you would like. How many rooms? A small or large garden? A garage? Central heating? In what area? What price would you pay?

 Game: Fire

Imagine that your house or flat is on fire. You only have time to save six of your things from the fire. Which six things would you save? Make a list and compare it with another student's. Say why you have chosen the six items.

 Complete

This is an insurance company form. How much do you think the contents of the average home or flat are worth? Complete the form and compare the result with other students' results. You can use pounds (£s) or your own currency.

CHECK LIST	Lounge	Dining room	Kitchen	Hall, stairs, landing	Main bedroom	2nd bedroom	3rd bedroom	Bathroom /Toilet	TOTAL
Carpets, rugs and floor coverings	£400	—	£150	£250	£145	£70	£70	—	£1,085
Furniture: tables, chairs, stools, suites, cabinets, sideboards, bookcases. Bedroom, bathroom and kitchen furniture									
Soft furnishings: curtains and their fittings, cushions									
Televisions, radios and similar equipment									
Household appliances: cooker, refrigerator/freezer, washing machine, vacuum cleaner, electrical goods, heaters									
Valuables: gold and silver articles, jewellery, pictures, clocks, watches, cameras, ornaments, collections									
Leisure: sports equipment, cycles, books, records, tapes, musical instruments, toys									
Household linen: bedding, towels, table linen									
Clothing									
Other Items									

 English for the classroom

Excuse me, what does ... mean?

Language Study Exercises 2.7 2.9 2.18 2.20 2.21 2.22

LESSON 9

Comparing the past and the present

Fred and Liz decided to buy the eight-bedroom house in the country. Soon after they bought the house, they were interviewed on the radio programme *Today's People*.

INTERVIEWER: Fred, can you tell us what effect winning the pools has had on your life?

FRED: Well, everything's different now, isn't it? We can do what we like, when we like. Just to take one example, when I was a milkman I used to get up at half past four in the morning. Now I don't have to get up at all if I don't want to.

INTERVIEWER: How about you, Liz?

LIZ: Living in the country's a big change. We used to live in a terraced house, but now we've got a big garden with a swimming pool. We're going to get our own tennis court, too.

INTERVIEWER: Any regrets?

LIZ: Well, I miss my old friends a bit. They don't come and see me any more...

FRED: Yes, but there's so much to do here. To start with, we play golf several times a week and Liz is having piano lessons. I've got a small plane of my own now. And then there's our social life. We eat out in restaurants a lot and usually have a party at home on Saturdays. Oh yes, we're very busy...

INTERVIEWER: And are you happier now than you used to be?

....

Two years after this interview there was a fire at the Mills' house. Fred and Liz were not hurt, but they lost everything they had. The house was not insured. Three months later, the lawyer who was looking after their money disappeared – with all the money. Exactly three years after winning the pools, Fred started work again, as a milkman. Liz and Fred had won, and lost, a million pounds.

 Ask and answer

What did Liz and Fred use to do when they were rich?

Example: Did they use to live in a big house?
Yes, they did.

 Questions

1. The interviewer says, 'How about you, Liz?' What does he mean?
2. 'Three months later'. Three months after what?
3. Do you think Liz and Fred were happier when they were rich?

Unit 2

 Tell each other

1. Tell another student about the things you used to do, wear and like.

Examples:
When I was at primary school, I used to wear school uniform.
Five years ago, I didn't use to smoke.
When I was young, I didn't use to like olives.

When I was a milkman, I used to get up at half past four in the morning.

2. Look at the pictures and tell each other about changes.

Examples:
Women used to wear bathing hats, but they don't any more.
It used to take ten and a half hours by train from London to Edinburgh. Now it only takes four hours thirty minutes.

London–Edinburgh
1863
10½ hours

London–Edinburgh
Now
4 hours 30 minutes

1890s

London–Paris
August 25 1919
2½ hours

London–Paris
Now
1 hour

London–New York
July 1 1946
19¾ hours

London–New York
Now
3 hours 45 minutes

Now

 Discuss

Think about changes in society in the last hundred years.
Think about medicine, transport, housing and food.
Make a list of the changes and discuss them with another student.
Have things got better or worse?

Examples:

CARS

There didn't use to be any cars.

NO SMALLPOX NOW

People don't die of smallpox any more.

 Project

In 1939, in Britain, you could buy ten cigarettes, a box of chocolates, a cinema ticket and a newspaper for two shillings (10p). Now you have to pay £3 for the same things. That's thirty times as much.

Do some things cost more in your country now than they used to cost?
Make a list of things which cost more. Talk about the differences in prices.

Language Study Exercises 2.10 2.12 2.13 2.23 2.24 2.25

22

LESSON 10

FOCUS ON WRITING

The structure of a letter of enquiry

1. Letters of enquiry

Look back at Jenny's letter on page 9. This is how she finished the letter.

I would be grateful for full details of scholarships to Mexico and an application form.

Yours faithfully,
J. Langley
JENNIFER LANGLEY

Conclusion: Jenny states clearly what she wants.

Write the conclusion to the letter to Britsell you started in Unit 1. Ask for details of summer courses and for an application form. Sign the letter.

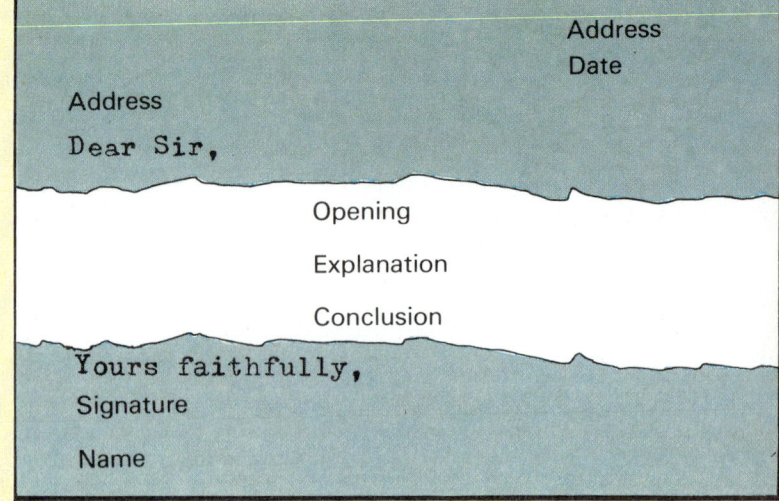

Address
Date
Address
Dear Sir,
Opening
Explanation
Conclusion
Yours faithfully,
Signature
Name

Write a letter of enquiry to the English Tourist Board, 4 Grosvenor Gardens, London SW1.

Opening Say that you are interested in youth hostels and cheap accommodation for young people.

Explanation Say that you're a student, say what country you are from and what you are studying. Say when you are visiting England and for how long.

Conclusion Ask for addresses of student accommodation and for details of any student discounts. (Student discounts = cheap prices for students.)

2. Report writing

When you have finished reading a book in English write a report for the other students. Say *what* the book is about and *if* you liked it.

BOOK REPORT

Author:

Title:

1. What kind of book is it? e.g. novel, detective story, biography, non-fiction, adventure story.
2. If a story:
   Where does the story take place? Who are the main characters?
3. What is the book about? (You can give a list of chapters.)
4. What did you like best?
5. How good is the book?
6. Any other comments.

Unit 2

FOCUS ON READING

This is a questionnaire. You need to read the questionnaire slowly. Then choose your answers carefully. If you are not sure what a word means, ask another student or your teacher for help.

Before reading
What is this questionnaire about?
Reading purpose
To find your score and what it means.

MONEY MAKES THE WORLD GO ROUND...OR DOES IT?

What is your attitude to money? Answer the questions below, and find out.

1. How would your describe your parents' attitude to money?
   a) very careful
   b) sensible
   c) generous
   d) extravagant

2. At the end of the week/month, have you usually
   a) spent all your money?
   b) borrowed some money?
   c) got a little left?
   d) got a lot left?

3. How often do other people ask you to lend them money?
   a) often
   b) sometimes
   c) rarely
   d) never

4. You lent a friend some money a long time ago. But the friend has not paid the money back. You think your friend has forgotten about it. Do you
   a) remind the friend?
   b) forget about it, too?
   c) feel too embarrassed to say anything?
   d) decide he/she isn't a friend anymore?

5. If you receive a sum of money as a present, do you
   a) spend it on something you really want?
   b) save some and spend the rest?
   c) put it all in your bank or savings account?
   d) spend it on a party for all your friends?

6. When your friends have birthdays, do you
   a) ask them what they'd like as a present?
   b) just send them a birthday card?
   c) buy something you know they want?
   d) buy the first thing you see, however much it costs?

How to score

1. a)4 b)3 c)2 d)1
2. a)2 b)1 c)3 d)4
3. a)1 b)2 c)3 d)4
4. a)3 b)1 c)2 d)4
5. a)2 b)3 c)4 d)1
6. a)3 b)4 c)2 d)1

What your score means

6-10
You love spending money and you are generous, even extravagant. Are you trying to buy friendship? Remember true friends like you for yourself, not for your money.

11-15
You are very generous, and you really enjoy life. You will probably never be rich, but you will be happy. You find it very difficult to save.

16-20
You organise your life carefully, and you are very sensible with money. When you go out with friends you always share the bill. You will always be able to buy the things you really want.

21-24
You are very careful with money. In fact, you hate spending money. You will be able to buy lots of things, but perhaps you would enjoy life more if you thought about money less. Remember that possessions aren't everything - your friends are very important, too.

Do these activities in pairs (A and B). A's instructions are below and B's instructions are at the bottom of the page.

Student A
COVER THE BOTTOM HALF OF THE PAGE. YOU MUST NOT LOOK AT B'S INSTRUCTIONS.

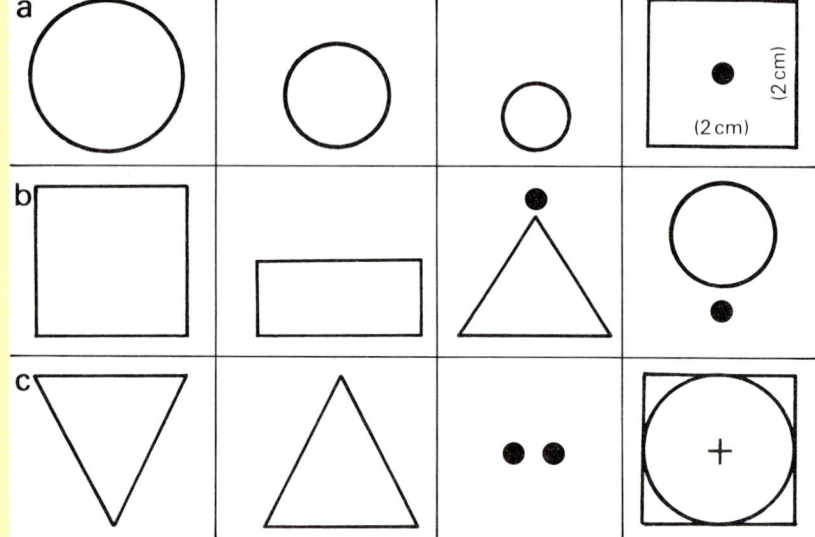

1. Describe these drawings to B. B will try to draw as you describe. Do not look at B's drawings.
   Begin like this: There are three sets of drawings, a, b and c. In the first set, set a, there are three circles and a square. The first circle is the biggest and the third the smallest. The square is the same size as the biggest circle. The square is 2 cm by 2 cm. There is a dot in the middle of the square.
2. When you have finished, compare the drawings above with B's drawings. Talk about any differences.
3. Now listen and draw as B describes three sets of drawings.
4. Then make some simple drawings of your own. Use circles, squares and triangles. Describe your drawings to B in the same way.
5. Listen as B describes his/her drawings.

KEY ◯ Circle △ Triangle ☐ Square + Cross ▭ Rectangle ● Dot

Student B
COVER THE TOP HALF OF THE PAGE. YOU MUST NOT LOOK AT A'S INSTRUCTIONS.

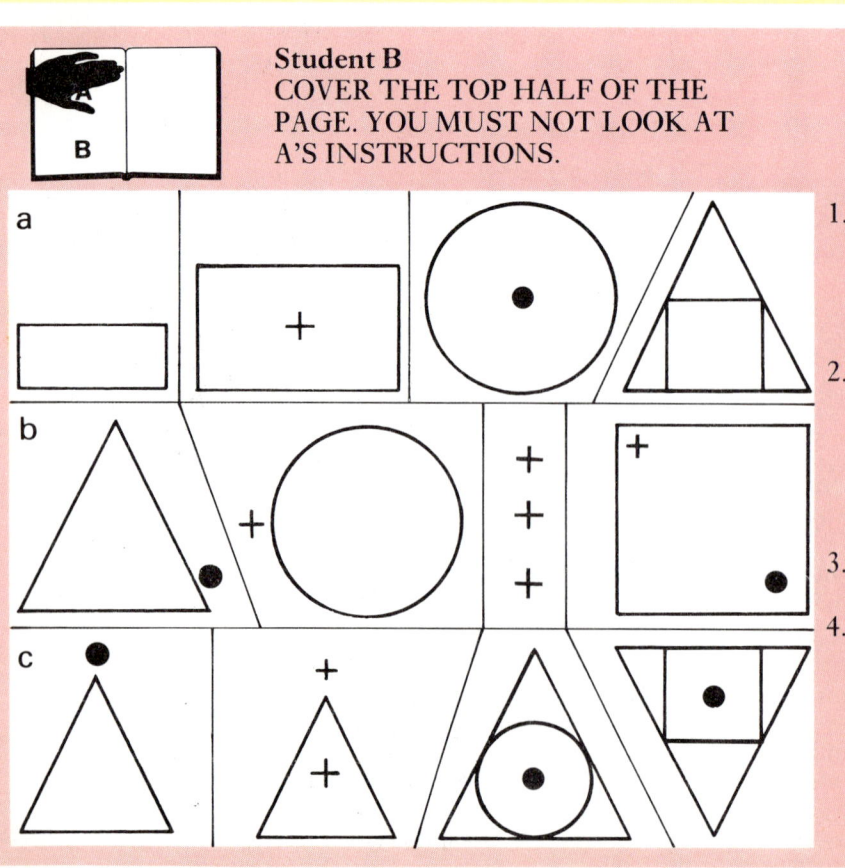

1. Listen to A. Draw on a piece of paper what A describes. Do not show A your paper until you have finished all three sets of drawings. Then compare your drawings with A's.
2. Now describe these sets of drawings to A in the same way.

   Begin like this: There are three sets of drawings, a, b and c. In the first set, there are . . .
3. A will now describe to you some drawings he/she has just done. Listen and draw.
4. Finally, make some simple drawings of your own. Use circles, squares and triangles. Describe them to A.

25

LANGUAGE STUDY

Lessons 6–10

STRUCTURE

EXPRESSING CONDITION

2.1 Study

CONDITIONAL SENTENCES: CAUSE and EFFECT

Examples: *If you've got* a million pounds, *you don't have to* count the pennies.
If they wanted something, *they bought* it.

Here, *if* means *when* or *whenever*.

⚠ In the first example, *both* verbs are in the present tense.
In the second example, *both* verbs are in the past tense.

2.2 Make sentences

Example: travel abroad/need a passport
If you travel abroad, you need a passport.

1. own a car/need insurance
2. press that button/start the machine
3. mix blue and yellow/get green
4. fly first class/get better food
5. not get enough sleep/feel tired

2.3 Answer the questions

Example: Where do you go if you want to catch a train?
You go to the station.

Where do you go if you want to:
1. see a film
2. borrow a book
3. see a play
4. catch a plane
5. have a swim
6. have a haircut

2.4 Study

CONDITIONAL SENTENCES: TYPE 1

Examples: *If we choose* the freezer, *we'll have* enough money for the refrigerator.
If we carry on spending like this, soon *there'll be* no money left.

These conditional sentences express *real possibilities or alternatives*.

⚠ *'If' Clause*   *Main Clause*
If + PRESENT TENSE ...,   FUTURE TENSE (or IMPERATIVE) ...

2.5 Complete

Example: If Jenny gets the scholarship ... (go to Mexico)
If Jenny gets the scholarship, she'll go to Mexico.

1. If Steve gives up teaching, ... (get another job)
2. If Jenny goes to Mexico, ... (travel a lot)
3. If Fred and Liz go to New York, ... (spend a lot of money)
4. If you follow the directions, ... (find the house)
5. If we buy a new car, ... (not have any money left)

2.6 Make sentences

Example: catch the train/hurry
You'll catch the train if you hurry.

1. feel better/give up smoking
2. have an accident/drive so fast
3. pass the exam/work hard
4. get a surprise/open the present
5. not meet people/stay at home

2.7 Study

CONDITIONAL SENTENCES: TYPE 2

These conditional sentences indicate that the situation is *unlikely*:

Example: *If we moved* from here, *we'd lose* all our friends.

or *impossible*:

Example: *If I were* Liz, *I'd give* some of the money to charity.

⚠ *'If' Clause*   *Main Clause*
If + PAST TENSE ...,   ... would/could ...

2.8 Drill

Give advice to a friend who can't sleep at night.

Example: go to the doctor
If I were you, I'd go to the doctor.

buy a new bed   try to relax
have a hot bath at bedtime   take more exercise
take a sleeping pill   stop worrying about it

2.9 Make sentences

Gloop is considering his career.

Example: study medicine
If I studied medicine, I could be a doctor.

study medicine   speak a foreign language fluently
learn to type   have driving lessons
join the army   learn to fly
go to a College of Education   be good at maths

STATE OR HABIT IN THE PAST: USED TO

2.10 Drill

Fred's life has changed since the Mills lost all their money.

Example: He's given up playing golf.
He used to play golf, but he doesn't any more.

He's given up   smoking cigars.
                  flying his plane.
                  eating in expensive restaurants.
                  driving a big car.
                  staying in expensive hotels.
                  spending a lot of money.

UNTIL

 2.11 Drill

Example: Fred Mills is a milkman (win the pools)
Fred Mills was a milkman until he won the pools.

1. Trevor Wilkinson has a sports car (get married)
2. Sue Matthews lives with her parents (go to university)
3. Steve teaches English (change his job)
4. Jenny works at the National Portrait Gallery (go to Mexico)
5. Liz has lots of friends (move to a new house)

2.12 Study

> **INDEFINITE PRONOUNS**
>
> anyone   anything
> someone something
> everyone everything
> no one   nothing
>
> *Examples:* Today I can buy *anything* I like.
> Do you want *something* to eat?
> *Everything*'s different now.
> *No one* can tell us what to do.
>
> ⚠ There *isn't anyone* there. = There's *no one* there.
> I *haven't got anything*. = I've got *nothing*.

2.13 Complete

Examples: The box is empty. There isn't ... in the box.
There isn't anything in the box.

A person stole his watch. ... stole his watch.
Someone stole his watch.

1. They're all dancing. ... is dancing.
2. The bottle is empty. There isn't ... in the bottle.
3. A person wants to see you. ... wants to see you.
4. I want a book to read. I want ... to read.
5. All the things are wet. ... is wet.
6. Are any of you coming? Is ... coming?
7. The refrigerator is empty. There's ... to eat.
8. They're away on holiday. There's ... at home.
9. I'm thirsty. I want ... to drink.
10. They're having lunch. There isn't ... in the office.

2.14 Study

> **COMPARISON OF ADJECTIVES**
>
> Two things: use the comparative form.
> Three or more things: use the superlative form.
>
> | | COMPARATIVE | SUPERLATIVE |
> |---|---|---|
> | *Examples:* cold | colder | coldest |
> | hot | hotter | hottest |
> | expensive | more expensive | most expensive |
>
> **IRREGULAR COMPARISONS**
>
> ⚠
> | good | better | best |
> | bad | worse | worst |
> | much/many | more | most |
> | little | less | least |

 2.15 Ask and answer

Example: train/fast
S1: *Is this train faster than the others?*
S2: *Yes, it's the fastest.*

room/quiet   cottage/old
suit/cheap   house/large
mountain/high   restaurant/good
book/funny   newspaper/bad

COMPARISON OF LONGER ADJECTIVES

 2.16 Drill

Examples: Is the freezer more important than the other items?
Yes, it's the most important.

Is the flat less convenient than the others?
Yes, it's the least convenient.

1. Is the Italian restaurant less expensive than the others?
2. Is this chair more comfortable than the others?
3. Is this painting more valuable than the others?
4. Is this magazine more interesting than the others?
5. Is this book less difficult than the others?

TOO/ENOUGH

2.17 Ask and answer

Example: the house is too small (big)
S1: *Don't you think the house is too small?*
S2: *No, it's big enough.*

the jacket is too short (long)
the car is too slow (fast)
it's cold in here (warm)
she's too young (old)
he's too short (tall)
it's too noisy to work in here (quiet)

COMPOUND ADJECTIVES

2.18 Drill

Example: It was a cheque for a million pounds.
It was a million-pound cheque.

1. The diamond ring cost a thousand pounds.
2. The car had four doors.
3. The house has three bedrooms.
4. The flight is two hours.
5. The journey is twenty minutes.
6. The race is five hundred metres.

VOCABULARY

SHOPPING

2.19 Complete

Fred and Liz went shopping. They had a long shopping list. Which items were for Liz? Which were for Fred? Which could be for Liz or Fred?

	Fred	Liz	Could be Fred or Liz
Example:	3 shirts	2 blouses	3 pairs of jeans

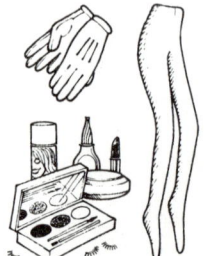

SHOPPING LIST
make-up
2 summer dresses
6 pairs of tights
vest and pants
after-shave lotion
bra and pants
2 suits (with waistcoat)
4 ties
swimming trunks
handkerchiefs
3 pairs of jeans
3 shirts
2 blouses
gloves
wallet
purse
2 belts
bikini
handbag
4 pullovers

Unit 2

WHAT DO YOU SAY?

 2.20 Listen and choose the most suitable

1. (a) I take a bus.
   (b) I'm fed up.
   (c) I'm late.
   (d) I'll catch the next one.
2. (a) Congratulations!
   (b) Good luck!
   (c) When will you get the results?
   (d) How interesting!
3. (a) Yes, it's too expensive.
   (b) I think so.
   (c) Yes, I've got a driving licence.
   (d) I haven't got a garage.

INTONATION AND STRESS

 2.21 Ask for repetition

Example: It cost twenty-eight pounds. (How much?)
           Sorry, <u>how much did you say it cost</u>?

1. She's gone to Acapulco. (Where?)
2. They left at three-twenty. (When?)
3. It went on for thirty minutes. (How long?)
4. He bought a dictionary. (What?)
5. She left because she felt ill. (Why?)
6. They met Paul McCartney at a party. (Who?)

Ask for repetition

Example: It cost twenty-eight pounds. (How much?)
           Sorry, it cost <u>how much</u>?

Do the same with the exercise above.

SENTENCE LINKING

2.22 Explain the meaning of the words in italics

Example: The house hasn't got a garden. That's why we didn't buy *it*.
           it = the house

1. I need some help to mend the motorbike. *It* won't take long.
2. I've found the soap and the toothpaste, but I can't see the towel. Do you know where *it* is?
3. 'Is the sheet cotton or nylon?' '*It*'s cotton.'
4. I'm going to wash the car. *It*'s terribly dirty.
5. Washing up isn't fun. But you have to do *it*.

2.23 Study

POSSESSIVE PRONOUNS	
mine	ours
yours	yours
his	
hers	theirs

2.24 Explain the meaning of the words in italics

Example: I failed my driving test, but Sue passed *hers*.
           hers = Sue's driving test

1. I've got my ticket, but Steve can't find *his*.
2. Margaret Wilkinson does her washing in a washing-machine, but Sue Matthews does *hers* by hand.
3. Your coffee's got sugar in it, but *mine* hasn't.
4. Fred and Liz invited some friends of *theirs* to a party.
5. My car's run out of petrol. Can I borrow *yours*?

2.25 Write a paragraph

Where did you use to live when you were a child? Describe the house or flat, and compare it with where you live now. Think about: kind of house/flat, number and size of rooms and kind of furniture. Say which house/flat you prefer and why.

Unit 3
LESSON 11

Discussing and comparing different customs

ANITA: Good evening. I'm Anita Lyons and this is the first of a new series of programmes called 'What do you think?' Our subject tonight is 'Living Abroad' and our first interview is with Hilda Lewis. Hilda's husband works for an oil company and they live in Saudi Arabia. Hilda, do you like living abroad?

HILDA: Well, that's a difficult question to answer. I certainly enjoy the variety. Everything's different, everything's new.

ANITA: How do you mean?
HILDA: Let me put it this way. You've got to change the way you live. It's not the same as living in Britain.
ANITA: What difficulties are there?
HILDA: The biggest, I suppose, is not being able to speak the language. And life can be more difficult for a woman than for a man.
ANITA: Really?
HILDA: Yes, for example, women are not allowed to drive cars.
ANITA: So it isn't easy to go out?
HILDA: Not really. But, if you live abroad, you must expect things to be different. You have to accept the customs of the country in which you live. There's no point in complaining all the time . . .
ANITA: Excuse me, Hilda, can I interrupt you for a moment? Now let's have a look at some of the differences between Britain and other countries. . . .

 Ask and answer

Make up questions about *What do you think?*
Ask another student your questions.

  Questions

1. Hilda says, 'Well, that's a difficult question to answer.'
   What does 'that' refer to?
2. Hilda says, 'The biggest, I suppose, is . . .' The biggest what?
3. Why can life in Saudi Arabia be more difficult for a woman than for a man? Because women
   (a) cannot speak Arabic
   (b) are not allowed to drive
   (c) complain all the time
   (d) have to change their clothes often

 Tell each other

Tell each other about differences between your country and Britain.
1. Look at the information on the TV screen.

Examples:

In Britain milk is sold in pints, *but* in my country it's sold in litres.
In Britain beer is sold in pints, *whereas* in my country it's sold in litres.

IN BRITAIN
- Milk and beer are sold in pints.
- Speed is measured in miles per hour.
- Small distances are measured in feet and inches.
- Longer distances are measured in yards and miles.
- People's weight is measured in stones and pounds.
- Pubs are closed in the afternoons.
- Milk and newspapers are delivered to your front door.
- Cars drive on the left.
- French is the most popular foreign language.

2. Look at this extract from a magazine for young people in Britain.
   Compare laws in Britain with laws in your country.

ARE YOU OLD ENOUGH?

There are laws which say how old you need to be to do certain things like see a film, vote, or start working. Here are the main ones.

The Law says you can	
vote at	18
smoke in public and buy cigarettes at +	16
drink alcohol in a pub at	18
drink beer or cider with a meal in a pub at	16
drink soft drinks in a pub at	18
work part-time (but your boss may need a permit) at	16
claim social security at	14
join the Army, Navy or Air Force at	13
join the Women's Army, Navy or Air Force at	16
drive a moped at	16
a car or motorbike at	17
a bus or lorry at	16
get married at	17
get married if your parents agree, at	21
	18
	16

Example:
In Britain you're allowed to drive a car when you are 17, but in my country you're not allowed to drive until you're 18.

Write sentences

Write five sentences about differences between your country and Britain.

Discuss

At what age should people be allowed to get married?
Look at the table and discuss this issue with three other students.

Example:
In Denmark men are not allowed to get married until they are 21. That's too old.

Country	Age at which marriage is allowed		Number of marriages per 1,000 population
	Men	Women	
Britain	16	16	7.7
Denmark	21	18	6.3
France	18	15	7.3
Federal Republic of Germany	21	16	6.2
Irish Republic	14	12	6.8
Italy	16	14	6.7
Japan	18	16	9.1
U.S.S.R.	18	18	10.1

Facts in Focus. Central Statistical Office 1980

Study

This is a *delaying expression*. It gives Hilda time to think about her reply. You can also say: 'It's difficult to say.'

Anita is asking Hilda to explain *exactly* what she means. You can also say: 'What exactly do you mean?' or 'Can you explain in more detail?'

Ask each other

A asks a question.
B uses a *delaying expression* then answers briefly.
A asks B to *explain*.
B explains in detail.
Start with these questions and then make up your own:
1. What is the biggest difference between your country and Britain?
2. What are the best and worst things about your job/school?

LANGUAGE STUDY Exercises 3.1 3.2 3.3

LESSON 12

Explaining what you mean and what you understand

> Good evening and welcome to 'What do you think?' again. This week our subject is 'Foreign Languages' and our first guest is Roger Shepherd, lecturer in Education at Thames University. Roger, why are the English so bad at foreign languages?

> I think that there are two main reasons. First of all, English is the most widely used language in different parts of the world. It is estimated that there are over 300 million native speakers of English. And, of course, English is also spoken as a second language by over 250 million people.

ANITA: So, in other words, the English don't need to learn foreign languages.

ROGER: I wouldn't say that. But they need a foreign language a lot less than Finnish speakers do, for example. Secondly, foreign languages are often taught badly in British schools.

ANITA: Is this because of old-fashioned methods?

ROGER: I'm afraid so. The textbooks used are often out of date. Not enough money is spent and not enough time is given to the study of languages.

ANITA: What you're saying is that more time and money should be spent on languages.

ROGER: That's exactly what I think.

ANITA: How interesting! But I'm afraid I must interrupt you there, Roger, and ask . . .

 Ask and answer

Make up questions about the interview with Roger Shepherd.
Ask another student your questions.

  Questions

1. How many people speak English as a first or second language?
2. What two reasons does Roger give for the poor teaching of languages in British schools?
3. Roger says, 'They need a foreign language a lot less than Finnish speakers.' Who are 'they'?
4. It is important for Finnish speakers to learn foreign languages because
   (a) there are over 300 million native speakers of English
   (b) the English do not need to learn foreign languages
   (c) few people outside Finland speak Finnish
   (d) foreign languages are taught badly in British schools

Unit 3

Complete: Agreeing and disagreeing

Put these phrases in the correct column.

Agreeing
1.
2.
3.

Disagreeing
1.
2.
3.

 Tell each other

Tell each other if you agree or disagree with these statements.

1. I think that smoking on buses should be stopped.
2. I think that English is a difficult language.
3. I think that taxes are too high.
4. I think that teachers should be paid more.

Make six more statements and talk about them in the same way.

 Tell each other: Summarising

In the television programme Anita summarises Roger's opinions to show that she has understood.

Use these expressions.

Example:
It only costs £90 for an air ticket to New York. But a ticket to Stockholm costs nearly twice as much. (*cheaper*)

So, in other words, it's cheaper to fly to New York than to Stockholm.

1. It takes me forty-five minutes to go to work by car. There's a lot of traffic and the car park is a long way from the office. By bicycle, on the other hand, I can get there in twenty-five minutes. (*quicker*)
2. Look, you need mathematics all day, every day; at work, shopping, everywhere. But when do you need a foreign language? Only when you go abroad. (*learning . . . more important*)
3. If you want to have a nice holiday, why go abroad? A holiday means trouble; passports, languages, food. Things always go wrong. But when you have a holiday in your own country everything's easy; no problems at all. (*better*)
4. Having your own car is very expensive. I only use my car at weekends. If you rent a car when you need one you save a great deal of money. (*more expensive*)

 Game: Quiz

Ask each other questions. A is the question master. B answers using one of these phrases:

I think . . ./I believe . . .
I'm not really sure. Was it . . .
I don't know. I'll guess. Was it . . . ?

Example:
Charles Dickens was born in
(a) 1712 (b) 1812 (c) 1912   (WHEN)
A: When was Charles Dickens born? 1712? 1812? or 1912?
B: I'm not really sure. Was it 1812?
A: That's right.

1. America was discovered in
   (a) 1776 (b) 1498 (c) 1000 (WHEN)
2. Printing was invented in
   (a) 1454 (b) 1554 (c) 1654 (WHEN)
3. The world's first railway was opened in
   (a) 1825 (b) 1855 (c) 1875 (WHEN)
4. Hiroshima was destroyed by an atom bomb in
   (a) 1944 (b) 1945 (c) 1946 (WHEN)
5. The world's first telephone conversation was held in
   (a) 1937 (b) 1876 (c) 1906 (WHEN)

Answers
1 (b), 2 (a), 3 (a), 4 (b), 5 (b).

Language Study Exercises 3.4   3.15   3.19

LESSON 13

Reacting to behaviour, opinions and advice

ANITA: It probably has. What really happened?
ZED: It was a New York–London flight. About two hours after leaving London, sorry, I mean New York, we got bored.
ZED: We?
ZED: Me and my friends. So we had a party – singing, dancing, you know. It was great. Then someone started throwing food.
ANITA: Was that you?
ZED: Well, airline food doesn't taste very nice. Anyway, after a while one of the passengers complained and the stewardess asked us to stop. That's all . . .
ANITA: Yes, but apparently the stewardess told a newspaper that your behaviour was disgusting.
ZED: I don't know what she means. There's nothing wrong with having a party.
ANITA: I suppose not. But a lot of people think you should behave more normally. Your fans imitate you, don't they?
ZED: That's none of my business. My fans can do what they like. I'm not going to tell them what to do.
ANITA: Actually, I didn't say you should . . .
ZED: Yes, you did.
ANITA: In fact, I said . . .
ZED: Rubbish! You journalists are all the same. I'm going.
ANITA: Well, thanks for talking to us. Goodbye.

 Ask and answer

Make up questions about the interview with Zed Hawks.
Ask another student your questions.

 Questions

1. Anita says, 'I suppose not.' Does Anita completely agree with Zed?
2. Zed says, 'That's none of my business.' What does 'that' refer to?
3. Anita says, 'Actually, I didn't say you should . . .' Can you complete her sentence?

Unit 3

 Complete

Usually people are formal and polite when they discuss or argue. When people are angry or when they know each other very well, they are often informal and less polite.
Find both a formal and informal expression for:
1. Disagreeing 2. Interrupting 3. Agreeing 4. Half-agreeing

Example:

	Function	Formal	Informal
	Disagreeing	I wouldn't say that.	Rubbish!

 Discuss

1. Discuss Zed Hawks' behaviour both on the plane and on the TV programme. Do you think he behaved badly?
2. What do you think of the behaviour in these photographs?

Example:
A: What about the first photograph?
B: I think it's disgusting!
A: Nonsense! There's nothing wrong with enjoying your food.

 Listening *Open Line*

People telephone the Open Line office for help with personal problems. Listen to three phone calls to Open Line. Then listen to the calls again, one by one.

1. Make notes about the problem.
2. Compare your notes with another student.
3. Discuss the problem. What is your opinion?
4. Decide what advice Open Line should give.

 Role Play

A works for Open Line. B has a problem.

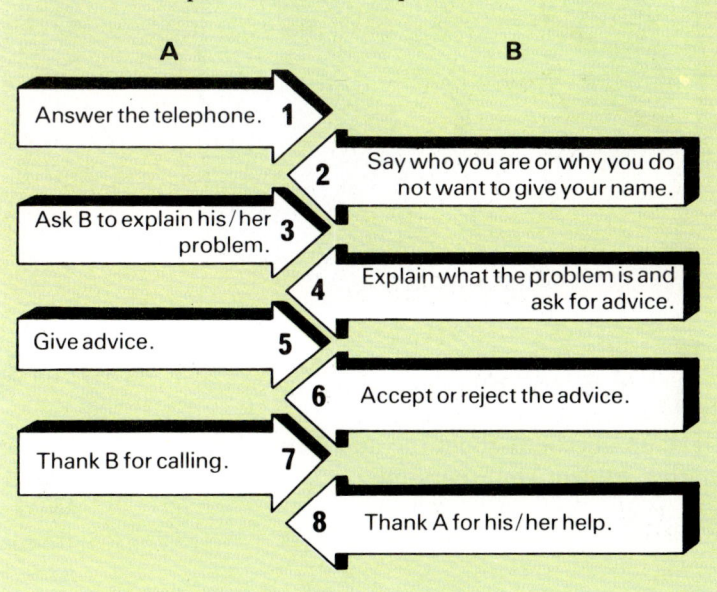

 Study

Giving advice	*Accepting advice*
Why don't you ……………?	That's a good idea!
You ought to ……………	Yes, I think I'll try that.
You should ……………	That's what I'm going to do.
If I were you, I'd ……………	
	Rejecting advice
Perhaps it would be a good idea to ……………	I've already tried that. I'm all right. I don't need ……………

LANGUAGE STUDY Exercises 3.5 3.6 3.7 3.8 3.11 3.12 3.13 3.16 3.17 3.18

LESSON 14

Stating and explaining your opinions

ANITA: Tonight's *What do you think?* is rather different. Everyone has heard about the terrible cyclone in India, in which many people were killed and injured. Well, we're out in the street watching a collection for the cyclone victims. We're asking people if they have given money to the appeal or not.

1 No, I haven't. These people are nothing to do with me. I'm not in favour of charity. The government ought to do something — the government should help. Don't ask me. There's nothing I can do.

3 No, I'm sorry. I haven't. We must remember that charity begins at home. I give money regularly to the local church. We should help our own people first.

5 Yes, I have. The survivors need the money more than we do. That's the main thing. We can do without something in order to help them.

4 I'm sorry. I'd like to help. There's no doubt that they need the money. But we're saving up for our summer holiday. Sorry.

2 Yes, of course I have. It seems to me that you've got to help. These poor people are dying. I mean, you never know, next time it could be us!

ANITA: And finally, could you tell us why you think people should give?
COLLECTOR: We're not saying that money will solve all the problems of those affected by the cyclone; it won't. But what we *are* saying is that people are suffering and dying and we should do all we can to stop it.

 Ask and answer

Make up questions about the interviews. Ask another student your questions.

 Questions

1. How many of the people interviewed gave money to the appeal?
2. Make a list of the different ways in which the cyclone victims are referred to in the interviews.
   Example: '*These people* are nothing to do with me.'
3. 'Next time it could be us.' What does the old lady mean?
4. 'We should do all we can to stop it.' What does 'it' refer to?
   (a) the cyclone (b) people suffering and dying (c) the appeal for the victims (d) money

Unit 3

  Make a list and discuss

Make a list of the arguments for and against giving money to charities like the Cyclone Victims Appeal. Use the opinions from the interviews and add your opinions.

Example: FOR AGAINST

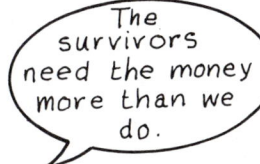

Role Play

A is collecting for a charity.

A
1. Explain what you are collecting for.
3. Try to persuade B.

B
2. Refuse to give money. Explain why.
4. Reply to A's arguments. Explain that you are busy. Suggest that A asks someone else.

It seems to me that....
We must remember that....
There's no doubt that....
I'm not in favour of....

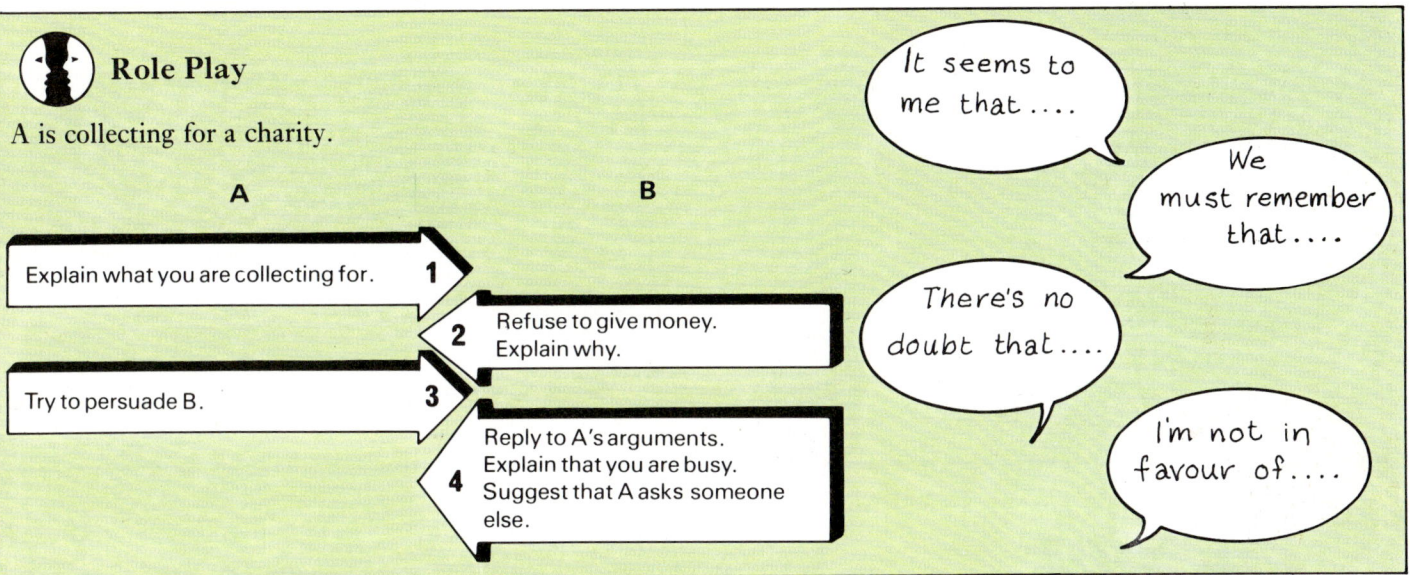

 Survey: Your opinions

Ask five other students their opinions on the statements below and complete the questionnaire.

Example:
Murderers should be executed.
I'm afraid I don't agree.

I quite agree.
I'm not sure.
I think it depends.
I'm afraid I don't agree.

	YES	NO	DON'T KNOW/ NOT SURE
1. Mothers should stay at home with their children and not go out to work.			
2. Old people should be put in special homes.			
3. Murderers should be executed.			
4. Young people today have too much freedom.			

Debate

Choose one of the statements from the Survey for debate.
Make notes on the arguments for and against.
Two students stand up and say why they agree with the statement.
Then two students say why they disagree.
Finally, the whole class votes.

Language Study Exercises 3.9 3.10 3.14 3.20

36

LESSON 15

FOCUS ON WRITING

1. Letters of enquiry

Read the advertisements and reply to two of them.

Opening: Open by stating what you are interested in.
Explanation: Give details of when you are going on holiday, who with (if not alone), and what kind of accommodation you would like.
Conclusion: Conclude by asking for a brochure and for a price list.

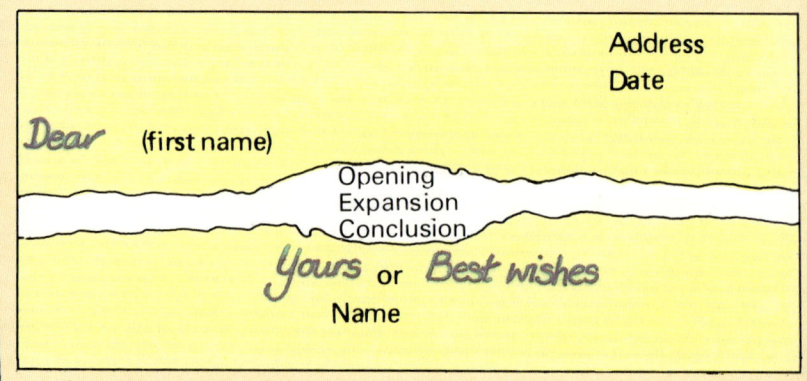

2. Personal letters

Read the list of people who want penfriends.
Choose a penfriend and write a letter describing yourself.

Opening: Open by saying who you are, where you live and how old you are.
Expansion: Give details about yourself: your family, your education and your interests.
Conclusion: Conclude by asking two questions about your penfriend.

The structure of a personal letter

3. Report writing

Write a **Reading Report** on an English book you have read. (See Lesson 10)

Unit 3

FOCUS ON READING

Before reading
Scan the first paragraph of the reading passage and decide if it is a true story or fiction.
Reading purpose
After each part of the story, decide what James England should do. If necessary, look back through the part you have just read to help you decide.

What should James England do?

Part One
James England is a salesman. He works for Fairbrother Engineering, a large company which makes engines for buses. Last year James spent two weeks in Skoll, the capital of Ruritania. He had meetings with government officials and with the state bus company.
During his stay in Skoll, James became friendly with Jan, one of the bus company executives. James spent a weekend with Jan's family.
The day before James left, the state bus company agreed to buy engines from Fairbrother Engineering and a contract was signed. There was a party at James' hotel that evening to celebrate the contract. The party finished in the early hours of the morning. James went to bed. But he didn't get to sleep. A few minutes later, there was a knock on his door. It was Jan. Jan opened a bag and took out a small, brown paper parcel.
Jan said that the parcel contained a book he had written. No one could publish the book in Ruritania because it criticised the Ruritanian government. He wanted James to take the book to a friend in England. The friend would publish the book in London. Jan asked James to put the book in his suitcase. Jan could not post the book.

*What should James do? Call the police? Take the book to England? Take the book and leave it in the hotel? Refuse to take the book?

Part Two
James told Jan he could not take the book. James said he was a guest of the Ruritanian government. He did not want to have any trouble. He told Jan to go. Jan asked James to see if there was anyone in the corridor outside the room. James looked. There was no one there. 'Goodbye Jan', he said. Jan left without saying anything. Then he turned in the corridor. 'Give my regards to your family,' he said.
The next morning at the airport there was a security check. A policeman searched James's briefcase. At the bottom of the briefcase was a small, brown paper parcel. 'It's Jan's parcel,' thought James.

*What should James do? Tell the police about Jan and his book? Say he has never seen the parcel before? Say that the parcel contains souvenirs? What else could he do?

Part Three
The policeman pointed at the parcel. 'It's a present for my mother,' said James. 'All right,' said the policeman. 'Thank you very much.'

As soon as his plane took off, James went to the toilet. He opened the briefcase and took out the brown paper parcel. James slowly opened the parcel. There was a small box inside. No book! James opened the box. There was a white powder inside. James was frightened now. He was sure that he was smuggling something. Something dangerous. But what was it?

*What should James do? Throw the parcel into the toilet? Call the air hostess and show her the parcel? Put the parcel back in the briefcase? What else could he do?

Part Four
James tasted a little of the powder. It tasted slightly sweet. He opened his briefcase and put the parcel away. The British Airways Trident Three landed at Heathrow Airport. The passengers went through passport control and collected their luggage. James England walked towards the customs.

*What should James do? Give the parcel to the customs? Ask to see a policeman? Find a toilet and throw the parcel away? Not say anything?

Part Five
James walked straight through customs and took a taxi home. His wife, Mary, and their two children were waiting. James kissed Mary and told her all about his trip.
James did not notice Mark, his son, open the briefcase. He did not see Mark take out the brown paper parcel and open it. Mark and his sister, Jane, started to eat the powder. They quickly ate all the powder.
Mark was sick on the floor.
James saw what had happened. 'Oh, no!' he said. James took the parcel away from Mark. A small piece of paper fell to the floor. James picked up the paper and read it:

> A present from Skoll. I hope your children like this traditional Ruritanian sweet.
> Jan

James told Mary about Jan and the parcel. Then he added, 'Jan must have had two parcels. He put the present in my briefcase when I was out in the corridor.'

 **COMMUNICATION ACTIVITY**

Do these activities in pairs (A and B). A's instructions are below and B's instructions are at the bottom of the page.

Student A
COVER THE BOTTOM HALF OF THE PAGE. YOU MUST NOT LOOK AT B'S INSTRUCTIONS.

1. **Press Conference**
You are a journalist. A famous person is visiting your town. B is the famous person and will tell you who he/she is. Today there is going to be a press conference. You are going to interview B.
Make a list of the questions you are going to ask.
   Ask whether he/she likes your town.
   Ask why he/she is visiting your town.
   Ask about his/her likes and dislikes (food, people, music, etc.)
   Ask about his/her opinion on important issues in your country now. (Ask several questions.)
   Use language you have learnt in this unit in your questions.

Examples:
Do you think the Government should .... ?
What do you think of .... ?
Could you tell my why .... ?
Ask for more explanation of some of B's answers.

2. **Holiday memories**
You and B used to be friends. Several years ago you went on holiday together. Now you meet again. You start to talk about the holiday. Here is an extract from your holiday diary. Tell B what you remember about the holiday and what you have forgotten.

Begin: Do you remember the holiday we had in London?

> July 10-16
> Holiday in London. Stayed at Hotel R.
> Terrible weather — rained every day.
> On Tuesday went to the theatre to see
> Thursday — wonderful day at the Zoo.
> Friday — last day — dinner at fish
> restaurant called

Afterwards, work with B to write a short account of the holiday.

Student B
COVER THE TOP HALF OF THE PAGE. YOU MUST NOT LOOK AT A'S INSTRUCTIONS.

1. **Press Conference**
Think of a famous person. Choose someone about whom you know a lot. You are going to be the famous person. Tell A who you have chosen to be. A is a journalist and is going to ask you lots of questions.
The journalist will ask you:
   whether you like the town you are visiting
   why you are visiting the town
   what your likes and dislikes are
   your opinion on some important issues in your country now
Think about your answers to these questions. Then ask A whether he/she is ready to start.
Use the language you have learnt in this unit (for example, Lesson 14) in your answers.

2. **Holiday memories**
You and A used to be friends. Several years ago you went on holiday together. Now you meet again by chance. A starts to talk about the holiday. But sometimes A cannot remember things or makes mistakes. Interrupt politely and correct A when necessary. Here is a postcard you sent while on holiday.

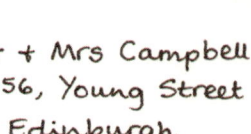

Hotel Royal   15th July
Having a good holiday. It's rained a lot, but yesterday was sunny. We went to the zoo and saw a baby giraffe. Saw the 'Rat Trap' at the Royal Theatre on Tuesday. Tonight going to Spokes Restaurant for a meal.
Love C.

Mr & Mrs Campbell
256, Young Street
Edinburgh

Afterwards, work with A to write a short account of the holiday.

LANGUAGE STUDY

Lessons 11–15

STRUCTURE

3.1 Study

> THE PASSIVE VOICE
> 'be' + PAST PARTICIPLE
>
> The passive tells us more about *what* happens, than about *who* makes it happen.
>
> *Examples:* Women *are not allowed* to drive cars.
> Present simple tense of 'be' + past participle = Present simple passive
>
> Many people *were killed*.
> Past simple tense of 'be' + past participle = Past simple passive
>
> You*'ve been criticised* a lot recently
> Present perfect tense of 'be' + past participle = Present perfect passive

3.2 Make sentences

Example: cotton/grow/Egypt
Cotton is grown in Egypt.

1. coffee/produce/Brazil
2. tobacco/grow/Virginia, USA
3. watches/manufacture/Switzerland
4. Spanish/speak/Chile
5. champagne/make/France
6. curry/eat/India
7. gold/find/South Africa
8. tea/drink/China

3.3 Drill

Example: *You're not allowed to cycle.*
No cycling

1.
   No overtaking

2.
   No stopping

3.
   No left turn

4. NO PARKING

5.
   No smoking

6. DO NOT TOUCH

7. SILENCE NO TALKING

8. DO NOT WALK ON THE GRASS

3.4 Make sentences

Example: 1863 The London Underground opened
The London Underground was opened in 1863.

1826 The first photograph taken
1879 The electric light bulb invented
1885 The motor cycle invented
1928 Penicillin discovered
1945 The atom bomb first used
1953 Mount Everest first climbed
1960 John Kennedy elected President of USA
1968 Martin Luther King killed

3.5 Drill

The police are called to a house that has been burgled. The occupants tell them what has happened.

Examples: They've stolen the television.
The television has been stolen.

They've taken all the records.
All the records have been taken.

1. They've stolen two cameras.
2. They've opened the window.
3. They've taken the radio.
4. They've opened the cupboards.
5. They've emptied the drawers.
6. They've damaged the furniture.

3.6 Ask and answer

Anita Lyons asked her secretary to do several things. Later she asked her secretary questions.

Examples: S1: What about the letters?
S2: *They've been posted.*

S1: What about the paper?
S2: *It hasn't been ordered yet.*

Things to do today

DATE 22 November

Urgent | | Done
☐ 1 Post the letters ✓
☐ 2 Order the paper ☐
☐ 3 Clean the typewriters ✓
☐ 4 Buy the stamps ☐
✓ 5 Send the telegram ✓
✓ 6 Photocopy the report ✓
☐ 7 Water the plants ☐
✓ 8 Book the flight ✓
✓ 9 Take the money to the bank ✓
☐ 10

NOTES

REPORTED REQUESTS AND COMMANDS

 3.7 Put the following requests and commands into indirect speech

Examples: The policeman said, 'Stop!'
He told me to stop.
The stewardess said, 'Please stop.'
She asked me to stop.
The robber said, 'Don't move!'
He told me not to move.

1. The director said, 'Please come in.'
2. The teacher said, 'Sit down!'
3. The lawyer said, 'Don't say anything.'
4. The doctor said, 'You must stay in bed.'
5. The old lady said, 'Would you close the window?'
6. The little boy said, 'Please don't go.'

 3.8 Complete

Example: 'Where shall I go?' 'Home.' She …
She told me where to go.

1. 'What shall I do?' 'Nothing.' He …
2. 'Who should I ask for?' 'Frank.' She …
3. 'What shall I buy?' 'Some food.' She …
4. 'Where can I sleep?' 'On the floor.' He …
5. 'When shall I come?' 'At two o'clock.' 'They …
6. 'How do I get there?' 'By bus.' He …
7. 'Which bus should I take?' 'The number 44.' He …
8. 'Where do I get off?' 'At the cinema.' They …

CRITICISM AND OBLIGATION

 3.9 Drill

Examples: Steve doesn't work hard.
He should work harder. or *He ought to work harder.*
Fred doesn't eat enough.
He should eat more. or *He ought to eat more.*

1. Nurses don't earn enough.
2. Zed doesn't sing well.
3. Sue Matthews doesn't save enough.
4. Anita's secretary doesn't type fast.
5. The government doesn't spend enough money on education.

 3.10 Drill

Example: Steve drives too fast.
He shouldn't drive so fast. or *He oughtn't to drive so fast.*

1. Liz spends too much money.
2. Zed talks too much.
3. Jenny works too hard.
4. Young people get married too early.
5. Steve smokes too much.

3.11 Study

> EXPRESSING AGREEMENT
>
> With positive statements:
>
> *Examples:* That's all been exaggerated.
> *I suppose so.*
> or *It probably has.*
>
> With negative statements:
>
> *Examples:* There's nothing wrong with having a party.
> *I suppose not.*
> or *There probably isn't.*

> ⚠ We use these expressions when we are doubtful, but want to be polite.

VOCABULARY

3.12 Study

Many adjectives are formed from the participles of verbs.

Examples:
boring	bored
disgusting	disgusted
exciting	excited
interesting	interested
surprising	surprised

> ⚠ Zed's *behaviour was disgusting*.
> The *stewardess was disgusted* by Zed's behaviour.
> (a feeling)

3.13 Complete

Put in the most suitable adjective from the list above.

1. Steve is … in football.
2. Fred was … to win the pools – he never expected to.
3. Skiing is a very … sport. I really love it.
4. Liz was very … about moving into a big house.
5. The food was so … I felt sick.
6. Jenny thinks Mexican art is very …
7. I fell asleep because the film was so …
8. Some TV viewers were … by Zed's behaviour.
9. Liz was a little … with life in the country.
10. It's not … that Steve didn't get a scholarship.

WHAT DO YOU SAY?

 3.14 Listen and choose the most suitable response

1. (a) It's difficult to say.
   (b) I'm afraid I don't think.
   (c) No, it's worse.
   (d) I think I'm afraid.
2. (a) What's the matter?
   (b) There's nothing to worry about.
   (c) In other words, you don't believe me.
   (d) I suppose so.
3. (a) Actually, it's in Italy.
   (b) Yes, we had a wonderful time.
   (c) Yes, we're flying next weekend.
   (d) I'm afraid so.

INTONATION AND STRESS

 3.15 Correct the statements

Example: S1: *The Second World War began in 1938.* (39)
S2: *I'm sorry, but did you say 1938? Wasn't it 1939?*

1. The First World War began in 1915. (14)
2. Elvis Presley died in 1980. (78)
3. Man first walked on the moon in 1971. (69)

Unit 3

4. The Battle of Hastings was in 1610. (1066)
5. India became independent in 1944. (47)

3.16 Correct the statements

Example: S1: *You're twenty-eight, aren't you?*
S2: *In fact, I'm thirty-one.* or *Actually, I'm thirty-one.*

1. Edinburgh is in England, isn't it?
2. You're speaking Spanish, aren't you?
3. The Taj Mahal is in Brazil, isn't it?
4. The capital of Portugal is Oporto, isn't it?
5. Dante was French, wasn't he?

3.17 Drill

Example: brown/green
I didn't say it was brown, I said it was green.

1. £15/£50
2. your fault/my fault
3. too expensive/not cheap
4. finished/nearly finished
5. raining/going to rain

3.18 Complete

Example: About two hours after leaving London (New York)
About two hours after leaving London – sorry, I mean, New York.

1. Brussels is the capital of Holland (Belgium)
2. The house is next to the pub (the post office)
3. I spoke to the manager (the director)
4. The train leaves at 2.55 (2.45)
5. Take this to the library (the laboratory)

SENTENCE LINKING

3.19 Ask and answer

Example: The price of oil is increasing.
  (a) There isn't enough oil.
  (b) The dollar is going down.
  (c) O.P.E.C. is very strong.

S1: *Why is the price of oil increasing?*
S2: *I think that there are three main reasons. First of all, because there isn't enough oil. Secondly, because the dollar is going down. And thirdly, because O.P.E.C. is very strong.*

1. House prices are going up.
   (a) More and more people want homes of their own.
   (b) The rate of inflation is high.
2. Hitler lost the Second World War.
   (a) He invaded the Soviet Union.
   (b) The Americans entered the war.
3. People smoke cigarettes.
   (a) They like the taste of tobacco.
   (b) Smoking is a habit.
   (c) It helps them to relax.

3.20 Write a paragraph

If you were prime minister of your country, what changes would you make?
Write a short paragraph about *three* changes you would like to make. *For example:* transport, education and national holidays.

Begin: First of all, I think that ... should ...
Secondly, ...
Thirdly, ...

Unit 4
LESSON 16

Discussing a job: advantages and disadvantages

Steve Wilson was still looking for a job. He went to Workwise, an employment agency, to ask for advice. After completing a form, Steve had an interview with a careers adviser, Mrs Page.

MRS PAGE: We'll find the right job for you, don't worry. Um ... it says here on your form that you want a job with variety and travel ...
STEVE: That's right. Perhaps I could work for a circus!
MRS PAGE: I'm afraid we can't help with that, but have you thought of being a salesman? I think that would suit you.
STEVE: Er ... but I don't know anything about selling ...
MRS PAGE: Well, most companies run training courses for new employees. In fact, English Transport, a local company, are looking for salesmen at the moment.
STEVE: Oh, is it well-paid? I mean, what kind of salary would I get?
MRS PAGE: It depends. As a trainee you would start at around £5,000. But within two or three years you could earn £10,000. Of course you'd have to work hard for that ...
STEVE: I suppose there would be long working hours ...
MRS PAGE: Look, English Transport are having an introductory course for salesmen next week. Why don't you go along? The career prospects are quite good. Salesmen are often promoted after a few years.

 Ask and answer

Make up questions about Steve's interview with Mrs Page. Ask another student your questions.

  Questions

1. Mrs Page says, 'I'm afraid we can't help with that ...' What does she mean?
2. What would Steve have to do to earn £10,000?
3. English Transport
    (a) are having a course at the moment
    (b) used to have courses every week
    (c) are going to have a course next week
    (d) will have a course in a few years

Unit 4

 Ask each other

A	B Example:
If you could choose, what kind of job would you like?	I'd like to be a doctor.
What kind of salary would you get?	The salary is quite low at first. But experienced doctors are very well-paid.
What would the working hours be like?	I'd have to work long hours, sometimes at night and at week-ends.
Would you need special training?	I'd have to study and train for seven years.
What are the career prospects like?	Very good. I'd like to be a heart surgeon.

 Write sentences

Write five sentences about the kind of job you would like.

 Study

Jobs in Britain

JOB	ADVANTAGES	DISADVANTAGES
Salesman	Well-paid. Good career prospects. Travel. Variety.	Long working hours. You have to work very hard to earn a lot of money.
Teacher	Long holidays. A very secure job. Enjoyable.	Not very well-paid. Some extra work in the evenings, preparing lessons.
Car factory worker	Well-paid. A discount on new cars (you can buy them more cheaply).	Tiring and boring work. Shift work. Dirty and noisy working conditions.

 Tell each other

Tell each other about the advantages and disadvantages of the jobs in the table and of the job you would like to have.

  Study and complete

```
WORKWISE QUESTIONNAIRE
Put the following items in        2. What are the most and
order of importance.              least important things for
1. What are the most and          you about a place of work?
least important things            Travelling time           □
about a job for you?              Personality of the boss   □
Security              □           Friendliness of other
Salary                □           people at work            □
Working hours         □           Clean and pleasant
Working conditions    □           place of work             □
Holidays              □           Free lunches              □
Promotion prospects   □           Good sports and social club □
```

 Ask each other

Compare your answers with another student's.
Discuss any differences.
Example:
A: Why did you put travelling time first?
B: Because I don't want to travel a long way to work.

 Discuss

Look at the table of unemployment statistics.
In which countries were the most and the fewest people unemployed?
Which countries had the highest and lowest percentage of unemployed?
If you can, find out what percentage of people are unemployed in your country.
Compare this with the percentages in the table.

UNEMPLOYMENT STATISTICS		
Country	Number of unemployed	Percentage of work force
Austria	69,295	2.4%
Belgium	471,600	11.6%
Germany (F.R.)	1,271,600	5.5%
Italy	1,913,000	8.4%
Japan	1,260,000	2.2%
Sweden	108,000	2.5%
United Kingdom	2,733,900	11.4%
United States	8,273,000	7.6%

I.L.O. Yearbook of Labour Statistics 1982

LANGUAGE STUDY Exercises   4.5   4.6   4.11   4.12   4.20   4.21

LESSON 17

Describing the qualifications and qualities needed for a job
Describing a work process

Steve went to the introductory course for salesmen at English Transport. The first speaker was Alan Pride, the Personnel Manager. Mr Pride spoke for nearly an hour.

Now I've been talking for far too long already...

MR PRIDE: But before I finish, let me . . . um . . . just sum up what I've been trying to say. Remember, you have to like meeting people in order to be a successful salesman. You are selling yourself as well as the product. You've got to be able to get on with all kinds of different people and work all kinds of hours. Being a good salesman is not easy, believe me. It takes a lot of energy and enthusiasm. Now are there any questions?

STEVE: This may sound silly, but . . . how much does a salesman need to know about the product he's selling?

MR PRIDE: That's a very good question. I think you need to know three things: you need to know what the product's best points are, you need to be able to answer basic questions on the product and be able to find out the answers to more technical questions. And it also helps to know how the product is made. In fact, we'll show you a film about our factories later today. Does that answer your question?

STEVE: Yes, thank you.

 Questions

1. Mr Pride is giving a lecture about being a salesman. But he also talks about himself and the way he is organising his lecture. For example, he says, 'Now I've been talking for far too long already . . .' Find other examples of how Mr Pride and Steve refer to the way in which they are talking.
2. Mr Pride says, 'It takes a lot of energy and enthusiasm.' What does 'it' refer to?
3. Steve says, 'This may sound silly, but . . .' Does 'this' refer to what Mr Pride has just said or to what Steve is going to say?

 Ask and answer

Make up questions about Mr Pride's talk. Ask another student your questions.

 Listening

Later in the morning Steve watched a short film about how cars are made at English Transport. Listen to the commentary on the film and put the pictures below in the right order.

a. The body is welded together.
b. The car is tested.
c. The other parts are added.
d. Steel for the body is pressed and cut into shape.
e. The body is sprayed with paint.
f. The body and engine are fitted together.
g. The engines are assembled.

Unit 4

Ask each other

Make a list of the jobs five other students would like. Then ask another student what *qualifications*, *skills* and *personal qualities* are necessary for the jobs.

Example:
A: What would you like to be?
B: A nurse.
A: What qualifications do you need?
B: You need five 'O' levels including English, mathematics and a science subject. Then there's a three year training course.
A: What kind of a person should you be?
B: You've got to have lots of patience.

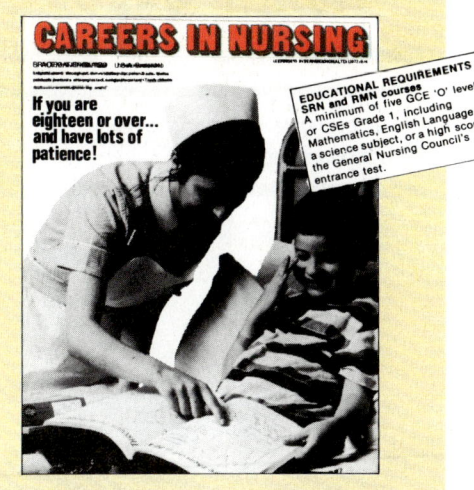

Make a list

Write down the qualifications and skills/personal qualities needed.

Job	Qualifications	Skills/Personal qualities
Nurse	3 year training course. 5 'O' levels including English, mathematics and a science subject.	Patience

Role Play

You are on holiday abroad. You are waiting at the station for a train. You start talking to the person sitting next to you.

*If you have not got a job, talk about the job you would like to have.

1–3 Starting a conversation
A: 1. Say something about the weather.
B: 2. Reply.
A: 3. Ask if B is waiting for the train.

4–6 Giving personal details
B: 4. Reply. Ask where A comes from.
A: 5. Reply. Say what your job* is. Ask what B does for a living.
B: 6. Reply. Say where you work.

7,8 Talking about your job
A: 7. Ask what qualifications are necessary for B's job.
B: 8. Reply. Ask if A enjoys his/her work.

9–11 Ending a conversation and saying goodbye
A: 9. Reply. Tell B that your train is coming.
B: 10. Say goodbye and that you hope to meet A again.
A: 11. Reply.

Project

Cars are an important product in Britain. They are made in factories all over the country.
What are your country's most important products?
Where are they produced?

Language Study Exercises 4.7 4.8 4.9 4.13 4.14 4.22

LESSON 18

Describing a day's work
Comparing pay

After the film Mr Pride introduced Peter Westbrook, an export salesman, for a question and answer session.

MR PRIDE: ... so he really knows what it's like to be a salesman. Now, it's up to you. Ask him whatever you like.

WOMAN: Mr Westbrook, can you tell us what a typical day is like for you?

MR WESTBROOK: A typical day? Yes. First of all, perhaps I ought to say that there is no such thing as a typical day; every day is different. As an export salesman I spend over two thirds of the year travelling abroad. In between trips I work in our Head Office ...

WOMAN: I really meant a typical day when you are abroad.

MR WESTBROOK: I suppose the day is divided roughly into four parts – travelling, waiting, seeing customers and entertaining. Which do you think takes the most time?

STEVE: Seeing customers?

MR WESTBROOK: I'm afraid not. It's getting from place to place that takes the time. I'm lucky if I spend more than three hours a day actually talking to possible buyers. After that comes waiting and then business lunches and so on.

This form shows how Peter Westbrook spends his time when he is at Head Office.

ENGLISH TRANSPORT

WORK ANALYSIS SHEET   Form 125/11/79

NAME: Peter Westbrook
Dept.: Export Sales
Working hours per week: 37½ hours
Times of starting and finishing work: 9 – 5.30
Time of lunch break: 12.45 – 1.45

Estimate the percentage of time you spend each day on the following activities.
Add any further activities which may be necessary.

Making phone calls: 15%
Dictating letters: 20%
Attending meetings: 25%
Seeing visitors: 5%
Writing reports: 15%
Training new staff: 10%
Planning trips abroad: 10%

 Ask and answer

Make up questions about the way Peter Westbrook spends the day. Ask another student your questions.

  Questions

1. Mr Pride says, 'Now, it's up to you.' Who is he talking to?
2. Approximately how many months a year does Mr Westbrook spend at Head Office?
3. What does Mr Westbrook spend *most* time doing when he is abroad? What does he spend *least* time doing?
4. Which of these statements about Mr Westbrook's work at Head Office is true (T) or false (F)?

   He spends more time dictating letters than writing reports.

   He spends least time training new staff.

   He spends as much time making phone calls as planning trips abroad.

   He spends most time attending meetings.

Unit 4

 Ask each other

How do you spend a typical day?
How many hours do you spend:

No. of hours

- Sleeping ☐
- Eating ☐
- Travelling ☐
- At work/school/college etc. ☐
- Cooking and cleaning ☐
- Reading ☐
- Watching TV ☐
- Listening to the radio ☐
- Looking after children ☐
- Talking to family or friends ☐

Add further activities where necessary.

> ⚠ I usually listen to the radio while I'm eating.

 Tell each other and write

Tell each other and write a short paragraph about at least five of the jobs in the table.

Example:
In São Paulo a secretary earns twelve thousand seven hundred dollars a year. She has to pay fourteen point nine per cent tax and social security contributions. She works forty hours a week.

 Questions

1. Find out in which cities secretaries, bus-drivers and primary school teachers have the highest and lowest salaries.
2. Find out in which cities tax and social security contributions are highest and lowest.
3. Find out which cities have the shortest and longest working hours for the different jobs.
4. Find out in which cities:
   (a) bus-drivers earn more than secretaries
   (b) secretaries earn more than teachers
   (c) teachers earn more than bus-drivers
   (d) teachers earn more than secretaries

 Write a paragraph

Write a paragraph comparing earnings and working hours in two of the cities in the table, and, if possible, with a city in your own country.

📖 **Study**

Earnings and Working Hours

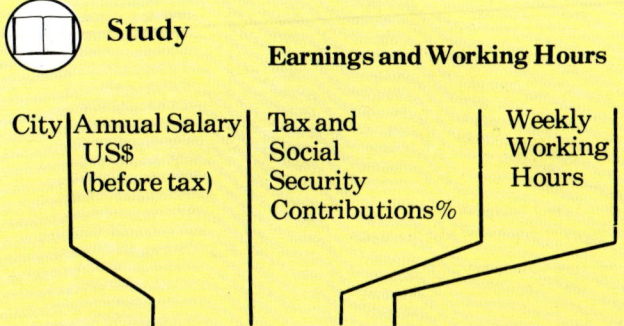

City	Annual Salary US$ (before tax)	Tax and Social Security Contributions %	Weekly Working Hours

1 The secretary of a manager in an industrial company with five years experience (shorthand, typing and one foreign language), about 25, single.

City	Salary	Tax %	Hours
Cairo	2600	26.5	42
Hong Kong	5400	0.7	40
London	10700	30.9	36
New York	17400	29.2	37
São Paulo	13100	18.0	48
Zurich	20800	24.7	43

2 A primary school teacher, with ten years experience, about 35, married, no children. (*Includes preparation.)

City	Salary	Tax %	Hours
Cairo	1000	11.5	30
Hong Kong	10100	0.4	22.5
London	13800	29.4	25
New York	24700	29.1	37*
São Paulo	3300	9.4	28
Zurich	32000	26.9	28

3 A bus-driver with ten years experience, about 35, married, two children.

City	Salary	Tax %	Hours
Cairo	1400	13.5	42
Hong Kong	3400	0	48
London	12700	26.3	39
New York	18700	20.7	40
São Paulo	3700	5.9	48
Zurich	25900	22.6	39

Source: Prices and Earnings Around the Globe
Union Bank of Switzerland. September 1982

LANGUAGE STUDY Exercises 4.1 4.2 4.3 4.16 4.17

LESSON 19

Talking about learning and using foreign languages

STEVE:	Do you need to speak a foreign language in your job?
MR WESTBROOK:	Most definitely. A good salesman ought to speak at least two foreign languages.
STEVE:	But don't a lot of the people you meet speak English?
MR WESTBROOK:	That's true, but of course many don't . . . It's also a question of politeness, of showing your customers that you're interested in them and in their country.
STEVE:	Excuse me asking, but what foreign languages do you speak?
MR WESTBROOK:	Oh, I speak French and German quite well and I've been learning Japanese for the last six months.

 Ask and answer

Make up questions about Steve's questions and Mr Westbrook's answers.

  **Questions**

1. Mr Westbrook says, 'But of course many don't . . .' Can you complete the sentence?
2. How can a salesman show his customers that he is interested in them and in their country?
3. How does Steve show that he is going to ask a personal question?

 Listening

Listen to this interview with an interpreter. Make notes about what her job involves. She has four main duties. What are they?

Unit 4

 **Complete**

Complete the questionnaire for your job or for a job you would like to have.

ENGLISH AT WORK

Your job:

Do you need to use English at work? Tick the activities which you need to carry out in English.
Do you need to:

Act as an interpreter.	
Be entertained when you are abroad.	
Entertain foreign visitors to your country.	
Give lectures or speeches.	
Listen to lectures or speeches.	
Make travel and hotel arrangements, buy tickets, etc.	
Read articles in scientific or technical magazines.	
Read instructions on how to operate machines, etc.	
Read letters or reports.	
Send telegrams or telexes.	
Talk to one person only.	
Take part in meetings of up to five people.	
Take notes at meetings.	
Translate letters or articles.	
Use the telephone.	
Write letters or reports.	
Write operating instructions or sales material.	
Add other activities where necessary:	

 Ask each other

Ask each other about learning English.
  How long have you been studying English?
  How much time do you spend studying English?
  Do you enjoy learning English?
  Why are you studying English?
  Ask about other languages.

 Project

Find some people in your town who use foreign languages at work. Interview them (using the English at Work questionnaire if you wish) and find out when they need to use a foreign language. Make notes and compare your answers with the other students.

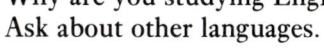
Language Study Exercises 4.4 4.10 4.15 4.18 4.19

 Discuss

What foreign languages are studied at secondary school in your country?
Which are the most popular languages and why?

Example:
Poland: Secondary schools
1st Foreign Language:
  Russian 100% of pupils
2nd Foreign Language:
  German   41% of pupils
  English   28%
  French   21%
  Italian ⎫
  Spanish ⎬ 10%
  Swedish ⎭

How about your country?

50

LESSON 20

FOCUS ON WRITING

Letters of application

1. Complete this application form.

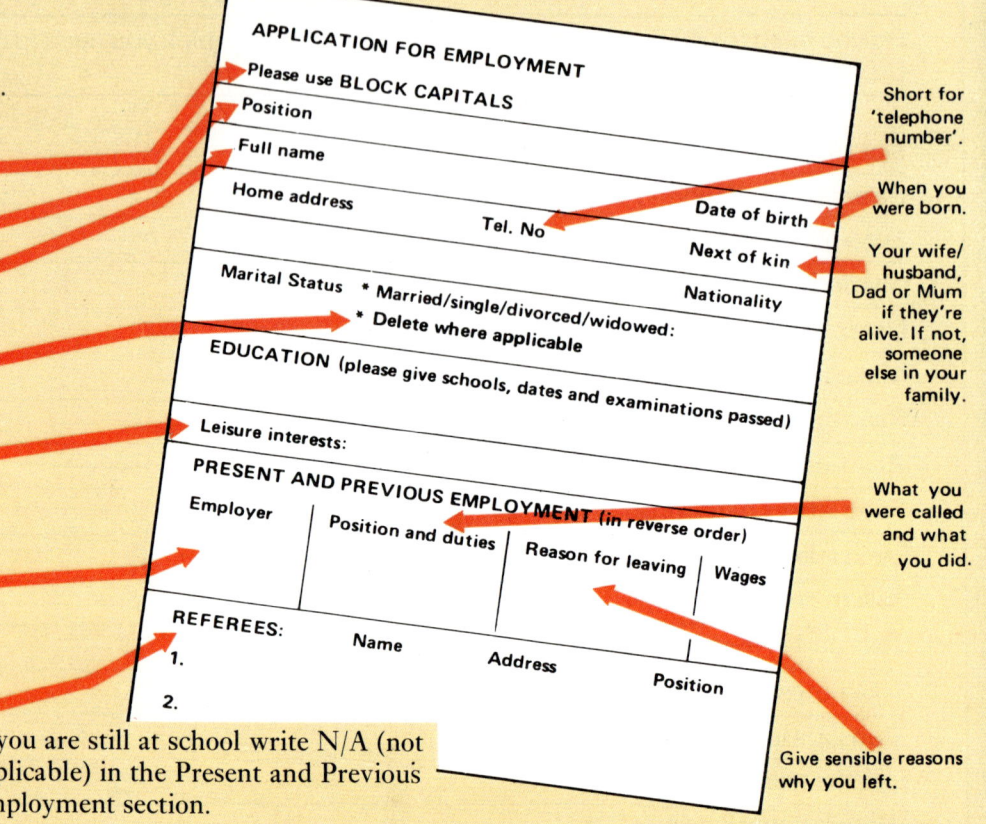

LOOK OUT for this before you start. It means use **capital letters**.

The job you are applying for.

Your first names and last name.

Means cross out the bits that don't apply to you.

Put anything you enjoy doing in your spare time: cooking, reading, swimming.

Start with the job you have now or your last job.

Choose someone who knows and likes you, e.g. teacher, employer, or anyone you have worked for. You can't use family.

Short for 'telephone number'.

When you were born.

Your wife/husband, Dad or Mum if they're alive. If not, someone else in your family.

What you were called and what you did.

Give sensible reasons why you left.

If you are still at school write N/A (not applicable) in the Present and Previous Employment section.

---

2. Reply to these advertisements. Lay out your letter like this:

In the *opening* say that you are interested in the job and would like to apply for it.

In the *expansion* state your qualifications and experience.

In the *conclusion* say you would be pleased to give more information about yourself or come to an interview.

A personal letter: narrative
The last letter from your penfriend asked you how you spent your day. Reply describing your daily routine.

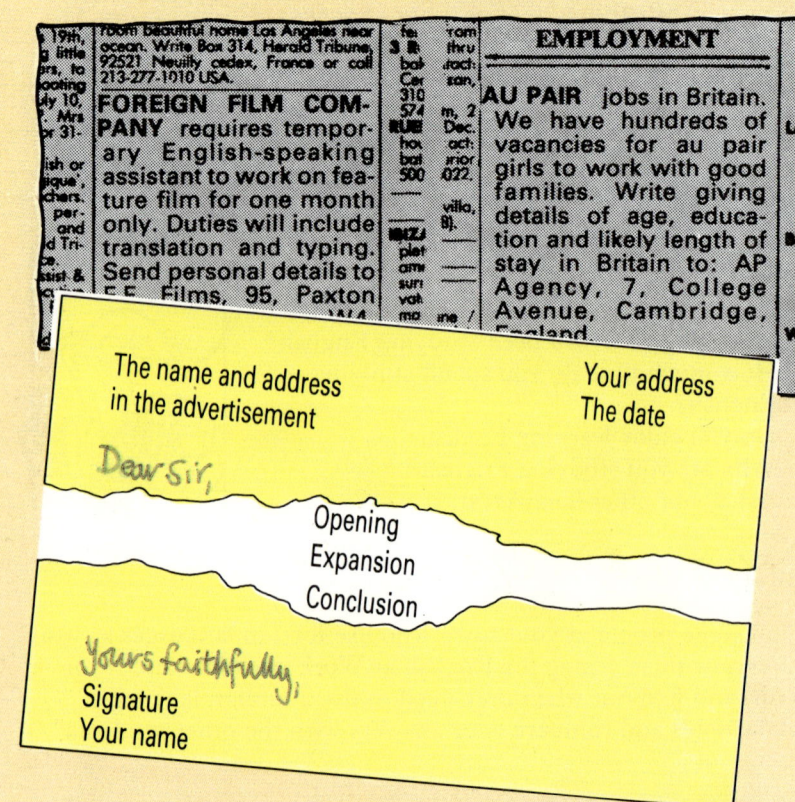

51

Unit 4

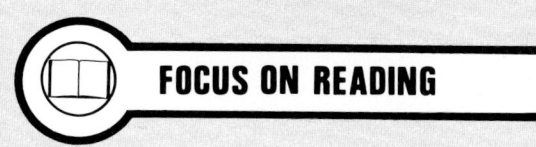

FOCUS ON READING

Before reading look through these two extracts and decide what kind of book or magazine they come from. In the extracts is the writer telling a story, reporting an event, giving advice, or giving invitations?

Reading purpose
Now read these questions and find the answers in the extracts.

For information
1. Should you smoke at an interview?
2. What questions might the interviewer ask you?
3. What should you do if you don't understand an instruction at work?

For deduction
4. Does Bert Green want the young worker to call him Bert or Mr Green?
5. Why does the man on the telephone ask for Bert and not Mr Green?

1.
THE INTERVIEW

- Be prepared to shake hands.
- Don't sit down until you're asked to.
- Don't smoke unless you are offered one.

QUESTIONS YOU MIGHT GET ASKED

What have you done in the past?

What do you know about this company?

Why have you applied for this job?

- Have some good answers ready.
- Be prepared to fill in an application form.
- Try not to answer with just YES or NO Think out the answers before you go.

ASKING QUESTIONS

They sometimes ask if you have any questions.
You could ask things like this:

Is there any training?
What is the pay?
What are the hours?
Is there a canteen?
Is there a union?
Do I have to work Saturdays?

IF you don't get this job don't worry —
- Someone may have been better than you.
- You may not have shown your best side.
- The job may not have been for you.

2.
HERE ARE SOME OF THE THINGS THAT MAY HAPPEN AT WORK:

I told you to pull the lever down when the machine stopped.

I'm sorry, I didn't understand what you said.

What does the boss mean?
ASK if you're not sure what the boss means or you might make an expensive mistake.

Work's different because
- Time is money.
- What you produce is valuable.
- Other people depend on you.
- You'll have to work on your own and be part of a team.

Go and tell Bert he's wanted on the phone.

O.K.

.... Bert, there's a call for you.

Mr Green to you, lad.

How was I supposed to know?

Putting your foot in it.
It's not always obvious what you're expected to do or say. You'll have to find out the hard way. Everyone does!

SO
- Have a sense of humour.
- If you have got a problem ask someone. Don't just walk out.

52

Do these activities in pairs (A and B). A's instructions are below and B's instructions are at the bottom of the page.

Student A
COVER THE BOTTOM HALF OF THE PAGE. YOU MUST NOT LOOK AT B'S INSTRUCTIONS.

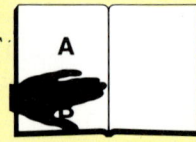

1. The appointment
You are a salesman for the Electronic Watch Company. You want an appointment with Mr Franks. He is the buyer for Great Worldwide Stores and you want to show him a new electronic watch. Telephone Mr Franks' office, say who you are and why you want an appointment. Here is your diary for the next two days.

Wednesday	Thursday
9.45–11 Sales Conference	10–12 Visit to watch factory
11.15 Meeting with Personnel Officer (about 1 hour)	1.00 Circle Club lunch
12.45 Lunch: Express Hotel	3.15 Trade Union meeting (45 minutes)
7.30 Theatre: The Wild Duck	

Remember it takes fifteen minutes to get from your office to Mr Franks' office.
Begin: Hello, is that Mr Franks' office?

2. Making paper
These three pictures show part of the paper making process.
B has three different pictures showing the rest of the process.
1. Describe your pictures to B.
2. Listen to B's description of his/her pictures.
3. *Do not look at each other's pictures.* Work together to find out the correct order for the pictures.
4. Finally, write a short paragraph describing the paper making process with B.

The finished rolls of paper are put on the lorries.

The crushed wood is mixed with water to make pulp.

The logs are crushed.

Student B
COVER THE TOP HALF OF THE PAGE. YOU MUST NOT LOOK AT A'S INSTRUCTIONS.

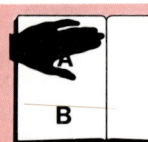

1. The appointment
You are a secretary. You work for Mr Franks, buyer for Great Worldwide Stores. Mr Franks is busy. He is in a meeting and must not be disturbed.
When people telephone for appointments you look at Mr Franks' diary and find a suitable time. You ask the caller to:
spell his/her name
say why he/she wants to see Mr Franks
Mr Franks usually sees each visitor for about 45 minutes.
His office hours are 9.15 a.m.–5.15 p.m.

Mr Franks' diary

Wednesday	Thursday
10.00 Hong Kong Toys Ltd.	9.15 New Kitchens Ltd.
2.00 Clothes International	12.30 Staff Meeting
2.45 High Fashion Ltd.	2.00 Interview candidates for job as trainee buyer (2 hours)
4.00 Fountain Books	

2. Making paper
These three pictures show part of the paper making process.
A has three different pictures showing the rest of the process.

Finally the pulp is pressed between heated rollers.

China clay is added to the pulp.

First, the logs of wood arrive at the factory.

1. Listen to A's description of his/her pictures.
2. Describe your pictures to A.
3. *Do not look at each other's pictures.*
   Work together to find out the correct order for the pictures.
4. Finally, write a short paragraph describing the paper making process with A.

LANGUAGE STUDY

Lessons 16–20

STRUCTURE

4.1 Study

> PRESENT PERFECT CONTINUOUS TENSE
> have been + PRESENT PARTICIPLE
>
> This tense emphasises the *duration* of a past activity up to the present.
>
> *Examples:* Let me sum up what *I've been trying* to say.
> Steve *has been looking* for a job.
>
> This tense is often used to describe a *very recent* activity where the result can be seen.
>
> *Examples:* Oh, look! *It's been snowing.*
> *She's been eating* too much.
> *Someone's been using* my pen.
>
> When 'for' and 'since' are used with the present perfect continuous tense, we understand that the activity continues into the present.
>
> *Example:* Peter's been working with us for over twenty years.
>
> *In other words:* Peter started working with us over twenty years ago and he's still working with us.
>
>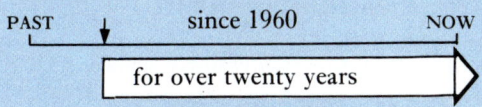

4.2 Find the answers in the second list

Example: Why are the streets wet?
Because it's been raining.

Why are the streets wet? 1
Why has Jenny got oil on her hands? 2
Why does Steve feel sick? 3
Why is Liz crying? 4
Why has Zed got a black eye? 5
Why is Fred worried? 6

Because she's been chopping onions. 4
Because he's been spending too much money. 6
Because it's been raining. 1
Because she's been mending the car. 2
Because he's been eating too many chocolates. 3
Because he's been fighting. 5

4.3 Drill

Example: Jenny started working at the gallery two years ago.
She's been working at the gallery for two years.

1. Jenny started learning Spanish six months ago.
2. Steve started looking for a job three weeks ago.
3. Mr Pride started talking nearly an hour ago.
4. Jenny started going out with her boyfriend a year ago.
5. Fred and Liz started playing golf two years ago.
6. It started raining a few minutes ago.

4.4 Ask and answer

Gloop works for a newspaper called *The Universal News*. He is at present studying English and writing a book about life on earth. Ask and answer questions about him.

Unit 4

1975 Started working for *The Universal News*.
1976 Started travelling through space.
1977 Came to live on this planet.
1978 Started learning English.
1979 Started writing a book about life on earth.
1980 Went to live in New York.

Example: S1: *How long has he been working for* The Universal News?
S2: *Since 1975.* or *For X years.*

4.5 Study

> FUTURE: WILL
>
> 'Will' is often used to show future offers, promises, and decisions.
>
> *Examples:* *I'll post* your letter. (Offer)
> *We'll find* the right job for you, don't worry. (Promise)
> *I won't take* the car, *I'll go* by train. (Decision)

4.6 Drill

Examples: Fred and Liz decided to go to New York.
'*We'll go to New York.*'
Steve promised not to be late.
'*I won't be late.*'

1. The student promised to work hard.
2. The taxi-driver offered to carry the case.
3. Fred and Liz decided to open a bank account.
4. The receptionist offered to call a taxi.
5. Jenny decided to write a letter.
6. Steve promised not to drive fast.
7. Liz decided not to take an umbrella.
8. The police promised to find the car.

4.7 Study

> OBLIGATION and NECESSITY
> MUST, HAVE TO/HAVE GOT TO, NEED TO
>
> *Examples:* You *must* expect things to be different. (*Personal necessity and Obligation*)
> You *have to* like meeting people. (*Obligation*)
> You've *got to* be able to work hard. (*Obligation*)
> You *need to* know three things. (*Necessity*)
>
> ABSENCE OF OBLIGATION and NECESSITY
> DON'T HAVE TO, DON'T NEED TO
>
> *Examples:* I *don't have to* get up early.
> You're saying the English *don't need to* learn foreign languages.
>
> 1. You *mustn't* smoke. = You're not allowed to smoke.
> 2. 'need' can be followed by an object.
> *Example:* You *need* qualifications to be a nurse.

54

4.8 Make sentences

Look at *Are you old enough?* on page 30.

Example: The Law says you can vote at 18.
You must be 18 to be able to vote.

Start your sentences with *you must*, *you have to* or *you've got to*.

Make twelve sentences.

4.9 Make sentences

Fred and Liz intend to spend a lot of money today, but they only have £250. Look at their budget, and decide which items they have to spend money on.

Examples: They have to pay the electricity bill.
They don't have to buy wine.

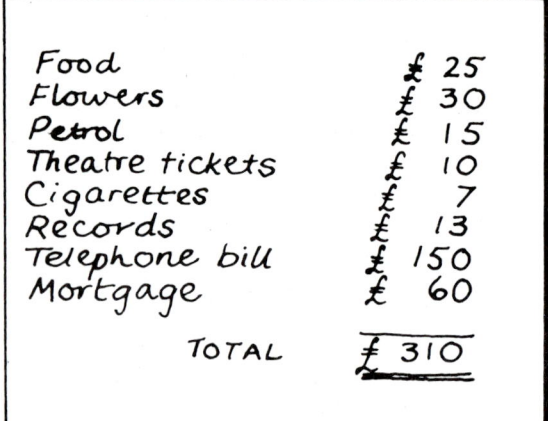

4.10 Make sentences

A friend is going to Jamaica for a summer holiday. She's made a list of things to pack, but she can't shut her suitcase. Tell her which items she needs to take.

Examples: You need to take your passport.
You don't need to take your skis.

```
THINGS TO TAKE
passport
skis
swimming costume
sunglasses
fur coat
summer clothes
3 raincoats
gloves
sun-tan oil
Greek phrase book
```

4.11 Study

> **CONDITIONAL WITHOUT 'IF'**
>
> *Examples:* What kind of salary would I get? (if I were a salesman)
> You would start at around £5,000. (if you were a salesman)
>
> These sentences are part of a conversation. The speakers don't need to add the 'if' clause.

4.12 Ask questions

Mr X has been offered a job as a spy. He isn't sure whether he wants the job, so he asks questions. The answers he receives are below. What questions has Mr X asked?

Example: Where would I have to go?

You'd have to go to Amsterdam. (Where)
You'd travel by plane. (How)
You'd meet Miss Y. (Who)
You'd have to deliver a letter. (What)
You'd stay in a hotel. (Where)
It would take about three days. (How long)
You'd earn £1,500. (How much)

4.13 Study

> **GERUND ('-ing' form)**
>
> The gerund can come at the beginning of a sentence and act as a noun or as part of a noun phrase.
>
> *Examples:* **Swimming** is good for you.
> **Being** a good salesman is not easy.
>
> ⚠ See **LS 1.11** for uses of the gerund after verbs and prepositions.

4.14 Drill

Example: It's useful to speak a foreign language.
Speaking a foreign language is useful.

1. It's convenient to be able to drive.
2. It's not cheap to eat in restaurants.
3. It's interesting to watch children grow up.
4. It's not easy to get up in the morning.
5. It's important to find the right job.

4.15 Complete

Example: Mrs Page is good at … people find jobs. (help)
Mrs Page is good at helping people find jobs.

1. Steve is interested in … a salesman. (be)
2. It's a question of … the right job. (find)
3. There's no point in … about tomorrow. (worry)
4. Have you thought of … to the doctor? (go)
5. There's nothing wrong with … television. (watch)

VOCABULARY

JOBS AND OCCUPATIONS

4.16 Complete

Steve is having great difficulty in deciding what he wants to do.

1. He doesn't play any instrument well enough to be a …
2. His voice isn't very good, so he can't be a …
3. He isn't good enough at maths to be an …
4. He gave up his job because he doesn't want to be a …
5. He'd have to study law to be a …
6. He doesn't like flying, so he can't be a …
7. He doesn't want to join the army, so he can't be a …
8. He'd have to go to dental school to be a …
9. He can't paint or draw well enough to be an …
10. He's decided he doesn't want to be a car …
11. He'd have to study medicine to be a …

*Look at the word down the centre. What does Steve finally decide to be?

Unit 4

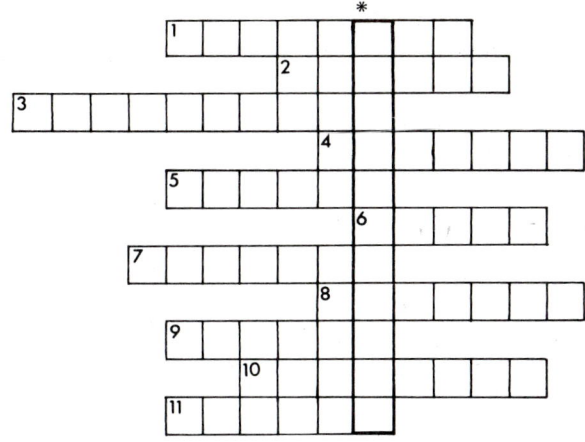

WHAT DO YOU SAY?

 4.17 Listen and choose the most suitable response

1. (a) Fifteen minutes ago.
   (b) Since half-past seven.
   (c) I'm here for a quarter of an hour.
   (d) I'm waiting for a friend.
2. (a) There's a café round the corner.
   (b) Thank you, I'd love some.
   (c) What did you get?
   (d) What did you forget?
3. (a) I catch the 7.54 train.
   (b) I've been travelling to the city every day for fifteen years.
   (c) The return fare is £2.47.
   (d) About an hour and a half.

INTONATION AND STRESS

 4.18 Give polite explanations

Example: You are waiting for the director. The receptionist asks you what you want. What do you say?
I was waiting for the director.

1. You are staying with a friend. You are looking for the milk in the refrigerator when your friend comes into the kitchen. What do you say?
2. You are having dinner when a friend arrives at the door. What do you say?
3. You've just started working in a big office block. You are looking for the lift when someone asks if he can help you. What do you say?
4. You are in a library trying to find a book about the car industry. The librarian asks if she can help you. What do you say?

4.19 Ask personal questions politely

Example: What foreign languages do you speak?
Excuse me asking, but what foreign languages do you speak?

1. What's your name?
2. Where do you come from?
3. What do you do?
4. Where do you live?
5. How old are you?

SENTENCE LINKING

4.20 Study

> RELATIVE CLAUSES
>
> Relative clauses tell us more about nouns or pronouns
>
> *Examples:* I've got all the information *I need*.
> Everything *they had* was bigger, better, and more expensive than before.
>
> These relative clauses define *which* information and *which* things.

 4.21 Join the sentences

Example: Jenny got the scholarship. She wanted it.
Jenny got the scholarship she wanted.

1. The stewardess dropped the glass. She was carrying it.
2. He's the man. I saw him on television.
3. People often say things. They don't mean them.
4. I enjoyed the book. You recommended it.
5. Fred and Liz lost all the money. They won it.

Example: The job was well-paid. Steve applied for it.
The job Steve applied for was well-paid.

1. The dress was expensive. Liz bought it.
2. The restaurant was full. We wanted to go to it.
3. The medicine was disgusting. I had to take it.
4. The house had eight bedrooms. Liz liked it.
5. The food was cold. The waiter brought it.

4.22 Write a paragraph

Look at the pictures and describe what happens when a letter is posted.
Use *first, next, then, after that, finally*

Begin: First the letter is collected from the post-box …

1.
Collected from post-box

2.
Taken to sorting office and sorted

3.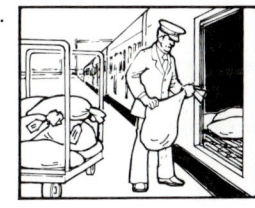
Put on train

4.
Taken to another post office

5.
Sorted again

6.
Delivered by postman

56

Unit 5
Lesson 21

Reporting public events

Sandra Mackenzie is a young journalist on the *Plymouth Evening Mail*. Her first job every morning is to make a summary of the most important news. Tom Franklin is the news editor.

Right, Sandra, what are the main stories today?

SANDRA: Well, there's been a big bank robbery in Birmingham. I telephoned the police there a few minutes ago. They said that it was one of the biggest robberies ever. I asked how much money had been stolen but they weren't sure.

TOM: Mm... which bank was it?

SANDRA: The General, in the city centre. The police said that the robbery had taken place some time during the night.

TOM: We'd better ring them again for more details in a minute. What else is there? It said on the radio that there had been a plane crash.

SANDRA: That's right. At a place called Paramaribo...

TOM: That's in Paraguay, isn't it?

SANDRA: Actually, it's in Surinam. The crash happened at about nine o'clock our time yesterday evening. There were 135 people on board. Apparently there were no survivors...

TOM: That's terrible. Any local news?

SANDRA: A fire at the primary school in Callington early this morning. One classroom was damaged.

TOM: O.K. Anything else?

SANDRA: Yes, a Plymouth woman had triplets last night in the City Hospital. The hospital said that they were all girls and that the mother was doing fine.

TOM: That'll make a good story. But we'd better start with the bank robbery.

 Ask and answer

Make up questions about Sandra and Tom's conversation. Ask another student your questions.

 Complete

Write down details of the news stories discussed by Sandra and Tom.

WHAT HAPPENED	WHEN	WHERE	COMMENT
Example: 1. A bank robbery	During the night	General Bank Birmingham	One of the biggest robberies ever
2.			
3.			
4.			

 Listening: The News

Listen to the radio news broadcast carefully and make notes. Then write down details of the four main news stories as in **Complete** above.

 English for the classroom: Revision

Ask your teacher how to spell difficult words in the radio news broadcast.
How do you spell ...., please?

Unit 5

 Tell each other

Use your notes to tell another student about:
1. The news stories discussed by Tom and Sandra.
2. The radio news broadcast.

 Ask each other

What are the main news stories today?
Have you read a newspaper today?
Have you listened to the news today?

Study

Direct speech	Indirect speech
 It's one of the biggest robberies ever.	The police said that it was one of the biggest robberies ever.
 They're all girls and the mother is doing fine.	The hospital said that they were all girls and that the mother was doing fine.
 How much money has been stolen?	I asked how much money had been stolen.
 Do you know when it happened?	I asked if he knew when it had happened.
 The robbery took place some time during the night.	The police said that the robbery had taken place some time during the night.

 Press Conference

Turn back to Press Conference in the **Communication Activity** section of **Lesson 15**.

Work in groups of three (A, B and C).
A is the journalist who asks the questions.
B is the famous person who answers the questions.
C is another journalist who writes the answers.
You then all work together to write a report on the press conference.

Example: *Interview*
A: Why are you visiting our town?
B: I'm having a holiday.
Report
A asked why B was visiting our town.
B said that he was having a holiday.

Language Study Exercises   5.1   5.2   5.3   5.4   5.5   5.6   5.7

LESSON 22

Reporting a sequence of events

Sandra telephoned the Birmingham police again and got more details of the robbery.

14 August 84

I know what — we'll have a series of drawings showing how the robbery was carried out. Have you got the details?

HOW THEY ROBBED THE BIRMINGHAM BANK

1 A few days before

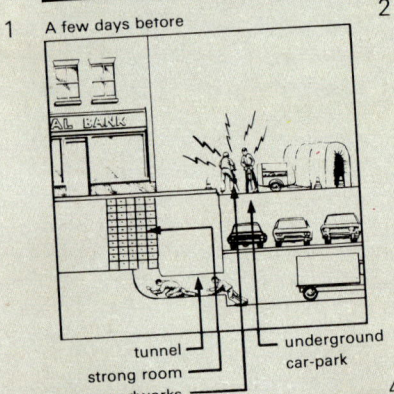

tunnel — underground car-park — strong room — roadworks

2 7 a.m.–Midnight

deposit boxes

3 During the night

£5,000,000
Police now believe that the armed gang who tunnelled their way into the General Bank in Birmingham yesterday got away with over £5,000,000. The total sum may be higher as not all deposit box holders have been contacted yet.

4 5 a.m.

Daring
Bank staff had no suspicions while the tunnel was under construction. A police spokesman thought that the noise had been masked by nearby road works.

SANDRA: Hang on a minute ... yes ... here we are. The robbers got into the bank through a tunnel from an underground car park. The police thought the tunnel had been dug a few days before ...
TOM: And no one heard anything?
SANDRA: No, there were road works outside the bank while they were digging the tunnel.
TOM: I see, go on.
SANDRA: Some time last night, after the bank had closed, the thieves cut a hole in the strong-room floor.
TOM: Do we know exactly when?
SANDRA: Not earlier than seven o'clock and not later than midnight. As soon as they were inside the strong-room, the gang started to open the deposit boxes. At the same time a lorry was driven into the underground car park. Then the gang carried the money through the tunnel to the lorry.
TOM: Mm ... and when was the robbery discovered?
SANDRA: At about 5 a.m. A security guard in the car park found the tunnel ...
TOM: What ... while the gang were still in the bank?
SANDRA: No, after they had left – with five million pounds!

 **Ask and answer**

Make up questions about the bank robbery. Ask another student your questions.

 Questions

1. 'The police thought the tunnel had been dug a few days before ...' Complete Sandra's sentence.
2. Why didn't anyone hear the tunnel being dug?
3. What two things happened when the thieves got into the strong-room?
4. The thieves broke into the strong-room
   (a) before midnight
   (b) after midnight
   (c) before 7 p.m.
   (d) at about 5 a.m.

Unit 5

 Role Play: Talking about a sequence of events

A and B are friends discussing the news of the Birmingham Bank Robbery.

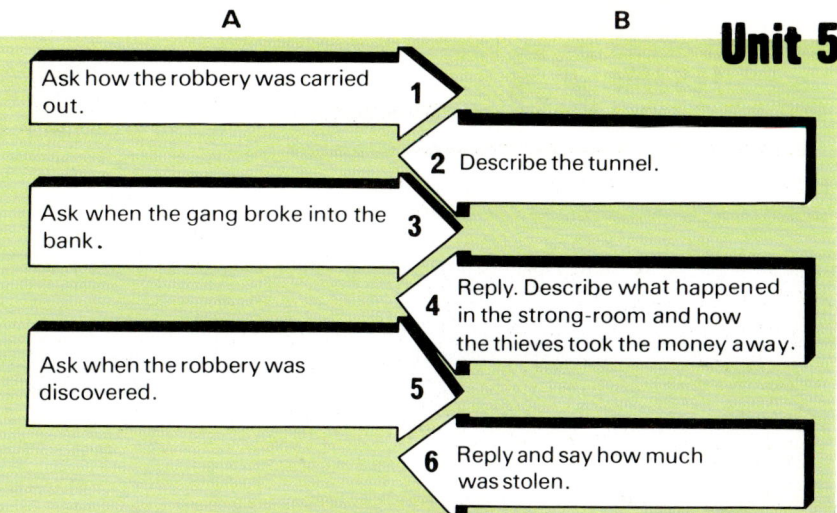

1. A: Ask how the robbery was carried out.
2. B: Describe the tunnel.
3. A: Ask when the gang broke into the bank.
4. B: Reply. Describe what happened in the strong-room and how the thieves took the money away.
5. A: Ask when the robbery was discovered.
6. B: Reply and say how much was stolen.

 Study and put in order

The sentences beside each picture describe what happened.
But the sentences are mixed up.
Put the sentences in the right order.

1.
- A. 5 Soon a crowd of people gathered and someone telephoned the fire brigade.
- B. 3 Then I noticed an open window. I tried to climb up a pipe to the window.
- C. 6 By this time I felt very cold and foolish. I wished the crowd would go away.
- D. 1 Last week I lost my front-door key and couldn't get into the house.
- E. 7 Finally, a fire engine came and I climbed down the ladder. The firemen helped me open the front door.
- F. 2 I rang the bell for a long time but there was no one at home.
- G. 4 But half-way up the pipe I got stuck. I couldn't go up or down. I shouted for help. I was too frightened to move.

2.
- A. 5 It was over twelve hours before the water went down.
- B. 2 Last night they had nearly ten centimetres of rain.
- C. 6 Then the police let everyone go back to their homes.
- D. 1 Have you heard about the floods in Colchester?
- E. 4 The police had to save some people who were trapped by the water.
- F. 3 Early this morning the river bank broke and the town was flooded.

 Study

Notice the use of these words and phrases in the stories above.
They tell us the order of events:
last week, last night, early this morning, before, soon, by this time, then, finally

 Tell each other

1. Tell another student about an important event you watched or took part in. Say what happened, when and where.
Begin: Let me tell you about . . .

2. Tell another student about:
The most exciting thing that has ever happened to you.
The most frightening thing that has ever happened to you.

Language Study Exercises   5.11   5.12   5.13   5.14   5.21   5.22

60

LESSON 23

Discussing possible explanations

Inspector Alex Crawford was the Press Liaison Officer at Birmingham Police Headquarters. Inspector Crawford's job was to give information to journalists.

1. Crawford speaking.

2. This is Sandra Mackenzie of the Plymouth Evening Mail again, Inspector. How is the investigation going?

3. Slowly, I'm afraid. We're still searching the bank and tunnel.

SANDRA: Do you know how many men took part in the robbery yet?
INSPECTOR: We're sure that there were at least six, maybe more. And it looks as if they were local men.
SANDRA: Really! Why do you think that?
INSPECTOR: It's quite simple. You see, a lot of the equipment used in the robbery was bought in local shops.
SANDRA: And are the robbers still in the Birmingham area?
INSPECTOR: It's difficult to say. They probably are, but we're not certain.
SANDRA: Do you think the gang may be part of an international group?
INSPECTOR: No. Definitely not. We're certain that no international group was involved.
SANDRA: Thank you, Inspector. And finally, how did the gang know there was so much money in the bank?
INSPECTOR: They . . . um . . . they may have had information . . . someone may have told them . . .
SANDRA: Someone working in the bank?
INSPECTOR: Perhaps . . . we just don't know.
SANDRA: Thank you very much indeed, Inspector.

 Ask and answer

Make up questions about the telephone conversation between Sandra Mackenzie and Inspector Crawford. Ask another student your questions.

 Questions

1. Inspector Crawford
   (a) was certain (b) thought (c) saw (d) hoped
   that there were at least six men in the gang.
2. Why do the police think the robbers are probably from the Birmingham area?
3. Find an expression meaning 'That's easy to explain,' and another one meaning 'It's not easy to give a simple answer.'
4. Crawford says, 'Someone may have told them . . .' Can you complete his sentence?

Unit 5

  Study and complete

Find these expressions in the telephone conversation. Then write down the Inspector's answers under the correct heading.

CERTAINTY	PROBABILITY	POSSIBILITY
We're sure that... We're certain that... *Example:* No international group was involved.	It looks as if... They probably are...	Perhaps Maybe...

 What is it?

What are the objects in the photographs?
Example:
A: What do you think it is?
B: I'm not sure. Perhaps it's a bridge.
A: I think it's probably a fork.

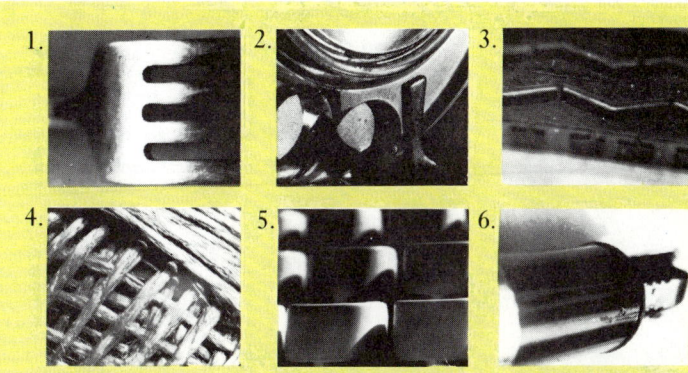

  Ask each other and write

Look at the illustrations. Ask each other what has happened and suggest an explanation. There are several possible explanations. Then write a short paragraph about two of the illustrations, saying what you think may have happened, and why.

Example:
A: What's happened?
B: I'm not sure. I think he's lost his keys.
A: It looks as if he can't get into his car.
B: Yes. Perhaps the keys are inside the car.
A: Or he may have dropped them somewhere.

1.
2.
3.  No one at home.
4.

 Discuss: The Mary Celeste

On November 5th 1872, the Mary Celeste, a 282 ton sailing ship, left New York on a voyage to Genoa. The ship's captain, Benjamin Briggs, took his wife and two-year-old daughter with him. There were eight men in the ship's crew.
One month later on December 5th, the Mary Celeste was found by another ship, the Dei Gratia, off the coast of Portugal. The Mary Celeste was sailing along but there was no one on board. Everything was in its place on the ship. There was plenty of food and water. All the crew's clothes were still on the ship. But the lifeboat was missing.
What do you think happened to the crew?
* The crew may have left the ship in a storm. But why did they leave their clothes behind?
* The crew may have jumped into the sea.
* The crew may have killed the captain and escaped in the lifeboat.
* Perhaps a sea-monster ate the crew?
* Perhaps the ship was attacked by men from outer space?
What do *you* think?

Language Study Exercises 5.15 5.17 5.18 5.20

LESSON 24

Discussing future possibilities

Two weeks after the robbery the Birmingham police arrested six men. At the trial, four months later, Albert Marconi was described as the leader of the gang. He was sentenced to twenty-two years in prison.

PLYMOUTH EVENING MAIL

BANK ROBBER ESCAPES

Albert Marconi, leader of the Birmingham bank robbers, escaped from the police after the end of his trial yesterday. Marconi jumped out of a courtroom window, after attacking two policemen.

WHERE IS HE NOW?

At a press conference this morning a police spokesman said, 'Marconi could be anywhere. He may still be in Britain, but it's very likely that he's now abroad.' The spokesman said that the police would watch all ports and airports carefully.

Top dog judges face

THIS IS HOW IT HAPPENED

Weather

Yesterday's weather report: Max. temp. 7°C. Min. temp. −2°C.
Rainfall: nil. Sunshine: 3 hours. Night frost. Wind: Light SW.

Today's weather report:

A DIAMOND almost as big as the Ritz, the largest uncut diamond in the world, goes on show at the Museum of Natural History in Washington tomorrow. It is 890 c...

 Ask and answer

Make up questions about Albert Marconi's escape. Ask another student your questions.

  Complete

1. Write a short account of Albert Marconi's escape.
   Begin: After attacking two policemen, Marconi jumped.........
2. The police spokesman made three statements about Marconi. Two were possible and one was probable. Put the statements under these headings:

   PROBABLE   POSSIBLE

Unit 5

 Listening

Look back at the report on yesterday's weather in the *Plymouth Evening Mail*.
Fill in the details in the table.
Now listen to the weather forecast on the radio for the same day and make notes in the table in the same way.

Weather	What actually happened yesterday	What the radio forecast said
Sunny/cloudy?		
Rain?		
Maximum temperature? Minimum temperature?		
Wind speed and direction?		
Fog?		
Frost?		
Snow?		
Thunder and lightning?		

 Tell each other

1. Compare yesterday's weather with what the radio forecast said. Use your notes. Talk about any differences and similarities.

Examples:
It said on the radio that there would be some rain but there wasn't any.
It said on the radio that there would be night frost and there *was*.

2. What is the weather like today? What did the weather forecast say it would be like?

 Discuss: Your opinion

What do you think will happen?
How sure are you?
1. *The weather* What will the weather be like tomorrow and at the weekend?
2. *Inflation* Will prices keep on going up and up?
3. *Oil* What will the world do when there is no oil left? What will happen to all the cars?
4. *Sport* Who do you think will win the football/tennis championships in your country?
5. *Your personal future in a year's time* Do you think you'll still have the same job? Do you think you'll still live in the same place?

   Example:
   Your personal future It depends. I may get a job abroad. But I'll probably still live here.

 Ask each other

Ask and answer questions about events in the future. Ask about:
Examinations Do you think you'll pass?
Birthdays What presents do you think you'll get?
Holidays Where do you think you'll go for a holiday next year?
Other events?

Language Study Exercises   5.8   5.9   5.10   5.16   5.19

LESSON 25

FOCUS ON WRITING

1. A simple narrative
Look at the picture story and write a short report of what happened.
Begin: Last Sunday at 10 p.m., Sally Pond was watching ....

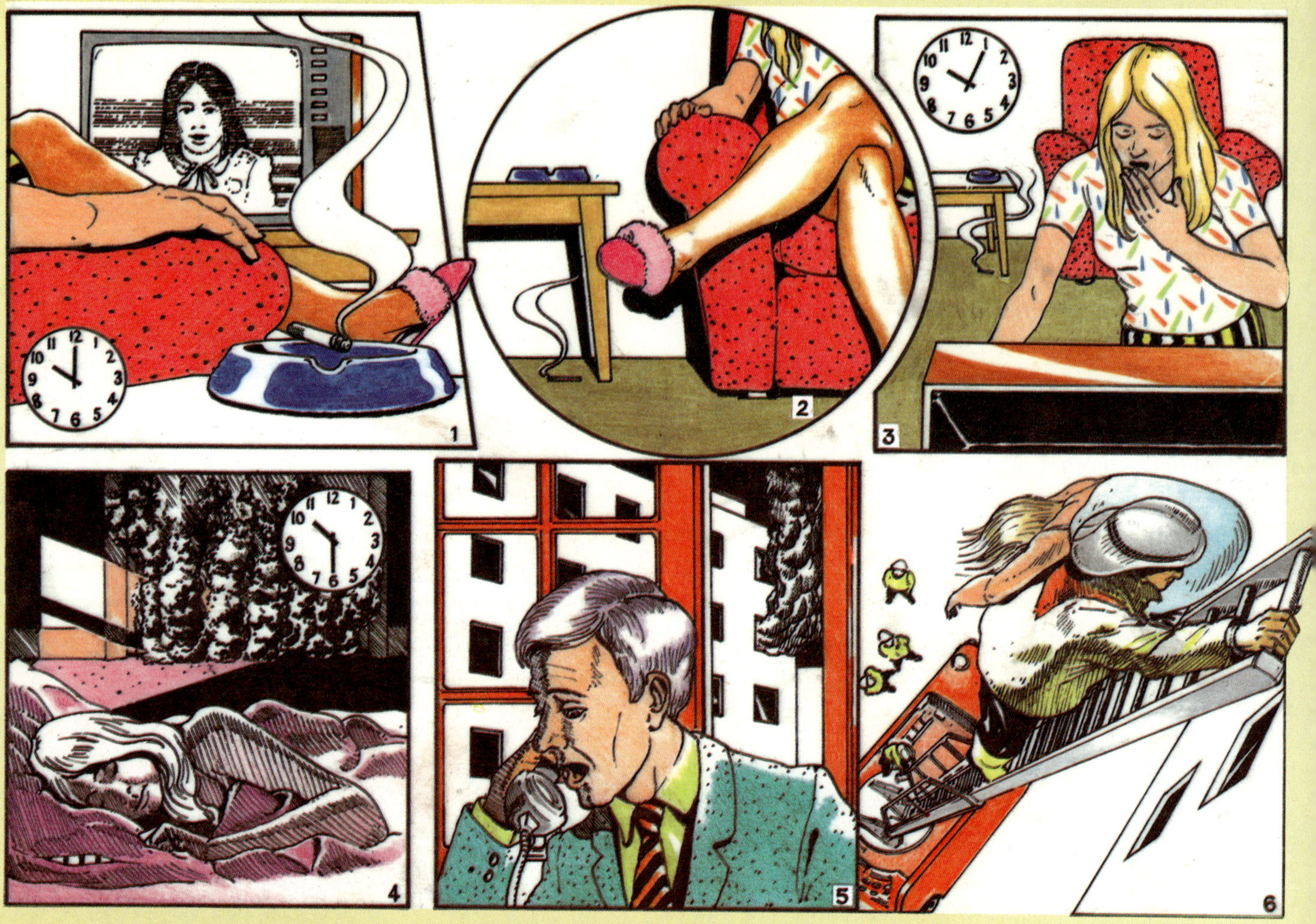

2. A personal narrative
Write a short report of something which happened to you: an accident you were involved in, a journey you made, a holiday you had, or a family event like a wedding or birth.

3. Personal letters: the future
Your penfriend writes:

Reply to the letter, thanking your friend for the description of the family party, and then describing your plans for next summer (perhaps I'll ...., or I may ...., ... it depends ....).

> Thank you very much for your last letter. It was very interesting to read about how you spend your day.
> Can you tell me about your plans for the future? What do you think you will do next summer? Will you be able to come and see me? Or do you have other plans?
> Now I'm going to tell you all about a family party we had last week

Unit 5

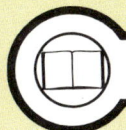

FOCUS ON READING

Before reading
Scan the first half of the reading passage, and decide whether it is a news report, a detective story, or a questionnaire.

Reading purpose
To decide who the murderer is. You should consider all the information you are given very carefully, and think like a policeman.

Arthur Evans
Age: 36 Driver

Mary Watson
Age: 29 Secretary

Jim Hare
Age: 35 Businessman

FIND THE MURDERER

Sir Frank Richards, a wealthy businessman, has been murdered. He was found dead in bed at eight o'clock this morning. Arthur Evans, his driver, found Sir Frank with a knife in his chest. The police were called, and Inspector Crawford arrived at ten o'clock. He interviewed the people who were in the house on the night of the murder. Here are his notes.

> Evans Says he spent the evening in the village pub. Returned to Sir Frank's house at eleven and went to bed. He knows *how* Sir Frank was killed. Watson and Hare don't know about the knife. Evans needs money to buy a house. A week ago he asked Sir Frank for higher wages.
>
> Watson Says she spent the evening working in her room. Went to bed early and was woken at midnight by the noise of an argument. Two men were shouting – one of the men was Arthur Evans. She's a very pretty woman – was there something between her and Sir Frank?
>
> Hare Says he spent the evening watching TV. Saw a film called The Wild Country. He didn't hear an argument. Hare wanted to leave Sir Frank and start his own business.
>
> Important: All three say Sir Frank went to bed at 8 p.m.

Discuss: Who do you think the murderer is? Why?

Inspector Crawford questioned the three suspects again. He asked them who the murderer was.

EVANS: I think it was Jim Hare. He used to argue with Sir Frank about business. And I'm fairly sure that Jim and Mary are in love.

WATSON: I think it was Arthur. I heard him arguing with Sir Frank. Arthur wanted higher wages, but Sir Frank refused. Have a look at the knife – are Arthur's fingerprints on it?

HARE: I'm sorry, but I've no idea who the murderer is. Perhaps it was someone from outside the house.

Inspector Crawford found out the following facts:

> 1. No fingerprints on knife.
> 2. Wild Country *not* shown on TV – cancelled because of football match.
> 3. 2 robberies at houses near Sir Frank's on night of murder.

Discuss: Who do you think the murderer is now?
Has each suspect got a motive (reason)?
Who has the strongest motive?

Inspector Crawford asked to see the three suspects together.

INSPECTOR: Mr Evans, I'm going to arrest you. I know what you did last night. You see, we found your fingerprints . . .

WATSON: I told you so, Inspector, I said he was the murderer . . .

EVANS: I didn't kill Sir Frank.

INSPECTOR: No, I don't think you did. I'm arresting you for two robberies last night. Your fingerprints were found in two houses near here and the stolen property is hidden in your room. Now, Miss Watson . . .

WATSON: Yes, Inspector.

INSPECTOR: Thank you for telling me to look at the knife. That was very helpful. It told me who the murderer was – you! Only Mr Evans and I knew that Sir Frank had been killed with a knife.

WATSON: All right, Inspector. I'm the murderer. But it wasn't my fault. I went to Sir Frank's room with some letters for him to sign. He . . . he . . . tried to kiss me . . . I pushed him away . . . then he hit me. I don't remember exactly . . . somehow I picked up the knife and . . .

HARE: Ah . . . Inspector. There's something I must tell you. Mary and I love each other. She is trying to protect me. I killed Sir Frank. We had an argument about business. After I killed him, I cleaned the knife. Then I went to see Mary. I told her what had happened. She's not the murderer, I am. Arrest me.

Discuss: Who did Inspector Crawford arrest for the murder?

66

Do these activities in pairs (A and B). A's instructions are below and B's instructions are at the bottom of the page.

Student A
COVER THE BOTTOM HALF OF THE PAGE. YOU MUST NOT LOOK AT B'S INSTRUCTIONS.

1. **The meeting**

> I'll meet you outside the station at 11.30. If I'm late can you ring 636162 that's my office number. If I'm not there I'll probably be at my lawyer's – 692 347. Try ringing there. If you can't contact me, take a taxi to my flat – 126 Carlton Drive and I'll be back by 1 p.m. at the latest. I'll leave the key under the mat.
> Yours,

You wait for your friend at 11.30 but no one comes.
You telephone, but 636162 is a shop, The Pink Boutique, and 692347 is the local police station.
There are twenty-five flats at 126 Carlton Drive and when you find the right one there is no key under the mat. You wait until 12.45 and then leave.
At 1.30 you telephone the flat. You are very angry. Remind your friend of what was said in the letter and say what actually happened. *Begin*: 'You said you would meet me at 11.30. But you didn't come.'
Continue, using: 'You said . . .'

2. **The accident**
You wake up one morning in hospital. A policeman (Student B) is sitting beside your bed. At first you can't remember why you are in hospital. Then you remember the accident last night. The drawings will help you to remember what happened.

Answer the policeman's questions truthfully. Say if you don't know or can't remember.

Student B
COVER THE TOP HALF OF THE PAGE. YOU MUST NOT LOOK AT A'S INSTRUCTIONS.

1. **The meeting**

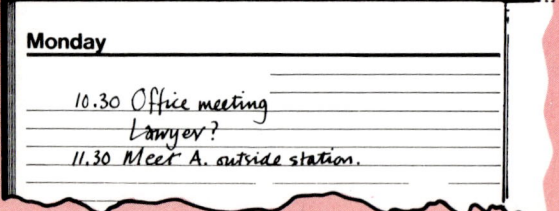

You have written a note to a friend. You have arranged to meet your friend outside the station at 11.30. You have told your friend to telephone your office (636261) or your lawyer (694732) if you are late. You promised to go straight to your flat by 1 p.m. if you were late.
Unfortunately, your office meeting goes on for a long time so you cannot go to the station. No one telephones. You go home at 1 p.m., but your friend isn't there. You feel rather angry. You don't know what has happened. At 1.30 the telephone rings.

2. **The accident**
You are a policeman. There has been a car accident and a cyclist has been killed. You are going to interview the passenger (Student A) who was in the car at the time of the accident. The passenger is in hospital and has just woken up. The driver of the car, Chris Johnson, is still unconscious.

You have instructions from the police station.

1. Introduce yourself.
2. Ask your questions.
3. Write down the answers.

Then, working with A write out a statement about the accident and ask A to sign it.

> *Find out:* who the passenger and driver are, what they did *before* the accident, exactly how the accident happened, and whose fault the accident was.

LANGUAGE STUDY

Lessons 21–25

STRUCTURE

5.1 Study

> **REPORTED STATEMENTS**
>
> | DIRECT SPEECH | INDIRECT SPEECH |
> |---|---|
> | *Examples:* | *Examples:* |
> | The police said, 'It*'s* one of the biggest robberies ever.' | The police said (that) *it was* one of the biggest robberies ever. |
> | The hospital said, 'The mother *is doing* fine.' | The hospital said (that) the mother *was doing* fine. |
> | 'I*'ve known* her for about a year,' said Jenny's boyfriend. | Jenny's boyfriend said (that) he *had known* her for about a year. |
> | 'The robbery *took place* some time last night,' they said. | They said (that) the robbery *had taken place* some time last night. |
>
> ⚠ 1. Notice the tense changes:
>
> | DIRECT SPEECH | INDIRECT SPEECH |
> |---|---|
> | Present simple | → Past simple |
> | Present continuous | → Past continuous (see LS 5.11) |
> | Present perfect | → Past perfect (see LS 5.13) |
> | Past simple | → Past perfect or no change |
>
> 2. Notice the pronoun changes:
>
> | I, you, we | → he/she, they |
> | my, your, our | → his/her, their |
>
> 3. 'that' is often not used.

 5.2 Put the statements into indirect speech

Example: 'I'm learning to fly,' said Fred.
Fred said (that) he was learning to fly.

1. 'I'm looking for a job,' said Steve.
2. 'I want to go to Mexico,' said Jenny.
3. Fred said, 'I don't want a big house.'
4. 'We've lost all our money,' said Liz.
5. Zed said, 'Someone started throwing food.'
6. 'Most companies run training courses,' said Mrs Page.
7. 'I don't like journalists,' said Zed.
8. Steve said, 'I haven't got a driving licence.'

 5.3 Put into direct speech

Example: The U.N. Secretary General said that man had to choose between peace and war.
'Man has to choose between peace and war,' said the U.N. Secretary General.

1. The prime minister said that education was very important.
2. The police said they did not know all the answers.
3. Steve said that he was living in Oxford.
4. Jenny said that she had been to Mexico.
5. The old lady said she wasn't feeling very well.
6. Steve said he had done Anthropology at university.
7. The man said that the boy had never stolen anything before.
8. Zed said that one of the passengers had complained.

5.4 Put the statements into indirect speech

Example: 'There has been a plane crash.' (on the radio)
It said on the radio that there had been a plane crash.

1. 'The house has eight bedrooms.' (in the advertisement)
2. 'Liverpool have won the match.' (in the newspaper)
3. 'The hotel is on the sea-front.' (in the brochure)
4. 'The police are still looking for the bank robbers.' (on television)
5. 'The government has not agreed to the pay-increase.' (on the radio)

5.5 Study

> **REPORTED QUESTIONS**
> The word order in indirect questions is the same as in statements.
>
> *Examples:*
>
> | DIRECT SPEECH | INDIRECT SPEECH |
> |---|---|
> | 'How much money *has been stolen*?' asked Sandra. | Sandra asked how much money *had been stolen*. |
> | '*Do* you *know* when it happened?' she asked. | She asked if he *knew* when it *had happened*. |
>
> ⚠ When the direct question does not begin with a question word, 'if' introduces the indirect question.

 5.6 Put the questions into indirect speech

Steve was looking worried, so his mother asked him questions.

Examples: 'What's the matter?'
She asked what the matter was.
'Are you all right?'
She asked if he was all right.

'Where did you lose it?'
'How much money was in it?'
'Have you told the police?'
'When did you have it last?'
'Do you know the number of the bus?'
'Why aren't you more careful?'

5.7 Put into direct speech

Examples: The student asked where the language laboratory was.
'Where's the language laboratory?'
The interviewer asked if there were any questions.
'Are there any questions?'

1. Anita asked why the English were so bad at foreign languages.
2. The teacher asked if anyone had read the book.
3. Jenny asked when the scholarship started.
4. Tom asked what had happened at the meeting.
5. Fred asked Liz how much money she was spending.
6. Mr Hyde asked Jenny if she had enjoyed being at art college.

5.8 Study

FUTURE: WILL

'will' is often used to express future intention. (See LS 4.5)

Example: The police will watch all ports and airports carefully.

'will' is also used to forecast the future.

Examples: The maximum temperature will be 10°C.

He probably won't take the job.

 'will' changes to 'would' in indirect speech.

Examples: The spokesman said that the police would watch all ports and airports carefully.

It said on the radio that the maximum temperature would be 10°C.

5.9 Drill

Why did people vote for the government?

Example: They said (that) they would build more houses.

WE WILL............
- ★ build more houses
- ★ increase wages
- ★ lower taxes
- ★ open more hospitals
- ★ spend more money on education
- ★ reduce unemployment
- ★ make the country strong again

VOTE FOR

5.10 Put into direct speech

A fortune-teller read Jenny's palm. What did he say?

Example: 'You'll travel across the sea.'

He said Jenny would travel across the sea and meet a tall, dark stranger. He said she would get married and have at least two children. He said that she would not come home for many years, but that she would be very happy.

5.11 Study

PAST CONTINUOUS TENSE
was/were + PRESENT PARTICIPLE

Examples:
1. I *was studying* last night.
   For a period of time: 'last night'

2. There were roadworks outside the bank while they *were digging* the tunnel.
   Two activities at the same time:
   1. roadworks ————————→
   2. digging the tunnel ————————→

3. The car *was turning* a corner when it crashed.
   Interrupted activity:
   ————————↓ when it crashed ————→

5.12 Put the verbs in brackets into the past simple or past continuous

Example: Fred (work) as a milkman when he (win) the pools.
Fred was working as a milkman when he won the pools.

1. Steve (work) as a teacher when he (meet) Jenny.
2. Fred (have) breakfast while Liz was reading the house advertisements.
3. 'What were you doing at eight o'clock last night?' 'I (watch) TV. I (go) out at about eight-thirty.'
4. Steve (go) to an employment agency because he (look) for a job.
5. The car (stop) suddenly and a man (get) out. He (hold) a gun.
6. While Zed (fly) to London, he and his friends had a party. The stewardess (ask) them to stop.

5.13 Study

PAST PERFECT TENSE
had + PAST PARTICIPLE

The *past simple tense* describes what happened at a time in the past. The *past perfect tense* is used for events that happened *before that time in the past*.

Examples:
       1   2
After the bank *had closed*, the thieves *cut* a hole in the strong-room floor.

                 2
A security guard *found* the tunnel after the gang *had left*.
                                        1

     1   2
The robbery *was discovered* at about 5 a.m. By this time, the gang *had left*.
                                                              1

 The following words and phrases are often used with the past perfect tense: *after, before, when, as soon as, by this time, because.*

5.14 Drill

1. Liz had a lot to do this morning.

First she made the beds.
Next she did the washing-up.
Then she went to the hairdresser.
After that, she bought some food.
Then she cleaned the house.
Finally, she cooked lunch.

Examples: After she'd made the beds, she did the washing-up.
After she'd done the washing-up, she . . .

Everything was done by one o'clock.

Example: *By one o'clock, she'd made the beds.*

2. Fred had a lazy morning.

First he had breakfast.
Next he read the newspaper.
Then he went for a walk.
After that he had a rest.
Then he listened to the radio.
Finally, he had lunch.

Example: *When he'd had breakfast, he read the newspaper.*
When he'd read the newspaper, he . . .

EXPRESSING PROBABILITY

 **5.15 Drill**

Examples: They were probably local men.
It looks as if they were local men.

We probably won't find them.
It doesn't look as if we'll find them.

1. The Inspector was probably right.
2. Jenny and her boyfriend probably won't get married.
3. It's probably going to rain.
4. Jenny will probably get a scholarship.
5. There's probably been a mistake.
6. Steve probably wasn't working very hard.
7. Fred is probably depressed.
8. I've probably found a flat.

 5.16 Drill

Examples: It looks as if they were local men.
It's likely that they were local men.

It doesn't look as if we'll find them.
It isn't likely that we'll find them.

Now do the same with the answers to the exercise above.

EXPRESSING POSSIBILITY

5.17 Drill

Last week, Zed Hawks completely disappeared. The police are looking for him, but no one knows where he is, or why he disappeared.

Example: Perhaps he took a holiday.
He may have taken a holiday.

Perhaps he had an accident.   Perhaps he's been ill.
Maybe he's left the country.   Maybe he's lost his memory.
Perhaps he wanted a rest.   Perhaps someone's killed him.

VOCABULARY

PHRASAL VERBS

5.18 Put in the correct word

Use *on, up, out, in*

1. The student looked ... the word in the dictionary.
2. It's very cold, so you should put ... a coat.
3. The robbers turned ... the TV to watch the news.
4. Could you fill ... this form, please?
5. That was a lovely meal – let me wash ...
6. It's a good plan, but it will be difficult to carry ...
7. I'd like to try ... these trousers.
8. O.K., I'll pass ... your message.
9. The police have given ... looking for the robbers.
10. I want to find ... when the house was built.
11. They can't afford a holiday because they're saving ... to buy a house.
12. The music stopped but they carried ... dancing.

WHAT DO YOU SAY?

 5.19 Listen and choose the most suitable response in each case

1. (a) I could meet you for lunch.
   (b) Oh, yes, I'd love to.
   (c) I don't like it at all.
   (d) How much does it usually cost?
2. (a) I'm terribly sorry.
   (b) I think we're near the station.
   (c) It doesn't matter.
   (d) Well, you can wear something else.
3. (a) I've read that one already.
   (b) I feel fine now.
   (c) I think this is the best one to buy.
   (d) No, we don't need to.

INTONATION AND STRESS

5.20 Respond to the questions with uncertainty

Examples: Is Marconi still in Britain?
He may be . . .

Has he already left the country?
He may have . . .

1. Is Liz looking for a job?
2. Has Jenny seen the film?
3. Is the bank still open?
4. Will you come to the party?
5. Have they missed the train?
6. Are the potatoes cooked?
7. Will the police find the robbers?
8. Have you got any aspirin?

SENTENCE LINKING

5.21 Join the following sentences to make a paragraph of no more than six sentences

Use each of the following words or phrases once only:
and, after, as soon as, because, but, so, when, while

Anita was going to Sweden for a holiday.
Her handbag was stolen on the underground.
She was travelling to the airport.
She realised what had happened.
She jumped off the train to phone the police.
She was very worried.
She had lost her passport, too.
She had reported the theft.
She went to the airport.
She spoke to an airline official.
She had told him the story.
He asked if she had any identification papers.
Luckily she had her driving licence.
She was able to fly to Sweden after all.

5.22 Write a paragraph

Write a short account of the most exciting/frightening thing that has ever happened to you. Use words and phrases like those above to connect your sentences. Look back at Lesson 22 for other expressions of time.

Test

Written Test – 1½ hours

Answer all the questions.

1. Ring the letter for the word or phrase that best fits the blank space.

    Example: He _____ in a big house in the country.
    A inhabits Ⓑ lives C rests D spends E exists

    (i) I haven't talked to Joan _____ a long time.
      A since B for C by D ago E after
    (ii) First open the packet and _____ pour out the flour.
      A so B after C for D to E then
    (iii) What a beautiful _____! It's so hot!
      A temperature B heat C sunshine D weather E day
    (iv) The children were making a noise. So I _____ them to go away.
      A demanded B told C spoke D said E talked
    (v) This coffee tastes funny. How _____ sugar did you put in it?
      A many B few C lot D much E some
    (vi) I was late _____ I took a taxi.
      A unless B that C so D only E for
    (vii) I'm afraid dinner isn't ready. I've _____ come in from the shops.
      A only B already C ago D now E just
    (viii) He _____ the plate and broke it.
      A dropped B let C fell D picked E put
    (ix) If I were you, I _____ go to the doctor.
      A will B shall C would D can E to
    (x) The house is _____ the end of the street.
      A on B in C to D at E of

2. Fill each of the blank spaces, writing only one word in each space.

    A: Yes, sir. Can _____ (1) help you?
    B: I _____ (2) like to make _____ (3) complaint about this shirt. When I washed _____ (4) the colour changed.
    A: At what temperature _____ (5) the shirt washed?
    B: About 60 degrees, I think.
    A: Ah, then the water was _____ (6) hot. This shirt _____ (7) be washed at forty degrees. Look, it says so _____ (8) the label. Of course we'll change the shirt. But next time, don't forget _____ (9) look at the washing instructions.
    B: That's very kind _____ (10) you.

3. Write a letter of about 120 words to The Worldwide Students Centre, Sea Walk, Bournemouth. You want to go to England to study English for one month next summer. Give details of your age, level of English and your plans.

4. Write the rest of this conversation. Your answer should be in about 100 words.
    Your friend: Did you enjoy your holiday?
    Yourself: Yes, very much. I went to ....

Oral Test – 30 minutes

LISTENING

(i) Someone says 'What's the right time?'. Of the four answers A, B, C and D below, only C is suitable.
A About four hours.
B The eighth of January.
Ⓒ Seven thirty.
D In about ten minutes.

Now you will hear ten test sentences like this. Choose the most suitable answer and put a ring around the letter.

1. A Do you go there often?
   B What are you going to study?
   C When did you leave school?
   D Can I come with you?
2. A You can always use our phone.
   B No one ever phones me either.
   C I'm glad you finally got it.
   D When did you book the call?
3. A Very well thank you.
   B What do you do?
   C I'm an engineer.
   D I'm going shopping.
4. A Don't be frightened.
   B Why not? There's plenty of room.
   C That's very kind of you.
   D I can't hear either.
5. A About half an hour by car.
   B I was looking for a job for six months.
   C There's a three-year training course.
   D I work an eight-hour day.
6. A Six months ago.
   B Until I was 16.
   C For three years.
   D In two years' time.
7. A I've lived there for two years.
   B About a month.
   C I spent six weeks.
   D About a hundred pounds.
8. A Where did you leave it?
   B Couldn't you find it yesterday?
   C I hope you find one.
   D Is a round one any good?
9. A Very much indeed.
   B Quite nice really.
   C Playing tennis.
   D A cup of tea.
10. A When is it going to happen?
    B Why doesn't someone stop it?
    C Why are they doing it?
    D Was anyone hurt?

(ii) The statements below are about the conversation you will now hear. There are four alternatives for each statement: A, B, C and D. Choose the correct one and put a ring around the letter.

1. The two people talking
   A are still at school   C left school some years ago
   B have just left school   D are school teachers
2. Chris
   A is a university student   C is a chemist
   B works in a travel agency   D works for a big company
3. Tommy
   A sells houses   C is a secretary
   B manages a hotel   D is a lawyer
4. Gareth
   A is a teacher   C is at college
   B is an actor   D works in a market
5. Frank
   A is unemployed   C works in a garage
   B is a pilot   D is a policeman

SPEAKING

Candidates are examined individually.
Part One: the teacher asks five questions.
Part Two: a role play exercise.

Songs

Unit 1 The Girl On The Poster

You're the girl on the poster
And I see you every day
I've told you what you mean to me
But there's nothing you can say.

Chorus I wish you could
Tell me about yourself
I'd love to hear you talking.

I've told you all my secrets
For more than a year
I've told you what I want to do
All my hopes and fears.

You're the best friend I have
Because you never let me down
Whenever I need your smile, it's there –
On every street, in every town.

You're the girl on the poster
And I don't know your name
I suppose I'm never going to meet you
But I want to thank you just the same.

Unit 2 Better And Better, Worse And Worse

We've got televisions, freezers and stereos
And machines that wash and dry
We've got helicopters waiting by the swimming pool
We've got everything money can buy.

Chorus Things are getting better and better
Every day there's something new
You think you miss the good old days
I'd think again if I were you.

We never used to travel much, we didn't have a car
We always used to stay at home
And we wrote a lot of letters in the good old days
Because we didn't have a telephone.

Traffic jams and blocks of flats
You see them every day
You think you've got a better life
But there's a price you've had to pay.

Unit 3 Talk It Over

In my life I've never worried for too long
I don't care who's right or wrong
Everybody's got their own opinion
It doesn't matter much to me
If people disagree
Just as long as they sit down
And talk it over.

Chorus So if you've been misunderstood
Don't walk away, you know you should
Talk it over.

There's a woman tired of waiting for her friend
But his work just doesn't end.
She gets home, the phone starts ringing
She lets it ring, he wonders why –
But he was only going to say 'Goodbye'
They've both got too much pride
To talk it over.

Unit 4 The Hotel Porter

Chorus It's been a typical day for a hotel porter
Waiting for something to do
It's been a typical day but I wish it were shorter
I want to go home soon.

I don't need to know about mathematics
But I've got to be smartly dressed
I'm not in the army any more
But my trousers are beautifully pressed.

I don't have to speak any foreign languages
But I've learnt a word or two
For a man like me, with a job like mine
'Hello' and 'Goodbye' will do.

The hotel guests often ask me
What to do and where to go
And in return they give me money
For telling them the things I know.

Unit 5 You've Got To Think Twice

Chorus You've got to think twice
About the news you hear
You know that it's up to you
You've got to think twice
And check the facts
Perhaps they're not quite true.

Who did it?
Where was it?
When did it happen and how?
The papers said it was a clever robbery
And it's under investigation
They're doing everything to get the facts
And they're looking for an explanation.

Who were they?
How many were there?
And how much did they take?
The radio said they'd caught one of the robbers
And he may have been the worst
But nobody'll ever know the full story –
The news not the truth comes first.

Listening Passages

UNIT 1 Lesson 4

1.
STEVE:	Hello, I'm ringing about your advertisement for English teachers. Can you tell me something about the job?
WOMAN:	Yes, we're looking for people to teach in Spain this summer.
STEVE:	Where exactly?
WOMAN:	In Cordoba and Cadiz. The salary is £185 a month. We're looking for people who can speak Spanish and who've got experience and qualifications in teaching English as a Foreign Language.
STEVE:	Oh, I've taught English, but I haven't got a qualification.
WOMAN:	Well, I'm sorry, but a qualification is essential.
STEVE:	I see. Well thank you, anyway.
WOMAN:	Not at all. Goodbye.

2.
STEVE:	I'd like to apply for a job as a tourist guide in Paris.
MAN:	Yes, I see. Do you speak French?
STEVE:	Oh yes, and Spanish and Portuguese.
MAN:	Good. Our guides must be at least 21.
STEVE:	Yes, I'm exactly 21. What is the salary, please?
MAN:	It's between £10 and £17 a day. It depends on how hard you work. And you'll also need a car.
STEVE:	Oh, it didn't say that in the advertisement. I haven't got a driving licence.
MAN:	I'm sorry. Thank you for calling.

UNIT 2 Lesson 8

LIZ: The first one is quite old. It's a terraced house built in 1897. It's in the city centre and has three bedrooms, bathroom, a modern kitchen, lounge, dining room, oil central heating and a big garden. The price is £38,500.

The second is very modern, 1978, but, oh dear, it's a city centre flat with electric heating – only one bedroom, too. And they want £27,000 for it.

The third one is a three-bedroom detached house in the suburbs. It's £48,000 and it's got a big lounge, dining-room and kitchen. There's a garden – doesn't say how big – and a garage. Oh yes, it's got gas central heating. Now how old is it? Here it is – 1958.

The last one looks lovely. It's an eighteenth-century country cottage. It's got four bedrooms. There's nothing about central heating, although they're asking £68,500 for it. But there's a big garden, a tennis court and a garage.

You see, dear, they're all far too small for us. Let's go and see the eight-bedroom house today.

UNIT 3 Lesson 13

First caller

OPEN LINE:	Hello, Open Line. Can I help you?
CALLER:	Er . . . my name's Sally, and I'm really calling about my son.
OPEN LINE:	Yes, I see. Can you tell me what the problem is?
CALLER:	It's . . . it's difficult to explain, I'm afraid, but I think he's taking drugs. He's got a lot of strange friends now and he's out at all hours of the night. I can't talk to him any more . . .
OPEN LINE:	Mm, go on . . .
CALLER:	. . . and last week I found some pills in his coat pocket. Some days he really looks strange . . . as if he wasn't here but somewhere else. But I don't know what to do.
OPEN LINE:	Have you discussed the problem with your husband?
CALLER:	No, I'm on my own you see, his father's dead . . . do you think I should ask the police to help?
OPEN LINE:	It's a difficult problem, isn't it? If I were you, I'd . . .

Second caller

OPEN LINE:	Open Line here.
CALLER:	Hello . . . I don't want to tell you my name but I'd like some help with a problem I've got.
OPEN LINE:	Yes, of course.
CALLER:	It's this . . . I keep on stealing things . . . nothing valuable you understand . . .
OPEN LINE:	Mm . . .
CALLER:	. . . when I'm out shopping. I don't mean to, but suddenly I take something. It's never anything I need. I don't know why I do this . . .
OPEN LINE:	Have you ever been . . .
CALLER:	No . . . no. But I know it's shoplifting really. I've got a whole room of things at home . . . small, silly things I've taken. You see, I'm afraid of being caught. . . . then I'd lose my job. You see, I work in a bank. What should I do?
OPEN LINE:	I think you ought to talk to someone in your family about your . . . your problem. Why don't you . . .

Third caller

OPEN LINE:	Good evening, Open Line. Can I help you?
CALLER:	Is that Open Line?
OPEN LINE:	Yes, that's right. What can we do for you?

CALLER: I'm sorry, my hearing's not very good. I'm a pensioner, you see. I'm telephoning about Arbury Road, that's where I live. There are lots of teenagers living near me . . . fourteen and fifteen-year-olds. And they're . . . they're driving me crazy. They're always knocking on my door . . . or just standing looking in the windows. And when I go out they follow me . . . they look so awful and their clothes are so strange . . .
OPEN LINE: Have you ever spoken to them?
CALLER: No, they never say anything. They just look at me.
OPEN LINE: Perhaps it would be a good idea to . . .

UNIT 4   Lesson 17

At English Transport cars are made on an assembly line over fourteen kilometres long. Each part of the car is assembled by a different worker as the car moves along the assembly line.

The many parts which make up a car are produced in specialised factories in different parts of the country.

First the steel for the body of the car is pressed and cut into shape in a body plant. Next the body of the car is welded together and then sprayed with paint in the paint shop.

Meanwhile engines are assembled in another workshop and electrical equipment is supplied by electricians.

Then the body and engine are fitted together and all the other parts of the car are added on the assembly line.

Finally, when the car is finished, it is tested. Then it leaves the factory to be sold.

UNIT 4   Lesson 19

Q: What do you do for a living?
A: At the moment I'm working at the film festival . . .
Q: In Krakow?
A: Yes . . . the Krakow International Short Film Festival. I'm an interpreter.
Q: How interesting! What exactly do you do?
A: Er . . . when we know that there's a foreign delegation arriving . . . a delegation that's English-speaking . . . I go out to the airport or to the railway station to meet them . . .
Q: Hm.
A: Then I take them back to the hotel where the film festival reception is.
Q: Which hotel is that?
A: The Cracovia – it's close to the Kiev cinema where the films are shown. At the hotel I help the delegation register and collect their festival programmes and badges . . .
Q: Like the one you're wearing?
A: . . . that's right – and then I show them to their rooms.
Q: How many delegations have you met so far?
A: Only two, because the festival doesn't start until tomorrow. An American delegation and one from Iraq.
Q: Really? The Iraqi delegation spoke English?
A: Yes, most of the foreigners who come to the festival speak English. The official festival newspaper is published in English.
Q: What else does your work involve?
A: Preparing translations of Polish films.
Q: How do you do that?
A: I have a script of the film in Polish and I translate it into English . . . um . . . then I see the film and make sure that . . . that my translation is accurate. When the film is shown at the festival I read my translation and . . . er . . . the people in the audience who want the translation listen to it on headphones.
Q: Is it difficult?
A: To listen on the headphones?
Q: No, to . . .
A: I'm sorry I don't understand what you . . .
Q: . . . to do the translation.
A: Sometimes I get native speakers to check the translations.
Q: What else do you do?
A: I have to sit at the information desk in the festival office.
Q: Mm . . .
A: And people come and ask questions. Silly questions sometimes.
Q: How do you mean?
A: Well, they ask questions to which they already know the answers.
Q: Such as . . .
A: Oh, they ask where the cinema is, when the films begin and so on.
Q: So that's about all, is it?
A: Yes . . . no . . . I forgot the most important part. When the jury meets I have to translate for the American judge . . . um . . . I tell him what the other members of the jury are saying.
Q: Do you translate every word?
A: No, not really – I summarise what they're saying. Then I translate the American judge's opinions into Polish. It's quite difficult, but lots of fun.
Q: What's the worst thing about being an interpreter?
A: Oh . . . I don't know . . . having to work late every evening.
Q: And the best thing?
A: Meeting lots of interesting people.

UNIT 5 Lesson 21

RADIO ANNOUNCER: And now it's almost five thirty and time to go over to David Knight in the news room.

NEWSREADER: Here are the news headlines at five thirty.

The United Nations Conference on World Peace opened this morning in New York. The conference was opened by the U.N. Secretary General who said that man had to choose between peace and war.

A West German airliner has been hijacked on an internal flight from Hamburg to Munich. The hijack took place at eleven thirty this morning. The hijacker, whose identity is not known, has demanded to see the West German President. The plane is at present at Munich airport where it has been surrounded by police.

Drugs Squad detectives found the largest quantity of illegal drugs ever in a London flat yesterday. A police spokesman said that the drugs were hidden in suitcases. He estimated the value of the drugs at over five million pounds.

Reports are coming in of a major accident in southern Sweden. The reports say that this afternoon a ship crashed into a bridge. Seven cars and two lorries are said to have fallen into the water from the bridge. We hope to have more details in our next news broadcast.

Those are the news headlines, and now at five thirty-two, it's back to Jo Vince and Rock of Ages.

UNIT 5 Lesson 24

NEWSREADER: And finally, the weather. Tomorrow is expected to be cloudy all day with some light rain showers in the afternoon. Winds will be light to moderate from the north-west and the maximum temperature will be 10°C, falling at night to zero or −1°C. There may be some frost in places in the early morning. The outlook for later in the week is for cooler weather with the possibility of some snow on high ground.

And now for the main points of the news again. The Birmingham Bank . . .

Irregular Verbs

The past simple and the past participle are the same in many verbs.
Those which are different are marked * below.

VERB	PAST SIMPLE	PAST PARTICIPLE	VERB	PAST SIMPLE	PAST PARTICIPLE
be	was, were	been*	see	saw	seen*
become	became	become*	sell	sold	sold
begin	began	begun*	send	sent	sent
break	broke	broken*	show	showed	shown*
bring	brought	brought	shut	shut	shut
build	built	built	sing	sang	sung*
burn	burnt	burnt	sit	sat	sat
buy	bought	bought	sleep	slept	slept
catch	caught	caught	smell	smelt	smelt
choose	chose	chosen*	speak	spoke	spoken*
come	came	come*	spell	spelt	spelt
cost	cost	cost	spend	spent	spent
cut	cut	cut	split	split	split
dig	dug	dug	stand	stood	stood
do	did	done*	steal	stole	stolen*
draw	drew	drawn*	swim	swam	swum*
drink	drank	drunk*	take	took	taken*
drive	drove	driven*	teach	taught	taught
eat	ate	eaten*	tell	told	told
fall	fell	fallen*	think	thought	thought
feel	felt	felt	throw	threw	thrown*
fight	fought	fought	understand	understood	understood
find	found	found	wake	woke	woken*
fly	flew	flown*	wear	wore	worn*
forget	forgot	forgotten*	win	won	won
get	got	got	write	wrote	written*
give	gave	given*			
go	went	been, gone*			
grow	grew	grown*			
hang	hung	hung			
have	had	had			
hear	heard	heard			
hide	hid	hidden*			
hit	hit	hit			
hold	held	held			
hurt	hurt	hurt			
keep	kept	kept			
know	knew	known*			
learn	learnt	learnt			
leave	left	left			
lend	lent	lent			
let	let	let			
lose	lost	lost			
make	made	made			
mean	meant	meant			
meet	met	met			
pay	paid	paid			
put	put	put			
read /ri:d/	read /red/	read /red/			
ride	rode	ridden*			
ring	rang	rung*			
run	ran	run*			
say	said	said			

Heinemann Educational Books Ltd
22 Bedford Square, London WC1B 3HH

LONDON   EDINBURGH   MELBOURNE   AUCKLAND
SINGAPORE   KUALA LUMPUR
NEW DELHI   IBADAN   NAIROBI   JOHANNESBURG
PORTSMOUTH (NH)   KINGSTON

© Philip Prowse, Judy Garton-Sprenger and T. C. Jupp 1980
First published 1980
Exchanges A reprinted 3 times, *Exchanges B* reprinted twice,
Exchanges Complete reprinted 3 times,
New colour edition first published 1985.
Reprinted 1986, 1987

Exchanges A Units 1–5	Students Book A	0 435 28435 5
	Workbook A	0 435 28441 X
	Test Book A*	0 435 28443 6
	Teachers' Book A	0 435 28437 1
	Cassettes (3)	0 435 28465 7
Exchanges B Units 6–10	Students' Book B	0 435 28436 3
	Workbook B	0 435 28442 8
	Test Book B*	0 435 28444 4
	Teachers' Book B	0 435 28438 X
	Cassettes (3)	0 435 28463 0
Exchanges Complete Edition Units 1–10	Students' Book	0 435 28434 7
	Songs and Dialogues Cassette	0 435 28459 2

* *Main Course Tests: Teachers' Guide* 0 435 28454 1 covers these titles

In the lesson material we have created characters in order to contextualise the language being taught. Where we have done this we have not intended to depict any person living or dead.

Acknowledgements

The authors would like to thank the students at Bell College, Saffron Walden (part of the Bell Educational Trust) for helping to try out *Exchanges* materials, and for acting as photographic models for the role play situations in this new colour edition of Main Course English.

While every effort has been made to trace the owners of copyright material in this book, there have been some cases where the publishers have been unable to find the sources. We should be grateful to hear from anyone who recognises their copyright material and who is unacknowledged. We shall be pleased to make make the necessary corrections in future editions of the book.
Illustrated by Chris Evans throughout. Other illustrations by Malcolm Bird, Brian Lee, Bill Le Fever, Linda Rogers Associates, David Lock, Oxford Illustrators and John Whittaker. Photographs by – Malvin van Gelderen (pp. 15, 17); Chris Gilbert (p. 62); Tony Payne (pp. 3, 19, 23, 34, 36, 66).
The authors and publishers would like to thank the following for permission to reproduce their material and for providing illustrations: pp. 2 & 3 thanks to the British Council for providing the material and information on Mexico on which these exercises are based; p. 10 Heinemann Educational Books Ltd, European Parliament and the Commission of the European Communities, Mr Alex Gordon, Sir Fred Catherwood MEP (all material refers to facts correct in 1979); p. 16 Barclays Bank plc; p. 22 Museum of Costume – Bath, Camera Press Ltd, Ian Allan Ltd, British Railways Board, Brenard Press Ltd, The Royal Aeronautical Society; p. 30 extract from *BBC Roadshow Guide* produced by National Extension College Basic Skills Unit for the Manpower Services Commission and the BBC (1980), marriage statistics from Central Statistical Office (1980); p. 34 Maggie Murray and Raissa Page, Format Photographers Ltd; p. 35 Camera Press Ltd; p. 36 Help the Aged; p. 40 road traffic signs reproduced with the permission of the Department of Transport and the Controller of Her Majesty's Stationery Office; p. 44 unemployment statistics from *Yearbook of Labour Statistics* (1982) published by International Labour Office; p. 46 Central Office of Information, British Leyland, Rolls-Royce Motors Ltd, Land Rover Group, Ford Motor Co. Ltd; p. 48 Tony Stone Photolibrary – London, J. Allan Cash Photolibrary, London Regional Transport Executive, Union Bank of Switzerland for information from *Price and Earnings Around the Globe* by M. Gutmann and Dr A. Kruck, September 1982; p. 49 Information Office of European Parliament; p. 52 extracts from *BBC Roadshow Guide* produced by National Extension College Basic Skills Unit for the Manpower Services Commission and the BBC (1980); p. 66 J. Allan Cash Photolibrary.

Note for teachers using this book in Spain:
Aprobado por el Ministerio de Educación y Ciencia, para su utilización en B.U.P., por orden ministerial del 1-12-83. B.O.E. 17-1-84.

Original design by Brian Lee
Cover design by Indent
Songs written and arranged by Russ Shipton and Kieran Fogarty
Set in Monophoto Ehrhardt by BAS Printers Limited,
Over Wallop, Hampshire
Printed and bound in Hong Kong
by Mandarin Offset

MAIN COURSE ENGLISH

EXCHANGES

Students' Book
Part B

Judy Garton-Sprenger   Philip Prowse

Project Adviser
T. C. Jupp

HEINEMANN EDUCATIONAL BOOKS
LONDON

Contents

Unit	Communicative aims	Key Structures
6 Personal feelings and information Lessons 26–30 page 73	Personal and medical details Describing feelings Personal and family habits Describing character, behaviour and attitudes *Spoken communication*: discussing personal feelings *Reading*: autobiography *Writing*: personal description reading report	Present perfect continuous tense contrasted with present perfect simple Present perfect tense contrasted with past simple Verbs not usually used in continuous forms Ability/permission with *can/could* *Make* + infinitive (without *to*) Prepositions and conjunctions: time Formation of adverbs of manner Idioms with *do* and *make* Pointing words: *this*, *that*, etc. Relative pronouns: *who*
7 Persuasion and complaints Lessons 31–35 page 87	Planning and describing Persuading and dealing with persuasion Complaining and dealing with complaints Making a written complaint Requesting something and offering alternatives *Spoken communication*: comparing costs *Reading*: information from a town guide *Writing*: your town guide	Conditional sentences (Types 2 and 3) Regret with *wish* Criticism with *should/shouldn't have* Causative verb: *have* Advice with *had better* Indefinite pronouns + adjectives *Both . . . and/not . . . and nor* *But, although, however* (contrast), *because* (reason)
8 Explanation and instructions Lessons 36–40 page 101	Explaining how to do something Information about how things work Understanding and giving instructions Asking for and discussing travel information *Spoken communication*: instructions *Reading*: consumer information *Writing*: instructions and information about your home	Present simple tense (giving instructions, describing habits, systems and processes) Passive + *by* + agent Relative pronouns: *who, that, which, where* Means with *by* + gerund Definition with *for* + gerund Words and phrases for expressing frequency Phrasal verbs and prepositions *Either . . . or/both . . . and*
9 Planning and co-operating Lessons 41–45 page 115	Making and accepting suggestions Discussing the best order Discussing changes of plan Commenting and criticising *Spoken communication*: discussing the best order *Reading*: how fast can you read? *Writing*: narrative description	Future in the past Future continuous tense Present perfect tense in time clauses Noun clauses introduced by *what* Suggestions and offers with *shall* Polite requests with *Would you mind . . .?/Do you mind if . . .?* Question tags Defining relative clauses ending in prepositions
10 Studying in English Lessons 46–50 page 129	Educational details and plans Using libraries and books Making notes Taking part in a discussion *Questionnaire*: Your English Course	Revision: tenses prepositions time-markers order of adjectives the article

Songs	142
Listening passages	143
List of irregular verbs	145
Structural reference list and summary	146
DIY Check-up: Key to answers	148

Key to symbols

 Oral work

 Written work

 Reading

 Listening

 Do-it-yourself English: Individualised activities

 Games, puzzles and crosswords

 Songs

 Important points to note

Unit 6
LESSON 26

Personal and medical details

Jenny Langley had won a scholarship to study in Mexico.
She received a letter about her scholarship.

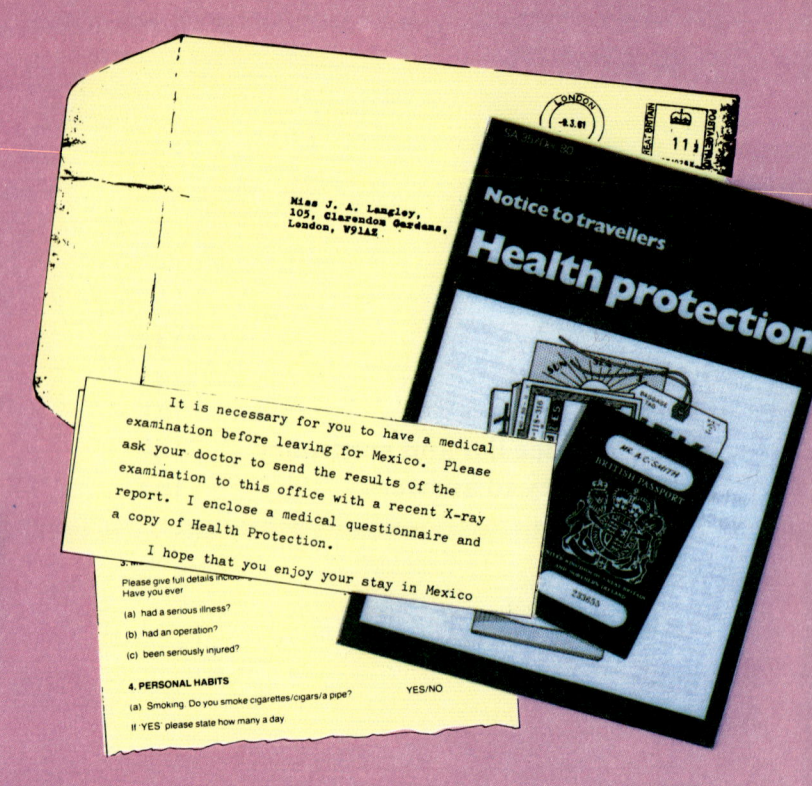

RECEPTIONIST: Dr Kemp's surgery. Good morning.
JENNY: Good morning. I'd like to make an appointment for a medical examination.
RECEPTIONIST: Certainly. Could you come on Wednesday afternoon at four?
JENNY: Yes, that's fine.
RECEPTIONIST: What's your name, please?
JENNY: Langley. Jennifer Langley.
RECEPTIONIST: Is that L-A-Y or L-E-Y?
JENNY: L-E-Y.
RECEPTIONIST: We'll see you next Wednesday then, Mrs Langley.
JENNY: It's Miss, actually.
RECEPTIONIST: I'm sorry. Goodbye, Miss Langley.
JENNY: Thank you. Goodbye.

Jenny filled in the questionnaire and took it to the doctor's.

 Ask and answer

Read the medical questionnaire and make up questions about Jenny.
Ask another student your questions.

Examples:

How tall is Jenny?
Has Jenny ever had an operation?

MEDICAL QUESTIONNAIRE

Complete this questionnaire and take it with you to your medical examination.

Full first names: *Jennifer Anne* (MR MRS MISS)

Surname: *LANGLEY* Age *23* Sex *F*
(BLOCK CAPITALS)

1. HEIGHT AND WEIGHT

(a) What is your height and weight in ordinary clothes?

Height *165* cm Weight *55* kg

(b) Has your weight changed in the last year? Has it stayed the same/been increasing/been decreasing?
It's been increasing. I used to weigh 50 kg.

2. FAMILY HISTORY

(a) Are your parents alive? Father *Yes* Mother *Yes*

(b) Has either of your parents been seriously ill at any time? YES/NO

If 'YES' please give full details:
My father had a heart attack in 1978. He is better now, but still has high blood pressure.

3. MEDICAL HISTORY

Please give full details including dates
Have you ever

(a) had a serious illness? *No*

(b) had an operation? *My appendix was taken out in October 1976.*

(c) been seriously injured? *Yes. I broke my right leg in May 1970.*

4. PERSONAL HABITS

(a) Smoking. Do you smoke cigarettes/cigars/a pipe? YES/NO

If 'YES' please state how many a day. *About 30 a day.*

Unit 6

 Study

Pains
She's got a pain in her ...... shoulder

Everyday illnesses		*Serious illnesses*	
I've got	a headache earache	He had	a heart attack pneumonia
	a stomach-ache toothache		a stroke cancer
	a sore throat backache		
	a cold flu		
	a cough		

 Ask each other: Enquiring about health

1. Look at the medical history section of the questionnaire. Ask another student questions.

Example:

A: Have you ever had an operation?
B: No, I haven't. But my father was in hospital for a long time.
A: What was the matter with him?.
B: He was in a motorbike accident and hurt his head badly.
A: How did he feel?
B: Terrible. He couldn't see properly and had a headache all the time.
A: Is he better now?
B: Yes, he's fine most of the time. But he still gets bad headaches.

2. Ask each other how you've been feeling recently.

Example:

A: How have you been feeling recently?
B: Not too bad. But I didn't feel well last Saturday.
A: What was the matter with you?
B: I had a sore throat and a cough.
A: Do you feel all right now?
B: Yes, fine.

 Listening: Advice and suggestions

Listen to the conversation about smoking between Jenny and the doctor. The doctor suggests five things that Jenny should do. Number these sentences to show the order of his suggestions.

- Don't breathe in the smoke.
- Smoke fewer cigarettes.
- Stop smoking strong cigarettes, start smoking mild ones.
- Only smoke half of each cigarette.
- Take the cigarette out of your mouth when you're not smoking it.

 Role Play: Making an appointment by telephone

A is a doctor's receptionist. B is not feeling very well.

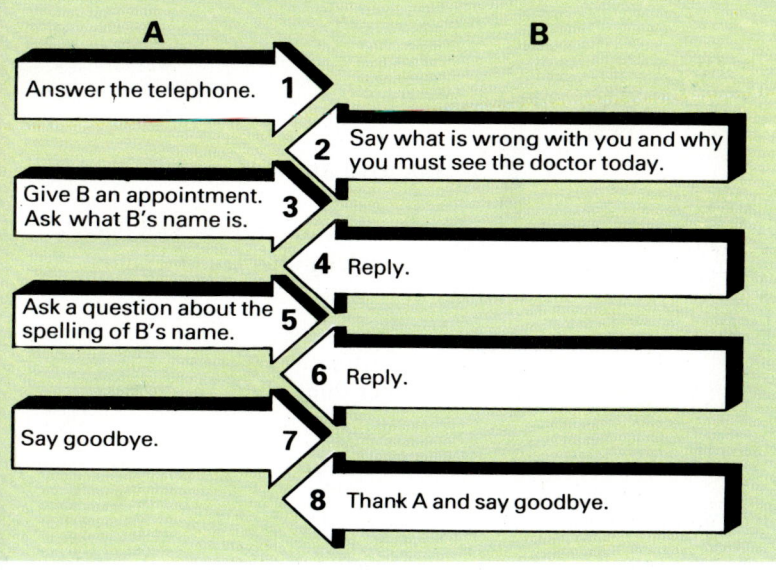

 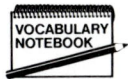

You should keep a vocabulary notebook for new words. Write down five words after each English lesson and learn them by heart.

Example:

In this lesson write down and learn some of the words for illnesses from the Study section.

LANGUAGE Study Exercises 6.1 6.2 6.6 6.7 6.9 6.10 6.11 6.12

LESSON 27

Describing feelings

Jenny and Peter, her boyfriend, went to an art gallery.

JENNY: Isn't this one marvellous? It really makes me feel great.
PETER: I don't know. It doesn't seem terribly good to me. In fact it makes me want to laugh. I suppose I don't know enough about modern art.
JENNY: Never mind, Peter! You won't have to go to boring exhibitions like this when I'm in Mexico!
PETER: That's true. But how do you feel about going away? You haven't talked about it very much.
JENNY: Well, of course I'll miss *you* – and my parents. But I'm very excited about going.
PETER: I wish I was going with you. Are you sure you'll be all right?
JENNY: Don't worry about me. I'm not afraid of anything.
PETER: No?
JENNY: All right. I *am* afraid of spiders!

 Ask and answer

Make up questions about Jenny and Peter's conversation. Ask another student your questions.

Example:

What does Peter think about the picture?

Unit 6

 Study

Describing feelings

| It makes me feel | bored. depressed. excited. embarrassed. frightened. |  | It makes me want to | cry. dance yawn. sing. |  |

 Tell each other: Feelings about pictures

Study the pictures on page 75 and tell another student about your feelings.
Say *why* the pictures make you feel the way you do.

 Writing: Doing and feeling

Make a diary for one day, showing what you were doing and how you were feeling.

Example:

Time	Place	Doing	Feeling
6 a.m.	In bed	Sleeping	Nothing
8 a.m.	In the kitchen	Having breakfast	Worried – I'd forgotten to do my homework
10 a.m.	At school	Geography	Bored
12 a.m.			

 Ask each other: Fears, likes and dislikes

1. *What are you afraid of?*
   Are you afraid of . . . having injections? flying?
   the dentist? the dark? snakes? spiders? meeting strangers?

Example:
A: Are you afraid of having injections?
B: No, not really. How about you?
A: I don't *like* having injections, but I'm not afraid of them.

2. *How do you feel about doing things?*
   How do you feel about . . .
   getting up in the morning? paying bills? staying up late?
   writing letters? cooking? washing up? buying clothes?

Example:
A: How do you feel about getting up in the morning?
B: I don't really mind. In fact, I quite like getting up early.

 Tell each other: Things you would miss

Imagine that you are going to live in another country.
What would you miss? Tell each other about the things you would miss most.
Example:
I'd miss my friends.

This is a good way to list new vocabulary:

Word	Meaning	Example
yawn	Open your mouth very wide when you are tired.	You're yawning all the time. Why don't you go to bed?

Language Study Exercises 6.4 6.5 6.8

LESSON 28

Personal and family habits

Before leaving for Mexico, Jenny went to see her parents. Jenny's parents live in Norwich, a city 178 kilometres north-east of London. Jenny hadn't seen her parents for nearly three months.

JENNY: How have you both been?
MOTHER: Oh, not too bad, dear. Your father's been feeling a lot better recently.
FATHER: Yes, the doctor's put me on a diet.
MOTHER: And you've been taking some exercise.
FATHER: Not a lot, just long walks. But you won't believe this – I've given up smoking!
JENNY: Really! That's wonderful. I've been trying to stop, but I haven't been able to. I'm so glad you're feeling better. Do you think you'll be able to go back to work again?
FATHER: I don't know. I'm quite happy to stay at home and do the housework, while your mother goes out to work.

Mr Langley's doctor gave him a leaflet about keeping fit. This is an extract from the leaflet.

"Yes, the doctor's put me on a diet."

THE TRAFFIC LIGHT GUIDE TO STAYING SLIM

Here is a very simple way to choose the foods that will keep you slim and feeling great. Use the three groups to discover a sensible balance which suits you.

Obviously, **how much** you eat is as important as **what** you eat. But even small quantities of RED-group food contain as many calories as quite large quantities of GREEN-group food.

 RED - stop and think

Sugar, sweets, chocolate, cakes, biscuits, honey, jam, marmalade, tinned and dried fruit, cream, butter, margarine, cooking oil, fat on meat, mayonnaise, chips, peanuts.

 AMBER - go carefully

Fatty meat (like bacon), sausage, liver paté, eggs, milk, cheese, thick soups, nuts, bread, cereals, rice, pasta (like spaghetti and macaroni), potatoes.

 GREEN - go right ahead

Fresh fruit, salads, green and root vegetables, fish, shellfish, chicken, kidney, yoghurt, clear soups, herbs and spices.

Remember, it is easier to stay slim than to lose weight once you have put it on. A little care in choosing what you eat and regular exercise will go a long way to keep you slim and healthy.

  Questions

Which of these statements about the guide are true and which are false?

1. Eating shellfish makes you fat.
2. You can eat as much cheese as you like and still stay slim.
3. Dried fruit is not fattening.
4. You will stay slim if you only eat food in the red group.
5. Peanuts are in the amber group.
6. You will get fat even if you only eat a very little of the red-group food.
7. You can eat as much chicken as you like without getting fat.
8. You should be careful how many eggs you eat.

Unit 6

  Ask each other and complete: Habits and food

1. Complete this section of the medical questionnaire for yourself and for another student. Compare the completed questionnaire with another student's.

2. What kind of food do you usually eat? Do you eat food in the red and green groups of the Traffic Light Guide? Have you ever been on a diet? If so, what did you eat?

> **4. PERSONAL HABITS**
>
> (a) Smoking. Do you smoke cigarettes/cigars/a pipe?   YES/NO
>
> If 'YES' please state how many a day.
>
> (b) Exercise. Do you take exercise regularly?   YES/NO
>
> If 'YES' state what kind of exercise (e.g. playing tennis, cycling) and how often (every day, twice a week, once a month).

 Survey: Work and decisions in the family

1. Make a list of jobs which someone has to do in every home. Make a list of decisions which someone has to take in every family.

I'm quite happy to stay at home and do the housework.

Examples:

do the shopping	do the washing	decide where to go for holidays
cook the food	do the ironing	decide what radio or TV programmes to watch
do the washing-up	do the cleaning	decide what clothes to buy
make the beds		

2. Use your lists to make a questionnaire. Ask other students about work and decisions in their families, and write down the answers.

Example:

Questions	Family members
Who does the shopping?	Mother, Father (sometimes)
Who makes the beds?	We all do.

3. Tell another student about work and decisions in your own family. Say who does what, and who you think should do what.

Example:

My wife does all the cooking. But I think I should help her more often.

You can make a list of words on a topic.

Example:

FAMILY		
Mother	Grandmother	Uncle
Father	Grandfather	Aunt
Brother		Cousin
Sister		

Make lists of words on these topics:
Kinds of sport, Parts of the body, Clothes

Language Study Exercises   6.3   6.15   6.16   6.19   6.20

LESSON 29

Describing character, behaviour and attitudes

190 Madron St.
NORWICH Y3 5BC

14th December

Dear Peter,

It's great to be at home again and I'm catching up on all the family gossip. The big news is that Uncle Fred and Aunt Jane are getting divorced. It's a terrible shock because they always seemed to get on so well together.

My father's feeling much better, but he's still not well. He says he's all right and he's very cheerful. But he's the kind of person who never complains.

I don't know what to do about the scholarship. I'd never forgive myself if he died when I was

Yes, I got your letter. Look, I think you should go. It'll do you good. Your trouble is that you're too unselfish. You think about other people far too much — and you don't think enough about yourself.

 Ask and answer

Make up questions about Jenny's letter and Peter's phone call beginning with WHO. Ask another student your questions.

Examples:

Who thinks it's great to be at home?
Who thinks about other people far too much?

Unit 6

 Reading: Describing character and behaviour

In a recent public opinion survey in Britain, nearly 2000 people were asked about changes in people's character and behaviour during the last ten years.

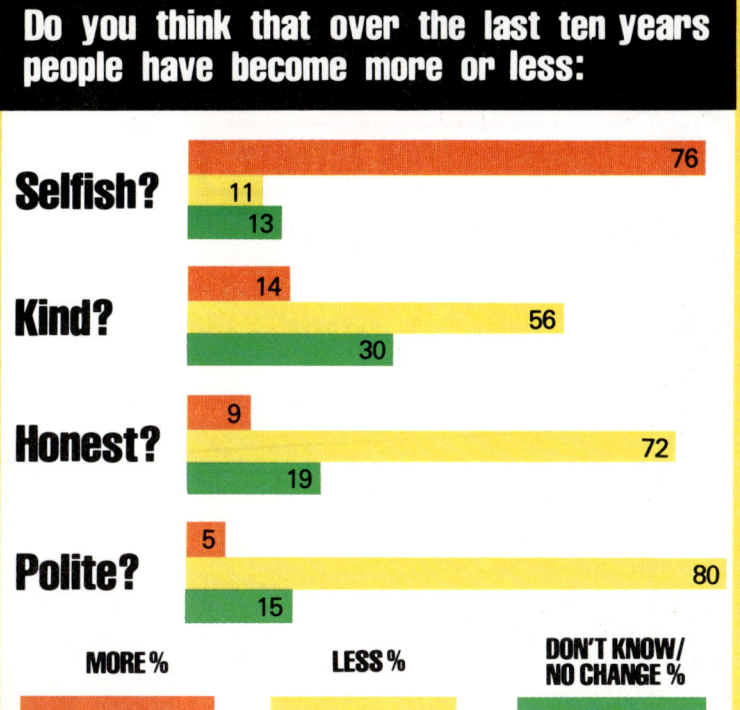

Do you think that over the last ten years people have become more or less:

	MORE %	LESS %	DON'T KNOW/ NO CHANGE %
Selfish?	76	11	13
Kind?	14	56	30
Honest?	9	72	19
Polite?	5	80	15

 Tell each other: Changes in character and behaviour

1. Tell each other about the survey.

Example:

The survey shows that seventy-six per cent think that people have become more selfish, eleven per cent think that people have become less selfish, and thirteen per cent don't know or think that there has been no change.

2. Discuss the results of the survey. Do you think there have been similar changes in your country?

 Study: Ways of describing character and attitudes

Good qualities		*Bad qualities*	
+	active	−	lazy
	cheerful		miserable
	clever		stupid
	friendly		unfriendly
	generous		mean
	honest		dishonest
	kind		unkind
	pleasant		unpleasant
	polite		rude
	sensible		silly
	unselfish		selfish

 Asking for definitions

Ask about the words in the Study section.

Example:

What's a cheerful person like?
The kind of person who always looks happy.

  Tell each other and write: My character

1. Tell each other about your good and bad qualities.
2. Write a paragraph describing your character. Do not put your name on the paper. Put all the papers together and see if you can guess who the descriptions are about.

In this lesson there is a list of ways of describing character and behaviour. Make lists of words which describe:

Personal appearance (e.g. slim, dark-haired)
Size, shape and colour (e.g. small, round, yellow)
Feelings (e.g. happy, excited)

Language Study Exercises   6.13   6.14   6.17   6.18   6.21

80

LESSON 30

 COMMUNICATION ACTIVITY

Discussing personal feelings
1. **Find a person who . . .**
Ask questions to find students who have these feelings.
Find a person who:

- is afraid of flying
- thinks motorbikes are exciting
- enjoys going to the dentist
- is feeling very happy today
- is frightened of the dark
- thinks watching television is boring
- hates eggs
- is always cheerful
- is feeling depressed today
- feels embarrassed about something

2. **My place in the family**
Do you have any brothers or sisters, or are you an only child?
- Make groups of students who have the same place in the family:

  ONLY CHILD   OLDEST CHILD   YOUNGEST CHILD
  MIDDLE CHILD

- Talk to other people in the group about your childhood and family.
  Do you think your place in the family has affected your life?
  Do the other members of the group think the same?
- Find out what the other groups think.

3. **Good things that have happened to me**
Make a list. Think about your life and the good things that have happened to you.
Make a list of ten of these events.

Examples:

Meeting someone special.
Winning a competition.

Compare your list with the other students' lists. Choose one event from your list and describe it. Say what happened and how you felt when it happened.

Example:

I'll never forget the day I passed my driving test. I wasn't very nervous before, but I made lots of mistakes in the test. After the test was over, I was sure that I had failed. I felt very depressed. But then the examiner told me that I had passed. I felt absolutely wonderful.

Unit 6

FOCUS ON READING

Autobiography

These extracts were not written specially for people learning English. So they contain some new and difficult words. But you do not need to understand all the words in order to understand what the writer means.

Before reading
Look quickly at these three extracts. One is a poem about a family visit. One is a man talking about what he did when he was young. One is a woman talking about the kind of person she is. Which is which?

Reading purpose
Find the answers to these questions:

Extract 1: Why was the writer able to look after herself?
Extract 2: Why was the writer going to university?
Extract 3: Why did the family feel alone?

After reading
1. Guess the meaning:
   (a) *a lighthouse keeper* is a person who ....
   (b) *an only child* does not have any ....
   (c) Does *elderly* mean fairly young, middle-aged, or fairly old?
   (d) Does *offered a place at* mean given a house to live in, given a chance to study at, or found a job in?
   (e) *dozens and dozens* means ....

2. In the first extract the writer gives four definitions of *a self-contained person*. What are the definitions?

1. In being a lighthouse keeper's wife what's important is the attitude. I'd say it was the most important thing of all, the attitude. You've got to be a self-contained person, someone who isn't miserable as soon as they are on their own, not needing the company of other people all the time. You've got to be able to do things for yourself, look after yourself. I've always been like that, so I don't have to make a lot of effort to change myself into somebody different. I should think it's because my parents both died by the time I was sixteen; I was the youngest of three girls, the other two married and had families of their own, so I had to learn to stand on my own feet.

   From *Lighthouse* by Tony Parker

2. I've eight 'O' levels and three 'A' levels. 'O' level English Literature, Language, French, German, Geography, History, Maths and Physics; 'A' level English, Geography and History. I was the only child of elderly parents; my father died when I was sixteen, my mother when I was nineteen. I was about to go to university when she died, I'd been offered a place at Birmingham. What exactly I was going to do when I got there I really don't know; take a degree and become a teacher, I suppose. I wasn't enthusiastic about the prospect; like a lot of young people I'd no specific ambition to do anything. I was going to continue in the educational system because I couldn't think of anything else.

   From *Lighthouse* by Tony Parker

Alison Slater

3. On Sunday last at half past three,
   All of our family came for tea,
   In cars and trains and buses they came,
   And our quiet house was not the same.

   My sister and I were expected to show,
   An example of good behaviour and so,
   We smiled and laughed and we joined in the fun,
   When we really preferred to play in the sun.

   Aunts, Uncles, Grandparents, Cousins,
   There were lots of us, yes, dozens and dozens,
   We all piled in to the little house
   And there wasn't room for even a mouse

   Everyone sat around the table,
   Eating as much as they were able,
   When at last they all went home,
   We all felt very much alone.

   Helen Chesworth, aged 12.   From *Happy Families* by Richard and Helen Exley

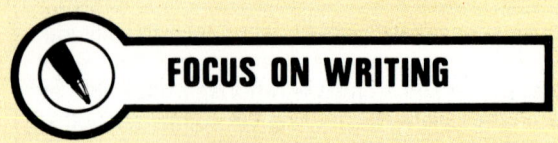

FOCUS ON WRITING

Personal description

One morning you receive this letter from an address in the United States.
Read the letter and reply to it.

> You don't know who I am, but I think we're part of the same family. I'm trying to find out more about the family, and that's why I'm writing to you.
>
> My grandfather came to the United States about eighty years ago, when he was a child. He didn't keep in touch with his family. All he knows is that the family come from the town where you live. So I'm writing to all the people with the same surname as me in your town. I looked you up in a telephone directory.
>
> Can you write to me describing yourself and your family? Then I'd know if we were related or not. I'd like to know what you look like (I've found some old photographs my grandfather had), something about you (where you went to school, what things you like doing, what your future plans are), and I'd like to know as much as possible about your family. I'm interested not only in you, but in all your relations. If you could tell me about all of them, their jobs, and their personalities, it would be wonderful. Then I could have a full picture of the family I've never seen.
>
> I'm hoping to come over from the States on vacation next summer, so perhaps we can meet then.
>
> Look forward to hearing from you,
>
> Yours sincerely,

Reading report

1. Write a list of the main characters in an English book you have read.
2. Then write descriptions of the characters. Use these headings to help you:

Name: Age: Occupation:

Physical description:

Personality:

My feelings (why I like or don't like the character):

---

3. Read through your descriptions and choose your favourite character.
4. Write a paragraph describing this character in detail and saying exactly why you like him/her so much.

Unit 6

LANGUAGE STUDY

Lessons 26–30

STRUCTURE

6.1 Study

PRESENT PERFECT CONTINUOUS TENSE
1. This tense can be used to describe a *recent* activity of *limited* duration. The activity is usually *incomplete*.
   Example: I've been reading 'War and Peace'.

   The present perfect tense describes a *completed* activity at an *indefinite time in the past*.
   Example: I've read 'War and Peace'.

2. The present perfect continuous tense is used for repeated actions in the recent past.
   Example: He's been going for long walks.

⚠ We do not use the present perfect continuous form when we are concerned with *how much* or *how many*. When we are talking about quantity, we use the present perfect tense.
Examples: 'What *have you been doing*?'
'*I've been writing* letters.'
BUT 'How many *have you written*?'
'*I've written* four letters.'

6.2 Put the verbs in brackets into the present perfect continuous

Example: Steve (look) for a job for several months, but he still hasn't found anything.
Steve has been looking for a job for several months, but he still hasn't found anything.

1. Jenny (eat) a lot recently. She's put on five kilos.
2. Mr Langley has given up smoking, and as a result, he (not cough) so much.
3. I (wait) for half an hour, but the bus hasn't come yet.
4. Jenny (get ready) to go to Mexico. She's stopped work and booked her flight.
5. The police (try) to catch the robbers for months, and at last they've arrested the leader.

6.3 Ask and answer

Example: Steve is applying for jobs. (for 3 months/6 jobs)
S1: *How long has Steve been applying for jobs?*
S2: *For three months.*
S1: *How many jobs has he applied for?*
S1: *Six.*

1. Fred is delivering milk. (since 6 a.m./400 pints)
2. Liz is watching TV. (for an hour/2 programmes)
3. Steve is saving money. (for 3 months/£200)
4. Sandra is typing letters. (since 9.30 a.m./5 letters)
5. The boy is selling newspapers. (for 10 minutes/50 newspapers)

6.4 Study

VERBS NOT USED IN CONTINUOUS FORMS
The following verbs are not *usually* used in continuous forms.

dislike	like	prefer	taste
hate	love	remember	think
hear	mind	see	understand
forget	need	seem	want
know	notice	smell	wish

6.5 Put the verbs in brackets into the present simple or present continuous

Example: 'I (make) some tea,' said Mrs Langley. 'You (want) a cup?'
'*I'm making some tea,*' said Mrs Langley. '*Do you want a cup?*'

1. 'You (remember) my Uncle Fred?' asked Jenny. 'He and my Aunt Jane (get) divorced. I (think) it's a terrible pity.'
2. 'You (like) travelling?' asked the doctor. 'Yes, I (love) seeing new places,' I replied.
3. 'I (buy) a new car,' said Liz. 'I (hate) the car I've got. It's so small.'
4. 'I (phone) about the robbery,' said Sandra. 'You (know) what happened?'
5. 'You (not like) your lunch?' asked Fred. 'It (not taste) very nice,' replied Liz.
6. 'You (listen) to the radio?' asked Jenny. 'No,' said her father. 'It's a pop music programme. That's all you (hear) on the radio now.'

6.6 Study

MODAL AUXILIARY: CAN

PRESENT AND FUTURE TENSE: CAN
PAST TENSE: COULD (often used as a polite form for *can*)

1. CAN often expresses *ability* and means BE ABLE TO
   Examples: Can you play any musical instruments?
   He couldn't see properly.
2. CAN often expresses *permission*.
   Examples: You can pay by cheque.
   Could I use your phone?

6.7 What do *can/could* mean in these sentences?

Examples: You can talk quietly. *Permission*
He could swim well. *Ability*

1. Steve can speak several languages.
2. Can you see my keys anywhere?
3. The police said the man could go.
4. You can get a bus from the airport to the city centre.
5. Can I turn on the TV?
6. You can borrow my car.
7. I couldn't understand a word.
8. Can I join you?
9. You can drive a car at 17 in Britain.
10. The old man couldn't read.

'MAKE' + INFINITIVE WITHOUT 'TO'

 6.8 Make sentences

How do the following things make you feel?
Find the answers in the second list.

Example: A hot bath makes you feel relaxed.

a hot bath	tired
the smell of food	sad
eating salt	worried
having a temperature	relaxed
a long journey	thirsty
saying goodbye to friends	happy
eating too much	hungry
losing your keys	hot
hearing good news	sick

PREPOSITIONS AND CONJUNCTIONS: TIME

6.9 Complete

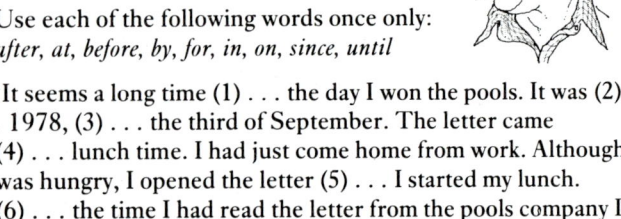

Use each of the following words once only:
after, at, before, by, for, in, on, since, until

'It seems a long time (1) . . . the day I won the pools. It was (2) . . . 1978, (3) . . . the third of September. The letter came (4) . . . lunch time. I had just come home from work. Although I was hungry, I opened the letter (5) . . . I started my lunch. (6) . . . the time I had read the letter from the pools company I didn't feel like eating! (7) . . . we got the news Liz and I gave a party for everyone in the street. But we had to wait (8) . . . nearly a week (9) . . . we got the cheque.'

VOCABULARY

When you are studying this vocabulary section, you will find a dictionary is very helpful.

WORD BUILDING

6.10 Study

> FORMATION OF ADVERBS OF MANNER:
> ADJECTIVE + SUFFIX '-ly'
>
> 1. Most adverbs are formed by adding the suffix '-ly' to adjectives.
>   *Example:* serious   seriously
> 2. In adjectives ending in '-y', the '-y' changes to an 'i'.
>   *Example:* happy   happily
> 3. Note the following exceptions:
>
> | Adjective | Adverb |
> | good | well |
> | early | early |
> | late | late |
> | hard | hard |
> | fast | fast |
> | straight | straight |
>
> ⚠ Some adjectives do not form adverbs with '-ly', e.g. big, fat, little, long, old, slim, small, tall, young and all colour adjectives.

 6.11 Drill

Agree with the statements.

Examples: Fred is a slow eater. *That's right. He eats slowly.*
Liz is a good dancer. *That's right. She dances well.*

1. Steve is a dangerous driver.
2. Sandra is a hard worker.
3. Tom is a heavy smoker.
4. Steve is a quick learner.
5. Jenny is a strong swimmer.
6. Mr Langley is a slow reader.
7. Liz is an extravagant spender.
8. Sandra is a fast typist.
9. Steve is a good teacher.
10. Tom is a bad writer.

 6.12 Drill

Combine the sentences by using an adverb formed from one of these adjectives:
amusing, angry, happy, hungry, quiet, slow

Example: Steve was singing. He felt fine.
Steve was singing happily.

1. Liz shouted. She was having an argument.
2. Jenny was learning Spanish. It was taking a long time.
3. The students were talking. They weren't making much noise.
4. Fred ate his breakfast. He hadn't eaten for a long time.
5. Sandra told the story. Everyone laughed.

6.13 Study

> PREFIX 'un-'
> The prefix 'un-' means *not*. It can be added to some words to make them mean the opposite.
> *Examples:* selfish   unselfish
> interesting   uninteresting

6.14 Add the prefix 'un-'

Put 'un-' in front of the adjectives to make them mean the opposite.

'I was a very happy child,' said Mr Successful. 'My parents were kind to me and interested in helping me. I enjoyed school – my parents said this was important. I think I was lucky. I was popular with other children at school, who said I was always friendly. Yes, life was pleasant when I was a child.'

WORDS OFTEN CONFUSED

6.15 Study

> IDIOMS WITH 'DO' AND 'MAKE'
> There are a number of idiomatic expressions with 'do' and 'make'.
> *Examples:*
>
> | do the shopping | make an appointment |
> | the housework | a complaint |
> | the washing-up | a mistake |
> | the washing | coffee |
> | your homework | the bed |
> | an exercise | friends |
> | damage | money |
> | well/badly | a noise |
> | you good | notes |
> | a course | an application |
> | your best | a phone call |

85

Unit 6

6.16 Complete

Put in the correct form of *do* or *make*.

1. Jenny . . . very well in the scholarship interview last month.
2. Ssh! Don't . . . any noise.
3. Steve . . . an appointment to go to the dentist yesterday.
4. The cyclone last month . . . a lot of damage to buildings.
5. Fred didn't . . . much money as a milkman.
6. During the lecture, the students . . . notes.
7. Fred wanted a dishwasher because he hated . . . the washing-up.
8. The customer called the manager to . . . a complaint.
9. The teacher asked if the students had . . . their homework.
10. The waiter . . . a mistake with the bill.

WHAT DO YOU SAY?

6.17 Listen and choose the most suitable response

1. (a) No, I feel fine.
   (b) The train's just left.
   (c) I really miss my friends.
   (d) Yes, my wallet's been stolen.
2. (a) I went by bus.
   (b) Much better, thank you.
   (c) I've been doing the shopping.
   (d) About six months.
3. (a) Yes, he's very kind.
   (b) He's rather lazy.
   (c) It's a black leather purse.
   (d) He's amused.

INTONATION AND STRESS

6.18 Listen and choose the most suitable stimulus for each response

1. (a) What do you like doing?
   (b) Do you like dancing?
   (c) Do you like swimming?
2. (a) What's the matter?
   (b) How do you feel?
   (c) Does it feel comfortable?
3. (a) What's the time?
   (b) Is it late?
   (c) Is it half past nine?
4. (a) Can you swim?
   (b) Have you been swimming?
   (c) Your hair's wet!
5. (a) Would you like to go to the cinema?
   (b) Are you afraid of snakes?
   (c) Can I ask you something?

SENTENCE LINKING

6.19 Study

POINTING WORDS	
'this' type:	'that' type:
this	that
these	those
here (at this place)	there (at that place)
now (at this time)	then (at that time)

Pointing words are used in three ways:
1. *Pointing out* to something in the world around the speaker.
   Example: I don't want *this* dress (the dress near me), I want *that* one. (the dress over there).
2. *Pointing backwards* to something which has been said.
   Examples: I've been saving up for years. *That's* why I can afford a holiday in Egypt. I've always wanted to go *there*.

   She's failed the exam. *This* is why she's unhappy.
3. *Pointing forwards* to something which is going to be said.
   Examples: *This* is how you work the dishwasher. First you plug it in . . .

   Here is the news. The Prime Minister flew to Washington this morning . . .

 Only 'this' type words can be used to point forwards.

6.20 Complete

Put in the correct pointing word.

1. Would you like to sit here or over . . . in the corner?
2. I used to live in Italy. . . .'s why I speak Italian.
3. . . . is very important: think before you drink before you drive.
4. Write down . . . things: your name, age, address, and occupation.
5. He visited me last month, but I haven't seen him since . . . .
6. Where's the bus? It should be here by . . . .
7. This is a nice restaurant – let's have dinner . . . .
8. This record is much cheaper than . . . ones in the shop window.
9. I can't find my keys. . . .'s the problem.
10. I only want to say . . . : don't come home late.

6.21 Write a paragraph

Write a short description of a person you admire. Describe the person's character and say why you admire him/her. Use the pointing words above to connect your ideas.

Example: A person who I admire very much is the Prime Minister. She is very sensible and clever. That is why she has been so successful . . .

DIY CHECK UP   Unit 1

Choose the most suitable word or put the verbs in brackets into the correct form.

Jenny is getting ready to go to Mexico. She (1) (*have*) her medical examination, and she (2) (*just book*) her flight. She is really looking forward to (3) (*go*) away. She (4) (*go*) to Mexico City two years ago, (5) *so/but* she couldn't speak Spanish. Now she is going to evening classes (6) *because/in order* to learn the language. She (7) (*be*) at the National Portrait Gallery (8) *for/since* two years, and she will be sorry to leave. She liked (9) (*work*) there, (10) *and/but* she would like (11) (*do*) something different for a while. She wants (12) (*travel*) all over Mexico.

* Look up the answers in the DIY Check-up Key. Discuss any mistakes you have made.
* Look up your mistakes in the Structural Reference List. Then turn to the Language Study exercises suggested.

Unit 7
LESSON 31

Planning and describing

Margaret and Trevor Wilkinson live in Clapham, in London. They have a fourteen-year-old daughter, Jane, and eight-year-old twins, David and Alan. The Wilkinsons have decided to have a holiday abroad for the first time. They are looking at holiday brochures.

TREVOR: I think it'd be lovely to get away from London. I'd like to go somewhere peaceful. Ireland might be nice.

JANE: Why can't we go somewhere exciting? How about Italy? Then I could get a suntan, and practise my Italian at the same time.

TREVOR: Actually, I don't know if we should have a holiday at all. Perhaps it'd be better if we stayed at home. Then we could buy new carpets.

MARGARET: Carpets! Forget about the house for a while! We're going to have a holiday abroad this year.

JANE: Yes, come on, let's talk about where we're going to go.

MARGARET: I don't really know. I think it'd be fun to go somewhere interesting – I don't want to sit on a beach all day. I'd like to be able to go to museums and art galleries, that sort of thing. But David and Alan wouldn't like that. They said they wanted a seaside holiday.

TREVOR: Quite right, too. We could all have a seaside holiday in Ireland – and then I'd be able to go fishing.

JANE: I know what – Mum and I can go to Italy, and Dad and the boys can go to Ireland!

 Ask and answer

Make up questions about the Wilkinsons' conversation. Ask another student your questions.

Example:

What kind of holiday does Jane want?

  Listen and complete: Describing different kinds of holidays.

1. Read the conversation again and fill in Part 1 of the table about the Wilkinsons' holiday ideas. What kind of holidays do they want?
2. Listen to the rest of the conversation and fill in Part 2 of the table.

	Margaret	Trevor	Jane
Part 1			
Kind of place	Somewhere interesting.	seaside	great big Hotel Italian speaking
Activity	Go to museums and art galleries.	Fishing	dancing + swimming
Part 2			
Accommodation	small family hotel	cottage by the sea	Hotel
Food	hotel food	Fish self-catering	little restaurants local food
Language	doesn't mind	somewhere English-speaking	practise her Italian

Tell each other and write: Comparing different kinds of holidays

1. Compare the kinds of holidays the Wilkinsons would like. Use the table to help you.

   Examples:
   Trevor wants to go somewhere peaceful, *but* Jane wants to go somewhere exciting.

   Jane *doesn't want* to go to museums and *nor does* Trevor.

   Both Margaret *and* Jane want to stay in a hotel.

2. Write a paragraph about the kinds of holidays the Wilkinsons would like.

   Begin:
   The Wilkinson family would all like to do different things on their holiday. Trevor would like..........

3. *Your ideal holiday*
   Ask each other about the kind of holiday you would like to have, if you had a lot of money.

   Examples:
   Where would you like to go?

   What would you like to do?

   Where would you like to stay?

4. Write a paragraph describing your ideal holiday.

   Begin:
   I would like to go somewhere..........

 Role Play: Describing what you want

A is a customer and B is a sales assistant in a shop.
A wants to buy a pair of jeans.

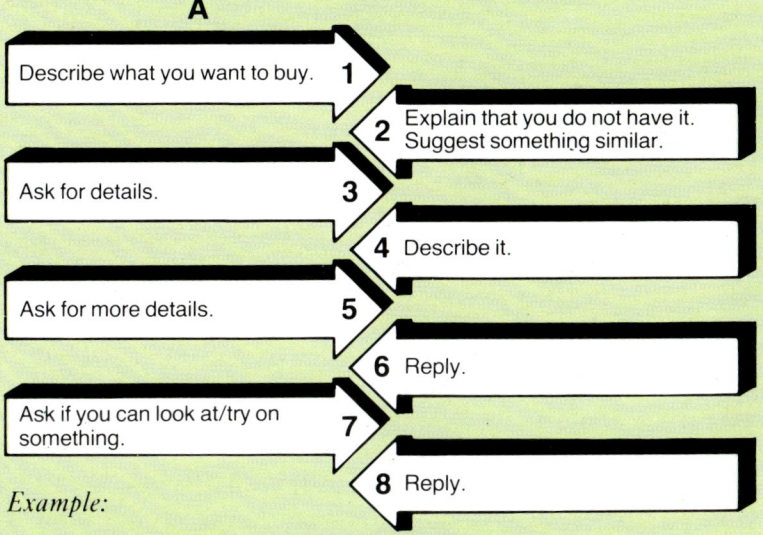

1. Describe what you want to buy.
2. Explain that you do not have it. Suggest something similar.
3. Ask for details.
4. Describe it.
5. Ask for more details.
6. Reply.
7. Ask if you can look at/try on something.
8. Reply.

Example:
1. A: I'm looking for a pair of light brown jeans – with narrow legs.
2. B: I'm afraid we don't have any light brown ones at the moment. But I think we've got a dark brown pair.
3. A: Are they wide or narrow?
4. B: Let me see. They're wide.
5. A: What narrow ones do you have?
6. B: Only blue, dark green and black.
7. A: Can I try on the dark green ones, please?
8. B: Yes, of course. The changing room is over there.

Further situations:
1. A wants to buy a guide book to Edinburgh, with a map and colour photographs.
2. A wants to buy a cheap 35 mm camera, with a flash and a case.
3. Make up your own situations.

 Project: **Your town guide**

In Lesson 35 you will write a guide to your town for English-speaking visitors.

Preparation:
Make notes answering these questions.
1. Do many English-speaking visitors come to your town? Do they come for holidays or work? Do they stay for a long time or just for a few days?
2. What places of interest are there in your town for foreign visitors? Museums? Important factories? Beautiful views? Old houses? Modern buildings?

Note:
If foreign visitors never come to your town, you can write about another town which you know.

LANGUAGE STUDY Exercises 7.1 7.12 7.13 7.14

LESSON 32

Persuading and dealing with persuasion

A place of your own in Ireland

HOLIDAYS IN MATONA

The new holiday centre with something for everyone. This Mediterranean island has everything: miles and miles of magnificent beaches, wonderful weather, marvellous museums, and now THE MATONA HOLIDAY VILLAGE. Stay in your own luxurious holiday cottage, eat in the superb restaurant, and dance the night away in the open-air disco. Lie on the beach all day, swim in the warm water, or enjoy the excellent fishing. Two swimming pools and a special children's playground make this the perfect place for a family holiday. And all the MATONA HOLIDAY VILLAGE staff speak English!'

The best climate in the world! Look at these weather statistics:

Month:	J	F	M	A	M	J	J	A	S	O	N	D
Average day temperature (°C)	24	24	25	26	26	28	30	32	30	26	25	24
Hours of sunshine a day:	7	7	8	10	11	12	12	12	11	9	7	7
Rainy days a month:	5	4	2	1	0	0	0	0	0	2	4	5

Note:
10% deposit must be paid when a booking is made. The total cost of the holiday must be paid 8 weeks before departure. Deposits cannot be refunded if holidays are cancelled.
I have read and understood the above information. I am over 18 years of age.
Signature........................ Date................

Italy

Trevor and Margaret go to a travel agency.

- Can I help you?
- We're thinking about a holiday. But we can't decide where to go.
- We've been looking at brochures for Italy and Ireland.

ASSISTANT: I'm glad you came to see me. I'm sure I've got the holiday you want. If I were you, I'd forget about Ireland and Italy. The place to go is Matona.
TREVOR: Hold on a minute. I've never . . .
ASSISTANT: You'll love it there. Matona's the place everyone's talking about.
MARGARET: Yes, but I don't even know where it is.
ASSISTANT: Have a look at the map in the brochure, madam. Look at the photographs. Isn't it the most wonderful holiday centre you've ever seen? But don't let me persuade you. Sit down and decide for yourselves.

Five minutes later

MARGARET: Well, it's got all the things we were looking for. But it's rather expensive, isn't it? It would cost over £1,200 for the five of us.
ASSISTANT: I'm not saying it's the cheapest holiday we've got, but it's certainly the best.
TREVOR: I'm not sure. We'd better think it over for a few days.
ASSISTANT: Of course, sir. But don't forget that Matona's very popular this year. To tell you the truth, if you came back next week it might be fully booked.
MARGARET: Perhaps we should book now.
ASSISTANT: I would if I were you, madam.
TREVOR: I'd like time to think about it.
ASSISTANT: If you book today, madam, I'll cut the price to £1,100.
MARGARET: All right. I hope we're doing the right thing.
ASSISTANT: I'm sure you are. Can I have a deposit of £110 please?

Unit 7

 Ask and answer

Make up questions about the holiday brochure for Matona.
Ask another student your questions.

Examples:
What are the beaches like?

Is there a swimming pool at the Matona Holiday Village?

What's the temperature in Matona in July?

 Questions

1. *Deciding if something is what you want:* Look at the holiday brochure for Matona, and at your notes in the table in Lesson 31. Would the Wilkinsons enjoy a holiday in Matona? Why or why not?
2. *Persuading someone to buy something:* The assistant says 'Don't let me persuade you.' But he does try to persuade them. Make a list of at least four ways in which he tries to persuade the Wilkinsons.
   Example: He says, 'The place to go to is Matona.'
3. *Dealing with persuasion:* Trevor does not like the way the assistant is trying to persuade them. Find three ways in which Trevor shows this.

Role Play: Persuading

A is selling his car.
B wants to buy a car and goes to see A.
A tries to persuade B to buy the car.

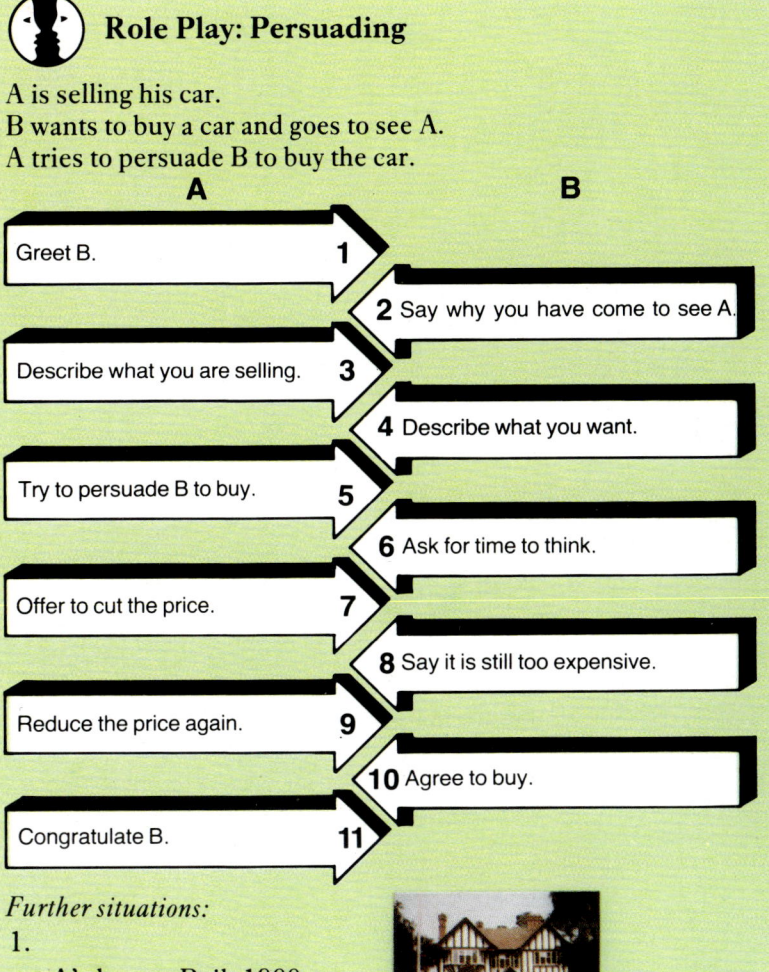

Example:

A's car: Twelve years old. £1,650.

B wants:
A small modern car costing about £1,000.

1. A: Good afternoon.
2. B: I'm thinking of buying a car. I see that yours is for sale.
3. A: I'm glad you came to see me. I'm sure this is the car you want. It's a marvellous car and the price is only £1,650.
4. B: I'm not sure. I'm really looking for a small, modern car.
5. A: I'm not saying this is the most modern car you can buy, but it's certainly the most exciting.
6. B: I don't know. I'd better think it over.
7. A: You can have it for £1,500.
8. B: No, I'm sorry, it's still too expensive.
9. A: Well, I'll cut the price to £1,200 if you buy now.
10. B: All right, I'll buy it. I hope I'm doing the right thing.
11. A: Yes, I'm sure you are.

Further situations:

1. A's house. Built 1900. 5 bedrooms. £80,000.

B wants: A modern four-bedroom house costing about £60,000.

2. A's dog. £250.

B wants: A dog. But B lives in a small flat without a garden.

3. A's colour TV. 5 years old. £200.

B wants: A portable black and white TV costing about £100.

 Project: **Your town guide**

Introduction: The Main Facts
Make notes for the introduction to the guide to your town. Use these headings to help you:

Position (Where is it?)
Character (Is it industrial, commercial, a tourist centre, a port, a market town?)
Appearance (Beautiful, peaceful, interesting?)
Population (How big is it?)
History (How old is it?)
People (What are they like?)

LANGUAGE STUDY Exercises 7.11 7.15

LESSON 33

Complaining and dealing with complaints

The Wilkinsons went back to the travel agency a week later.

> We're worried about the holiday we booked in Matona. In fact, we'd like to cancel it, and get back the £110 we paid you.

ASSISTANT: I see, sir. Of course you can cancel the holiday, but I'm afraid we can't give you back your deposit. It says so in the brochure.

MARGARET: I don't believe what it says in the brochure. We saw a television programme about Matona last night. You told us we'd love it there. But it said in the programme that the holiday village hasn't even been built yet. And there aren't any museums on the island.

ASSISTANT: Now, madam, you shouldn't believe everything you see on television. If the village isn't ready, I'm sure you'll stay somewhere just as nice. But if you cancel your holiday, you lose your deposit. It's as simple as that.

TREVOR: You should have listened to me, Margaret. If we'd thought about it for a few days, we wouldn't have booked the holiday. I wish we'd never heard of Matona.

ASSISTANT: I'm sorry, but there's nothing I can do to help you. Why don't you write to the 'Holidays in Matona' company about it?

  Questions

1. *Making sure of the facts:* The assistant says, 'It says so in the brochure.' What does it say about a deposit in the brochure on page 89?

2. *Criticising:* Trevor says, 'You should have listened to me.' What does he mean? What did Trevor say on page 89?

  Listen and write: Comparing different descriptions of the same thing

1. Listen to the television programme about Matona. The programme is called 'What Do You Think?' and Anita Lyons is interviewing the Director of Tourism for Matona. Anita asks questions about three different topics. Note down the topics of Anita's questions and the director's replies.

   Anita's topics   *The director's replies*
   a) The brochure   a)
   b)   b)
   c)   c)

2. Listen to the last part of the interview again. Write down the differences between what Anita says, and the weather statistics in the brochure on page 89.

3. Listen to the first part of the interview and read the conversation between the Wilkinsons and the assistant again. Make a list of the differences between what it said in the brochure about Matona, and what Matona is really like.

4. Then write sentences like this:

   It said in the brochure that.........., but in fact.........

   Although it said in the brochure that ...., the truth is that..........

   The brochure said that.......... However, in fact..........

Unit 7

 Role Play: Complaining

A is an assistant at a travel agency.
B has just been on holiday.
Lots of things went wrong on the holiday.
B is very angry and wants his money back.

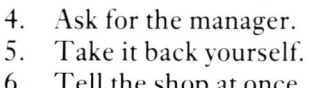

A	B
1. Greet B and ask if you can help.	
	2. Explain that you want your money back.
3. Ask B what was wrong with the holiday.	
	4. Tell A about three things which went wrong.
5. Explain that there is nothing you can do.	
	6. Ask for your money back.
7. Refuse politely. Suggest that B writes to the holiday company.	
	8. Agree and say goodbye.

 Tell each other: How to make a complaint

Match the instructions with the pictures, and tell each other what to do if something you buy is no good.

Example:
I. Keep calm. F.
'You should keep calm.'

1. Keep calm.
2. Stop using it.
3. Keep the receipt.
4. Ask for the manager.
5. Take it back yourself.
6. Tell the shop at once.

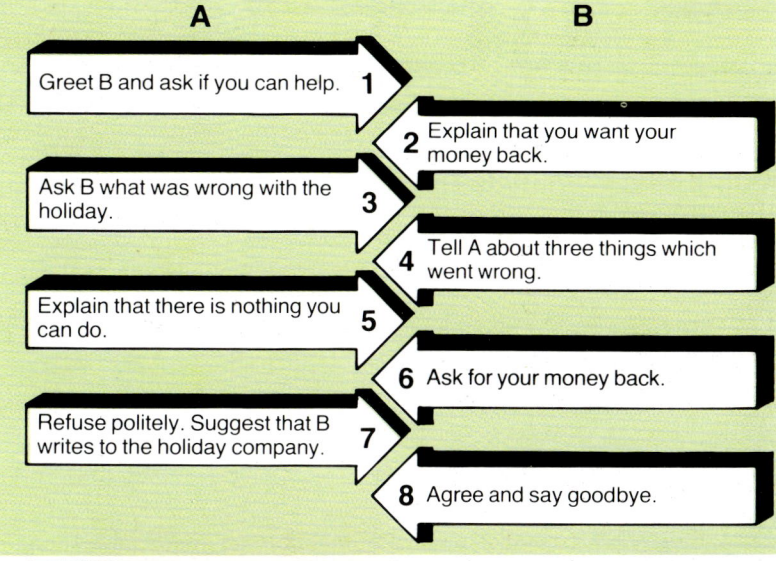

 Study

Last week, Margaret Wilkinson bought a pair of shoes. When she got home, she took the shoes out of the bag and threw it away. The receipt was in the bag. The next day, she wore the shoes to work. While she was at work, one of the heels broke off. Margaret mended the heel with some glue, and wore the shoes the next day. Then the heel broke again. A few days later, she went back to the shop to complain. She was very angry, and shouted at the assistant who had sold her the shoes. Margaret didn't get her money back. When she got home, she told Jane what had happened. 'But, Mum,' said Jane, 'you shouldn't have......'

 Tell each other

1. What should Margaret have done and what shouldn't she have done? Use the instructions from 'How to make a complaint' to help you.

   Example:
   Margaret should have kept the receipt.

2. Margaret would have got her money back if she'd........

   Example:
   Margaret would have got her money back if she'd kept the receipt.

 **Project:**  **Your town guide**

1. Look at the table on page 89 about the weather in Matona. Make notes about the weather in your town.

2. What kind of clothes does a visitor to your town need at different times of the year?

   Example:
   It's very wet in November, so you need a raincoat.

Language Study Exercises   7.2   7.3   7.4   7.6   7.7   7.8   7.9   7.17   7.18

LESSON 34

**Making a written complaint
Requesting something and offering alternatives**

The Wilkinsons wrote a letter of complaint to the 'Holidays in Matona' company.

> 'Holidays in Matona',
> Cheshire Road,
> Manchester.
>
> 23 Bunyan Road,
> London SW11
> 20th February
>
> Dear Sir,
> We are writing to you about your 'Holidays in Matona' brochure. We have cancelled a holiday in Matona, and we want our deposit back.
>
> Two weeks ago we booked a holiday in Matona at the Super Tours Travel Agency, 620 Oxford Street, London W.1. We went there to enquire about holidays in Italy and Ireland. The assistant showed us your brochure, and persuaded us to go to Matona. He offered to reduce the price if we booked at once. We decided to book, and paid a deposit of £110.
>
> After we had made the bookings, we found out a lot more about Matona from a T.V. programme. Your brochure gives a completely false picture of the island. If we had known the truth, we would not have booked a holiday there. We went to the agency, and asked for our money back. The assistant refused to return the deposit, and suggested that we write to you.
>
> We feel that you should return our deposit, because the brochure is completely inaccurate. We enclose a copy of the booking form, and the receipt for the deposit.
> Yours faithfully,
> T. Wilkinson   M. Wilkinson
> Trevor Wilkinson   Margaret Wilkinson

 Ask and answer

Make up questions about the Wilkinsons' letter and the reply to it. Ask another student your questions.

Example:
Why did the Wilkinsons go to the travel agency?

Here is part of the reply to the Wilkinsons' letter.

> wish to apologise for what has happened. We are producing a new brochure about Matona because of complaints about the old one. I enclose a cheque for £110.
>
> Yours faithfully,
> P. Barnwell
> P. Barnwell
> Managing Director

  Questions: Reporting

1. 'He offered to reduce the price if we booked at once.' What did the assistant actually say? Look at page 89.
2. 'The assistant refused to return the deposit.' What did the assistant actually say? Look at page 91.
3. 'The assistant . . . suggested that we write to you.' What did the assistant actually say? Look at page 91.

Writing: A letter of complaint

1. Note how the Wilkinsons begin and end their letter.
2. There are four paragraphs in the Wilkinsons' letter. Label the paragraphs:
   OPENING   WHAT HAPPENED   WHY WE ARE COMPLAINING   CONCLUSION
3. Look at the picture and conversation on the right. Imagine that you are the customer. Write a letter of complaint to the manager of Storehouse Ltd, Knightsbridge, London SW1.

CUSTOMER: I bought this cassette recorder here last week. It worked all right for a few days, but now it won't work at all. Here's the receipt.
ASSISTANT: It looks as if you've dropped it on the floor. Have you?
CUSTOMER: Certainly not.
ASSISTANT: Well, it looks as if you have. I'm afraid there's nothing we can do. We can't repair it.

Unit 7

 Role Play: Having something done

A is a sales assistant and B is a customer.
A works at a dry-cleaner's and B wants to have a pair of trousers cleaned.

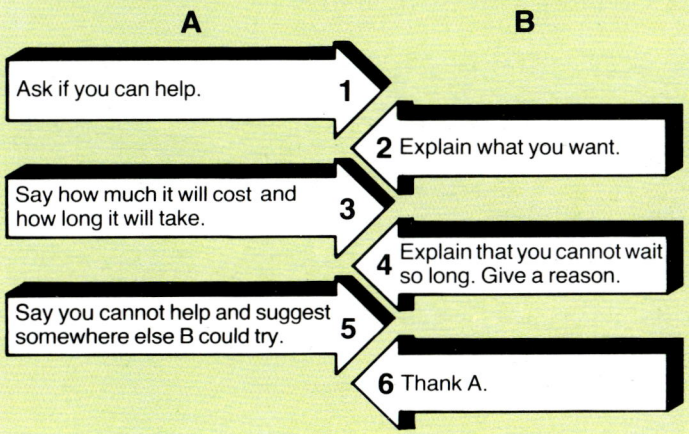

Example:

1. A: Can I help you?
2. B: I'd like to have these trousers cleaned.
3. A: That'll be £2 and they'll be ready tomorrow afternoon.
4. B: I'm afraid that's too late. I need them tonight, because I'm going to a party.
5. A: I'm sorry, but there's nothing I can do about it. Why don't you try ABC Dry-Cleaners round the corner? They might be able to help you.
6. B: Thank you very much. That's very kind of you. Goodbye.

Further situations:

1. At a photographer's. B wants to have a passport photograph taken.
2. At a garage. B wants to have a car serviced.
3. At an optician's. B wants to have a pair of glasses mended.
4. At a jeweller's. B wants to have a watch mended.
5. At an electrical shop. B wants to have a radio repaired.
6. At a camera shop. B wants to have a colour film developed and printed.
7. Make up your own situations.

 Project: **Your town guide**

Tourist services in your town

1. Discuss which services a visitor to your town might need.
   For example:
   A bank, shops, the post office, the tourist information office, a dry-cleaner's.

2. Make notes. Write down the addresses, opening hours and any other important details of these services.

3. How much do you know about hotels and restaurants in your town? Make two short lists, one of hotels and one of restaurants. Divide the lists into:

   EXPENSIVE   MEDIUM-PRICED   CHEAP

4. Make notes on entertainment facilities in your town: cinemas, theatres, concert-halls, etc. Give the usual starting times of performances and say whether it is necessary to book.

LANGUAGE STUDY Exercises   7.5   7.10   7.16   7.19

LESSON 35

COMMUNICATION ACTIVITY

Comparing costs

Do this activity in pairs (A and B). A's instructions are below and B's instructions are at the bottom of the page.

PRICES AROUND THE WORLD: LIVING COSTS FOR BUSINESSMEN

One night in a room with private bathroom, including breakfast

Dinner for one in a good restaurant

A five-kilometre taxi ride

One hotel night, one restaurant dinner and one taxi ride

Student A
COVER THE BOTTOM HALF OF THE PAGE. YOU MUST NOT LOOK AT B'S INSTRUCTIONS.

City	Hotel £	Restaurant £	Taxi £	Total £
Amsterdam	45.14	6.16	2.27	53.57
Bangkok	24.87	11.40	0.62	36.89
Copenhagen	49.74	8.80	2.31	60.85
Jakarta	31.32	12.97	0.74	45.03
Jeddah	76.92	15.11	2.75	94.78
London	64.02	7.75	1.80	73.57
Los Angeles	35.93	7.83	1.77	45.53
Madrid	34.54	5.57	1.39	41.50
Rio de Janeiro	35.93	10.81	0.36	47.10
Tokyo	66.33	15.67	1.69	83.69

Prices and Earnings Around the Globe: Union Bank of Switzerland, Dec. 1979

1. Tell B which city is the most expensive and the cheapest for a hotel room, a restaurant meal and a taxi ride. Which is the most expensive and the cheapest city *in total*?

   Example:
   The most expensive city for a hotel room is Jeddah and the cheapest is Bangkok.

2. B also has a table of living costs. Compare your table with B's. *Do not show B your table.*

   Examples:
   My table says a taxi ride in Rio de Janeiro costs thirty-six pence. What does your table say?
   What does it say in your table for a hotel room in Amsterdam? In mine it says forty-five pounds fourteen pence.

3. Why do the tables give different prices? Ask what B thinks.

Student B
COVER THE TOP HALF OF THE PAGE. YOU MUST NOT LOOK AT A'S INSTRUCTIONS.

City	Hotel £	Restaurant £	Taxi £	Total £
Amsterdam	38.63	14.22	2.37	55.22
Bangkok	29.93	5.13	2.33	37.39
Copenhagen	37.45	12.50	3.57	53.52
Jakarta	29.64	7.58	1.14	38.36
Jeddah	62.06	13.40	2.12	77.58
London	65.50	11.00	2.50	79.00
Los Angeles	34.60	7.58	2.37	44.55
Madrid	27.82	6.04	1.07	34.93
Rio de Janeiro	38.20	7.64	0.76	46.60
Tokyo	38.52	19.17	2.68	60.37

A Businessman's Guide to Living Costs: Financial Times, Jan. 26, 1980

1. Decide which city is the most expensive and the cheapest for a hotel room, a restaurant meal and a taxi ride. Which is the most expensive and the cheapest city *in total*? Listen to A, who also has a table of living costs. Tell A if you do not agree.

   Example:
   Just a minute, it says here that the most expensive city for a hotel room is London, not Jeddah. A room in London costs sixty-five pounds fifty pence.

2. Compare the prices in your table with A's prices. *Do not show A your table.*

   Example:
   My table says a taxi ride in Bangkok costs sixty-two pence. What does yours say?

3. Do you think the prices in the table are high? How do they compare with prices in your town?

Unit 7

FOCUS ON READING

Information from a town guide

Reading purpose
Here are some extracts from a guide to Hanover in English. Find the answers to these questions:

1. How long does it take to travel by bus from the airport to the railway station?
2. Can you take a city sightseeing tour on a Sunday at 2 p.m.?
3. When is the Hanover Trade Fair held?
4. Are the banks open on Saturday mornings?
5. Are the theatres open in August?

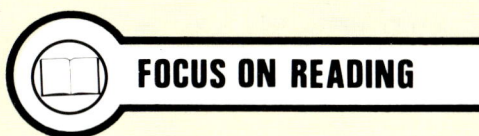

SAS CITY PORTRAIT

Hanover

SAS SCANDINAVIAN AIRLINES

Introduction
Hanover (spelt 'Hannover' in the German language) is the capital of the German state of Lower Saxony. A lively, modern city of almost 550,000 inhabitants, it is an important business and communications centre.
Not much is left of the old Hanover; in fact, an almost entirely new city welcomes visitors. The modern buildings, busy traffic, elegant shops, and beautiful parks appeal to practically everyone.
The people of Hanover make friends quickly and you will find them eager to help make your stay a pleasure.

Your arrival in Hanover
You arrive at Langenhagen Airport, 8 miles (13 kms) from the city centre. At the airport there is an Information Desk, restaurant, souvenir shop, post office and travel agency. Outside the main hall is a taxi rank and bus stop. The bus takes 20 minutes to the Central Railway Station.

Hotels
Hanover's hotels, most of which are modern and comfortable, provide excellent service. During the Hanover Trade Fair in April, and also during July and August, it is advisable to book accommodation well ahead. The following list of hotels is divided into three groups:
Expensive   Medium priced   Cheap

Restaurants and food
International dishes can be ordered at any good restaurant. If, however, you would like to try a typical local speciality, try 'Labskaus' (a traditional dish consisting of pork, mashed potatoes, and sometimes fish. It is served with egg and cucumber).
Listed below are a few suggestions for places to eat.

Sights and places of interest
For a comprehensive look at the city, take a sight-seeing coach tour: departure point the Tourist Office opposite the Central Railway Station. Tours run from June to September, daily at 10 a.m.; Wednesday and Saturday at 10 a.m. and 2 p.m. The trip lasts about 2 hours.
The main city sights are:

Entertainment
The theatre and concert season runs from early September to late June. Hanover has quite a number of big cinemas showing German films and foreign films dubbed into German. The following cinemas and theatres are close to the city centre:

Tipping
A service charge of 15% is usually added to hotel bills; in restaurants 10% is included in the total figure. People usually tip taxi-drivers, hairdressers and cloakroom attendants, as well as porters at stations and hotels.

Shopping and souvenir hunting
Shopping in Hanover is always a pleasure. Walk into any shop and you will find superb service. Among the many articles on sale, leather and glass are especially reasonably-priced. Other good buys include cameras and toys. The main shopping streets are

Business hours
Banks: open weekdays between 9 a.m. and 1 p.m., and on Fridays between 4 and 6 p.m. Closed all day Saturday and Sunday.
Shops: open Monday-Friday from 9 a.m. to 6.30 p.m., and on Saturdays until 2 p.m.
Offices: open 8 a.m. to 5 p.m., Monday to Friday. Closed Saturday.

Transport
The bus service is excellent, and there are plenty of taxis, which can be hired in the streets, or by telephone (tel. 6811). Coaches depart from the Central Railway Station (tel. 1981), or the Coach Station, (tel. 197 3911).

Sport
Football and rugby are Hanover's most popular sports. Important matches are held at the Niedersachsen Stadion, which can accommodate up to 74,000 spectators.

Climate and clothing
Hanover's climate is pleasant for most of the year. During the summer months the temperature averages 20-25 °C. An overcoat is necessary during the winter months (October to March), and a raincoat is useful all year round. Average monthly temperatures are

FOCUS ON WRITING

Your town guide

Writing purpose
To write a short guide for an English-speaking visitor to your town.

1. *Headings:* These are the headings for the sections of the guide to Hanover.
Can you use these headings in your guide?

Introduction	Tipping
Your arrival	Shopping and souvenir-hunting
Hotels	
Restaurants and food	Business hours
Sights and places of interest	Transport
	Sport
Entertainment	Climate and clothing

   Do you need any new sections? For example: Parks or Beaches

2. *Contents:* Before writing make sure that you have all the information you need.

   Introduction: See your notes in Lesson 32.
   Your arrival: If there is no airport, you can describe the way to the town centre from the railway station, or the nearest main road.
   Hotels, restaurants and food: See your notes in Lesson 34. Recommend one restaurant which you like very much. What local dish are you going to describe?
   Sights and places of interest: See your notes in Lesson 31.
   Entertainment, shopping and souvenir-hunting, business hours: See your notes in Lesson 34.
   Tipping: Do you need this section? How much do people usually tip in your town?
   Transport: What are the main forms of public transport in your town?
   Sport: What are the most popular sports and where are they played?
   Climate and clothing: See your notes in Lesson 33.

3. *Language preparation:* Do these three exercises before writing your guide.

   (a) *Example:*
   If you want a comprehensive look at the city, take a sightseeing tour.
   For a comprehensive look at the city, take a sightseeing tour.

   Now do the same with these:
   1. If you need further information, contact the Tourist Information Office.
   2. If you're interested in classical music, go to concerts at the Opera House.
   3. If you want local food, visit some good restaurants in the old part of the town.

   (b) *Example:*
   If you walk into any shop, you will find superb service.
   Walk into any shop and you will find superb service.

   Now do the same with these:
   1. If you climb up to the castle, you will have a good view of the city.
   2. If you buy a Tourist Ticket, you can travel on all the city's trains and buses.
   3. If you get up early, you can find bargains in the antique market.

   (c) *Example:*
   Hanover's hotels provide excellent service. Most of Hanover's hotels are modern and comfortable.
   Hanover's hotels, most of which are modern and comfortable, provide excellent service.

   Now do the same with these:
   1. Souvenir shops sell postcards and films. Most souvenir shops are open on Sundays.
   2. Taxis can be hired in the street or by telephone. Most taxis are black.
   3. Sightseeing coach tours usually take three hours. Most sightseeing coach tours leave from the City Hall.

4. *Writing:* Using your notes and the guide to Hanover as a model, write the guide to your town on your own or in a small group. Show the guide to other students when you have finished.

Unit 7

LANGUAGE STUDY

Lessons 31–35

STRUCTURE

EXPRESSING CONDITION
CONDITIONAL SENTENCES: TYPE 2 WITHOUT 'IF'

 7.1 Make sentences

Imagine that you are going to the seaside for your summer holiday. Say what you would or would not be able to do.
Examples: I'd be able to lie on the beach all day.
I wouldn't be able to walk in the mountains.

lie on the beach all day	go ice-skating
swim in the sea	play tennis
walk in the mountains	make sandcastles
go skiing	throw snowballs
go water-skiing	have a picnic

Imagine that the holiday is in the mountains in the middle of winter.
Say what you would or would not be able to do.

7.2 Study

CONDITIONAL SENTENCES: TYPE 3
Examples: If we'd thought about it for a few days, *we wouldn't have booked* the holiday.
(We didn't think about it for a few days, so we did book the holiday.)
If I'd known, I'd have phoned you.
(I didn't know, so I didn't phone you.)

⚠ 'If' Clause   Main Clause
If + PAST PERFECT ..., would/could have
+ PAST PARTICIPLE ...

 7.3 Drill

The Wilkinsons did not go to Italy. Jane is thinking about what would have happened if they had.
Example: go dancing every night
I'd have gone dancing every night.

meet a handsome Italian	eat lots of sea-food
get a good suntan	visit Rome
make lots of new friends	practise speaking Italian
learn how to eat spaghetti	play tennis every evening
go swimming every day	have a wonderful holiday

 7.4 Drill

Mr Contrary never agrees with anyone. His friend is telling him what she did last night. What would Mr Contrary have done?
Example: I went to the theatre last night. (cinema)
I'd have gone to the cinema.

Then I went to a restaurant. (café)
I ordered steak and chips. (fish and chips)
I had a cup of tea after the meal. (coffee)
Then I walked home. (catch a bus)
At home I had a bath. (shower)
And then I watched TV. (go straight to bed)

 7.5 Drill

Say what would have happened if things had been different.
Example: The Wilkinsons complained, so they got their money back.
If they hadn't complained, they wouldn't have got their money back.
Steve didn't have a driving licence, so he didn't get the job.
If he'd had a driving licence, he would have got the job.

1. Jenny spoke Spanish, so she got the scholarship.
2. Fred won the pools, so he stopped working.
3. The Wilkinsons saw the TV programme, so they didn't go to Matona.
4. Steve didn't win a scholarship, so he didn't go to Mexico.

7.6 Study

EXPRESSING REGRET WITH 'WISH'

When 'wish' is followed by a verb in the past tense, it expresses a regret about the present.

Examples: I wish *I was/were going* with you. (I'm sorry I'm not going with you).
I wish *I could swim.* (Unfortunately, I can't swim.)

When 'wish' is followed by a verb in the past perfect tense, it expresses a regret about the past.

Examples: I wish *we'd never heard* of Matona. (I'm sorry we ever heard of Matona.)
Steve wishes *he hadn't given* up his job. (He's sorry he gave up his job.)

⚠ Do not confuse this usage of 'wish' with 'wish' + infinitive ('wish to') which is a very formal way of expressing 'want to'.
Example: I wish *to apologise* for what has happened.

 7.7 Drill

Gloop is unhappy because he is different from people on Earth. What does he wish?
Examples: I can't swim. *I wish I could swim.*
I haven't got any hair. *I wish I had some hair.*
I feel sad. *I wish I didn't feel sad.*

I can't sing.	I haven't got a girlfriend.
I can't play the guitar.	I can't speak English fluently.
I'm made of metal.	I feel lonely.
I haven't got eyes.	I'm not happy.
I look different from other people.	I don't know what to do.

98

7.8   Drill

Mr Regretful is in prison. What does he wish?
Examples: I took the money.
   I wish I hadn't taken the money.
   I didn't tell my wife.
   I wish I'd told my wife.

I broke into the house.
I stole the money.
I dropped my driving licence.
I didn't pick it up.
The police found it.

I didn't leave the country.
The police caught me.
I've lost my job.
My wife has left me.
I wasn't sensible.

EXPRESSING CRITICISM

    7.9   Drill

Things always go wrong for Mr Unlucky. Mr Criticism tells him about the mistakes he has made. Find the clues in the list below. They are not in the correct order.
Examples:

try it on
You should have tried it on.

not open the door
You shouldn't have opened the door.

1.
2.
3.
4.
5.
6.

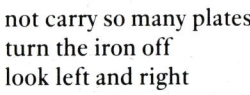

not carry so many plates
turn the iron off
look left and right

remember your parachute
learn to swim
not put in so much salt

CAUSATIVE VERB: 'HAVE'

    7.10   Make sentences

When Fred Mills was a millionaire, he never did anything himself.
He always *had things done* for him.

Example: Those shoes are dirty. (clean)
   I must have them cleaned.

1. The car is dirty. (wash)
2. That wall looks terrible. (paint)
3. The TV isn't working. (repair)
4. That suit is dirty. (dry-clean)
5. This room is very untidy. (tidy up)
6. The window is broken. (mend)

ADVICE: 'HAD BETTER'

    7.11   Give advice

Example: Steve wants to find a job. (go to an employment agency)
   He'd better go to an employment angency.

1. Fred and Liz have lost all their money. (start working again)
2. I'm absolutely exhausted. (go to bed)
3. Jenny's passport is out of date. (get a new one)
4. Steve has an interview in the morning. (not be late)
5. We've run out of coffee. (buy some more)
6. You look ill. (not go out)
7. Zed was very rude. (apologise)
8. My hair is too long. (have it cut)

INDEFINITE PRONOUNS FOLLOWED BY ADJECTIVES

    7.12   Drill

Use: *someone, somewhere, something, anyone, anywhere, anything*

Example: I'd like to go to an exciting place.
   I'd like to go somewhere exciting.

1. Have you met any famous people?
2. I've never been to an interesting place.
3. I'd like to talk to an amusing person.
4. We want to stay in a cheap hotel.
5. I'd like to be a successful person.
6. Do you want to go to a quiet place?
7. I can't afford an expensive thing.
8. I'd like to buy a useful thing.

VOCABULARY

When you are studying this vocabulary section, you will find a dictionary is very helpful.

WORD BUILDING

7.13   Study

> FORMATION OF ADJECTIVES:
>
> SUFFIXES '-ful' AND '-less'
>
> '-ful' and '-less' can be added to some words to form adjectives.
>
> *Examples:*   use   *useful* (of use)   *useless* (of no use)
> Some words, like *use*, can take both '-ful' and '-less'. Many others take either '-ful' or '-less'.
>
> *Examples:*   beauty   *beautiful*   (no adjective with '-less')
>   sleep   *sleepless*   (no adjective with '-ful')

7.14   Make adjectives

Make adjectives from these words and match them with the definitions below.

end   truth   price
pain   colour   play
peace   hate   success
taste   help   forget

1. Something without colour.
2. Something that has succeeded.
3. Something quiet.
4. Something that never finishes.

Unit 7

5. Someone who always helps.
6. Something so valuable that it cannot be given a price.
7. Someone who often doesn't remember.
8. Something you dislike very much.
9. Something that hurts.
10. Someone honest.
11. Something that has no taste.
12. Someone who likes playing.

WORDS OFTEN CONFUSED: SAY/TELL

7.15 Complete

Put in the correct form of *say* or *tell*.

'Excuse me, sir' (1) . . . the customs officer. 'Can you (2) . . . me what's in this suitcase?'

I didn't know what to (3) . . . . I opened the case.

The customs officer looked inside and (4) . . ., 'Perhaps you'd better (5) . . . me why your case is full of watches.'

'I've got a big family,' I explained, 'and all the children are learning to (6) . . . the time.'

'So what you're (7) . . . is that these watches are presents for your children!' exclaimed the customs officer.

'That's right.'

The customs officer laughed. 'I don't think you're (8) . . . me the truth. And you know what it (9) . . . in the customs regulations. I think you'd better (10) . . . me your name and address.'

WHAT DO YOU SAY ?

7.16 Listen and choose the most suitable response

1. (a) The gold rings were too expensive.
   (b) I wish I hadn't.
   (c) I'm sorry, I shouldn't have done that.
   (d) I tried to phone several times.
2. (a) Yes, he hit me.
   (b) No, I didn't touch him.
   (c) He's a journalist, isn't he?
   (d) No, I can't hear what he's saying.
3. (a) Yes, it would.
   (b) Yes, I would.
   (c) I like it.
   (d) I would have.

INTONATION AND STRESS

7.17 Respond with indignation

Example: The film starts at seven-thirty. (eight o'clock)
   But you said it started at eight o'clock!

1. The rent is £25 a week. (£20)
2. Steve lives in Oxford. (Leeds)
3. Jenny is going to Mexico. (Brazil)
4. I want a motorbike. (car)
5. Fred and Liz are poor. (rich)

Example: The shops close at lunchtime. (five-thirty)
   But you told me they closed at five-thirty!

1. The Wilkinsons are going to Ireland. (Matona)
2. Zed is very rude. (polite)
3. I want a cup of coffee. (tea)
4. The holiday costs £350. (£250)
5. Steve likes rock music. (jazz)

SENTENCE LINKING

7.18 Join the sentences

Use *although* or *because*

Examples: Fred Mills wasn't very happy. He'd won a million pounds.
   Fred Mills wasn't very happy, although he'd won a million pounds.
   Liz spent a lot of money. She was extravagant.
   Liz spent a lot of money because she was extravagant.

1. Jenny was worried. Her father wasn't very well.
2. The Wilkinsons decided to go to Matona. They had never heard of it before.
3. Steve became a salesman. He really didn't like the work.
4. Jenny had an interview. She wanted to study in Mexico.
5. The police didn't catch Marconi. They searched everywhere for him.
6. Jane wanted to go to Italy. She was learning Italian.

7.19 Write a paragraph

Write a description of a place you have visited, and say why you liked it, or didn't like it. You should mention both good and bad points in your description. Use *although* and *because* to connect your ideas.

Examples:

You can begin like this: *Although I don't speak Arabic, I enjoyed visiting Cairo.*
   or like this: *I liked Lisbon because it was a very friendly city.*

DIY CHECK UP   Unit 2

When they were discussing their holiday, the Wilkinsons made a list of advantages and disadvantages. Put the words in brackets into the correct form or fill in the missing words.

ADVANTAGES AND DISADVANTAGES

* If you (1) (stay) in a hotel, you don't have to do any cooking.
* If Jane (2) (go) to Italy, she'll be able to practise her Italian.
* If we were rich, we (3) (be able) to have two holidays.
* If we went to Ireland, Trevor (4) (can) go fishing.
* Camping is much cheaper. We (5) (use) to go camping every summer.
* We should find out more about Matona. We don't know (6) . . . . . at all about it.
* The holiday in Matona is the (7) (expensive) one we've talked about.
* Jane thinks Ireland would be (8) . . . . . exciting than Italy.

* Look up the answers in the DIY Check-up Key. Discuss any mistakes you have made.
* Look up your mistakes in the Structural Reference List. Then turn to the Language Study exercises suggested.

Unit 8
LESSON 36

Explaining how to do something

Tom and Sandra Mackenzie are discussing future articles for the Plymouth Evening Mail.

We need someone to do a report on the Summer Festival next month.

SANDRA: I'm afraid I'll be on holiday, so I won't be able to do it.
TOM: Yes, of course. I'd completely forgotten. You're going to Sweden, aren't you?
SANDRA: That's right. I'm exchanging my flat for one in Stockholm.
TOM: Really? How do you arrange something like that?
SANDRA: It's very easy. I contacted an agency which specialises in home exchanges. It publishes a home exchange directory.
TOM: What's that?
SANDRA: It's a list of houses and flats which people want to exchange. What you do is advertise in the directory. You describe your flat or house, saying exactly what it's like and where it is.
TOM: Then what happens?
SANDRA: People who are interested in exchanging with you write and describe their homes.
TOM: How long does all this take?
SANDRA: Well, I found an exchange in just under a month, but I was a bit lucky, I think. I got lots of replies, and chose to go to Stockholm. So I wrote to Henrik – he's the person I'm exchanging with – to arrange the exact dates.
TOM: It sounds easy.
SANDRA: I've got to leave lots of instructions for him of course – how things in the flat work, and so on.

 Ask and answer

Make up questions about Tom and Sandra's conversation. Ask another student your questions.

Example:
Where is Sandra going for her holiday?

  Questions: Explaining

1. Sandra explains how a home exchange works. Put these sentences in the correct order to show that you have understood Sandra's explanation.
   A. You describe how things in your flat work.
   B. You get letters describing other people's flats.
   C. You agree on when the exchange will take place.
   D. You advertise your flat in a directory.
   E. You decide which flat you prefer.

2. When Tom asks Sandra to explain, he says, 'How do you arrange something like that?'. By 'you' he is referring not to Sandra, but to people in general. Find three more examples in the conversation of 'you' used in this way.

 Listening: How to get a British passport

Sandra needed a passport to go to Sweden, so she telephoned the Passport Office in London. Listen to the telephone conversation and complete the diagram.

 Tell each other: How to get a passport

1. You are over 16 and were born in Britain. Use the diagram you completed in the Listening section to tell each other how to get a British passport.
   Begin: First you ask at any..........
2. What do you do to get a passport in your country? Tell each other and draw a diagram.

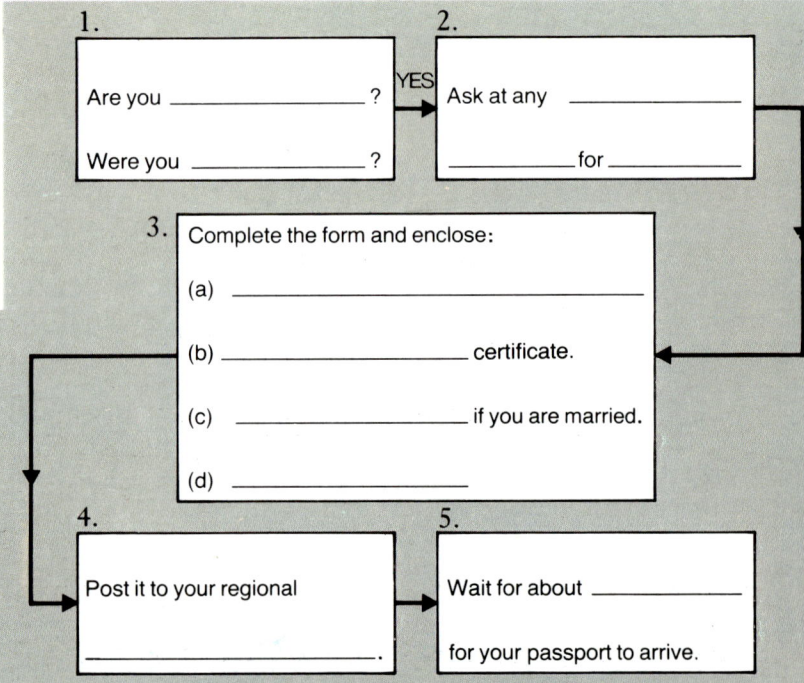

Unit 8

 Writing: Putting instructions in the correct order

Put these instructions for making a telephone call from England to Sweden in the correct order.

Sweden
To make a call

A. Do not replace your receiver: give the equipment time to connect the call.
B. Please dial carefully without long pauses between numbers.
C. Write down the complete number first.
D. For example, to call Stockholm 239500 dial 010 46 8 239500.
E. After dialling you may have to wait up to a minute before hearing a tone.
F. This consists of the code followed by the subscriber's number.

 Study and complete: Putting instructions in the correct order

The boy's instructions to his sister are listed below, but they are not in the correct order. Match each instruction with the correct illustration. Bruce is the name of the dog.

The Green Cross code ✗ and how to use it.

A. And let traffic pass.
B. Stop and wait near the kerb.
C. No traffic near.
   Go straight across.
D. Look all around and listen.
E. Keep looking and listening.
F. Find a safe place away from parked cars.

After each word in an English dictionary you will usually find:

1. How the word is pronounced.
2. What part of speech it is.
3. What the word means and how it is used.

dic·tion·ary /ˈdɪkʃnrɪ/ *n* a book listing words in alphabetical order with their meanings, use and pronunciation.

Look up at least five words from this lesson in your dictionary and complete the table.

WORD	PRONUNCIATION	PART OF SPEECH	MEANING
directory	dɪˈrektrɪ	noun	a book with an alphabetical list of names or subjects: 'a telephone directory'

Language Study Exercises 8.4 8.5 8.6 8.7 8.8

LESSON 37

Information about how things work

Before Sandra went to Sweden, she left these notes about her flat for Henrik.

MEMOS

Milk
The milk is delivered every morning at about 8.30. The milkman leaves one pint a day. If you want to change this put out a note. The milkman also delivers eggs and butter so order if you want. He rings the bell on Thursdays with the bill.

Papers
You can have daily papers delivered by Preston's, the newsagent's on the corner. They send you a bill once a fortnight.

Rubbish
The dustmen collect the rubbish twice a week, on Tuesdays and Fridays.

Post
The post is usually delivered at about 9 every morning except Sunday. The post is collected from the postbox outside Preston's at 9.30 a.m. and 4 p.m. Monday to Friday and at 11 a.m. on Saturdays.

Hot water and central heating
Hot water is heated by a gas boiler near the back door in the kitchen. This boiler also heats the radiators. The boiler is controlled by a thermostat and time switch. The time switch is set for hot water all day. The central heating is turned off at the moment but please turn it on if you feel cold. The controls are on the wall behind the boiler and the thermostat is above the bookcase in the living room. I've left the instruction booklet if you need more details.

Fuse box
This is in a cupboard in the hall. The mains switch is on the left of the fuse box. Down = ON. The meter is read every three months.

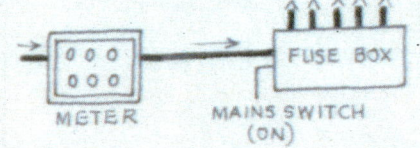

Water
The mains tap is under the sink in the kitchen. If you need to turn it off, turn it anti-clockwise (it's very stiff).

Useful telephone numbers
Doctor 20392   Electricity 23642
Police 999   Gas 27911
T.V. rental 23232   Mrs. Evans 262573 (she lives round the corner and will help if there are any problems.)

103

Unit 8

 Ask and answer

Make up questions about Sandra's list. Ask another student your questions. Ask *when* things are done, and *where* things are.

Examples:
When is the milk delivered?
Where is the gas boiler?

 Questions

What should Henrik do if:
1. He wants to have eggs delivered?
2. He wants to have newspapers delivered?
3. He wants to turn off the electricity?
4. He wants to turn off the water?
5. The television goes wrong?
6. He doesn't understand how something works?

 Study and complete: How a refrigerator works

When a liquid evaporates (i.e. changes to gas), (it) takes in heat. In a refrigerator, the heat is taken from the food compartment (which) is therefore cooled. When the gas changes back to a liquid in the condenser, heat is given out. (This) does not raise the temperature of the cold storage compartment because the condenser is always situated outside (it).

Explain the meaning of the ringed words:

it =   which =   This =   it =

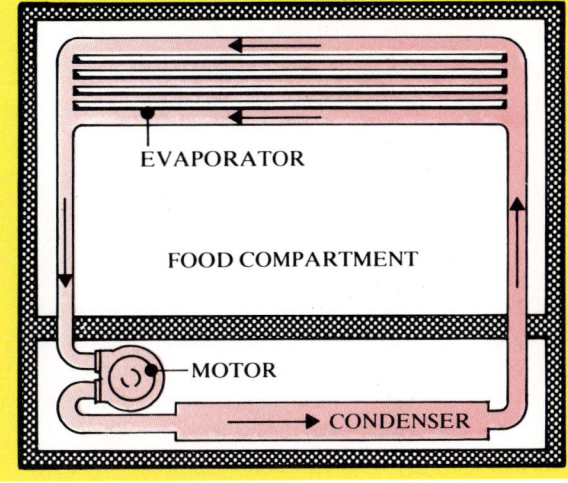

 Tell each other: Explaining how things work

Look at this diagram, and tell each other how a ball point pen works.

Ball point pen
First describe the parts of the pen, and then say how it works. Use a real pen if possible.

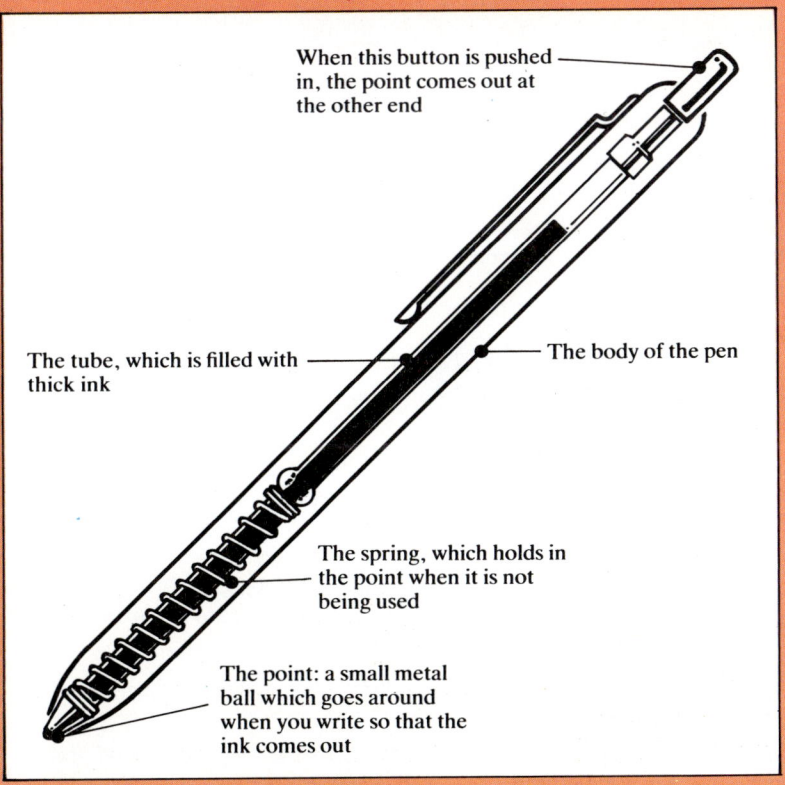

- When this button is pushed in, the point comes out at the other end
- The body of the pen
- The tube, which is filled with thick ink
- The spring, which holds in the point when it is not being used
- The point: a small metal ball which goes around when you write so that the ink comes out

 Tell each other and make notes

1. Say what things are delivered to your home (e.g. letters) and when they are usually delivered.
2. Describe the heating in your home. How is the water heated? Is it necessary to heat the rooms? If so, how are they heated?

1. *Alphabetical order:* Put these words in alphabetical order.
   change   central   controlled   cold
   control   collected   cupboard   corner
   condenser   cooled   compartment
2. *Guessing spelling:* Guess the spelling of these words from Lesson 36 and then check in a dictionary.

   ____lustration   ____tructions
   ____habetical   ____lanation

3. *Making up words:* How many different words can you make up from the letters in INTERESTED?

   Examples: IN   TIE   RED   NEED

LANGUAGE STUDY Exercises   8.1   8.2   8.3   8.12

104

LESSON 38

Understanding and giving instructions

Sandra bought a camera to take to Sweden. She asked the shop assistant how to use the camera.

ASSISTANT: It's really very easy. Look, hold it in your left hand. O.K.? See this little black thing on the side here?
SANDRA: Yes.
ASSISTANT: Well, push it down. Gently – not too hard.
SANDRA: Like this? Oh, the back's opened.
ASSISTANT: That's right. Now, take the film out of the packet, and take off the paper. See, the film's in a kind of plastic box. Now, pop it into the camera.
SANDRA: It won't go in like this.
ASSISTANT: No, that's because you've got it the wrong way round. The big bit goes in at this end.
SANDRA: I see.
ASSISTANT: Now, shut the back of the camera carefully. That's it, and turn the camera over. See this funny-looking thing here – it's for winding on the film. Move it backwards and forwards. That's right, keep on until it won't move any more. Fine. Now, look at the back of the camera again. You can see the film through the little window.
SANDRA: It says 'one'.
ASSISTANT: So now you're ready to take your first picture. Hold the camera carefully . . .
SANDRA: I think I'll take one of you!

Sandra got an instruction book with the camera. Here are four pictures from the book.

How to load the camera

1 — Catch   2 Cartridge   3 — Slider   4 KODACOLOR II

 Questions

1. Look at the illustration and match the instructions on the right with the numbers on the pictures.
2. Look at the *catch*, the *cartridge* and the *slider* in the illustration. What words does the shop assistant use to describe these three things?
3. How does Sandra say: 'How do I load the camera?'?
4. How does the shop assistant say: 'Drop in a film cartridge'? '. . . close the camera.'? '. . . until it locks.'?

A Wind on the film by pushing the slider several times *until it locks*. This advances the film ready for the first exposure.
B Drop in the film cartridge and close the camera.
C The number 1 and the type of film will appear in the camera-back window.
D Open the camera back by pressing the catch on the end of the camera.

105

Unit 8

 Tell each other: Giving instructions

1. *How to take a film out of a camera*
   Read the conversation in the camera shop again. Then read the instructions below on 'Unloading the camera' and look at the illustration. Tell each other how to take a film out of a camera.

Begin:
When the film is finished, you..........

> **Unloading the camera**
> When the film is completely exposed, operate the wind-on slider several times until it locks. Open the camera back by pushing the catch. Remove the cartridge and replace it with another.

 remove = take out
replace it with another = put another one in

2. *How to use a cassette recorder*
   Look at the illustration of a cassette recorder and the instructions.
   Tell each other how to record a conversation.

Begin:
When you want to make a recording, first you..........

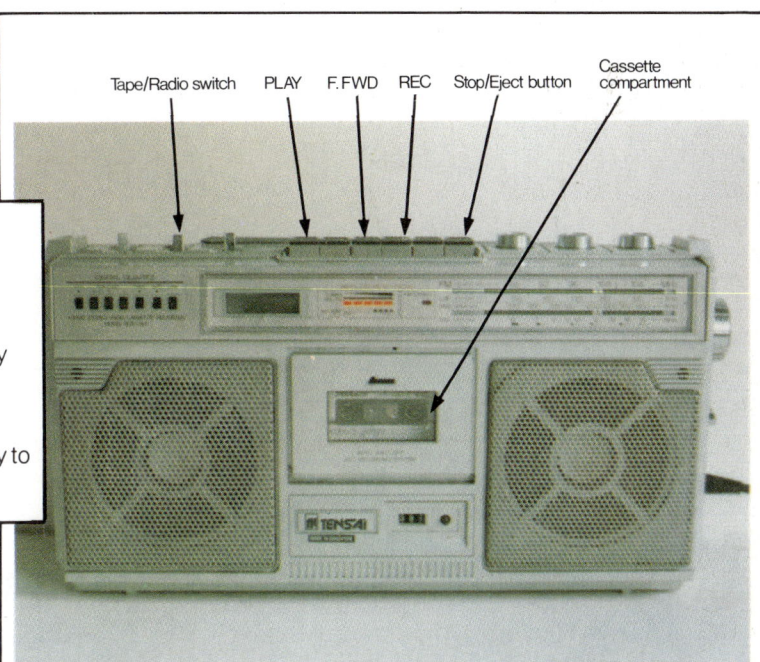

> **Recording with built-in microphone**
> 1. Depress the Stop/Eject button to open the compartment.
> 2. Insert a cassette and close the compartment gently and firmly.
> 3. Set the Tape/Radio switch to Tape.
> 4. Depress the REC and PLAY buttons simultaneously to record.

 depress = push down
insert = put in
simultaneously = at the same time

 Writing: Instructions

Someone is coming to stay in your home when you are away. Write short notes explaining how to use two household machines.

Example:
How to use the television set and the washing-machine.

Abbreviations: Dictionaries often start with a list of abbreviations used in their definitions. What do these abbreviations stand for?

   adj   adv   n   pl   prep   pron   sing

If you are not sure, look them up.

LANGUAGE STUDY Exercises   8.9   8.10   8.11   8.14   8.16

106

LESSON 39

Asking for and discussing travel information

Sandra wrote to Henrik with information about getting to Plymouth from Heathrow Airport, outside London.

Underground timetable

Average Journey Times and Fares to Heathrow from Central London

Station	Approximate Journey Time to Heathrow (Minutes)	Route	New Low Fare (One Way)
Hammersmith	32	DIRECT	£1.30
Earl's Court	36	DIRECT	(£1 Sunday)
Gloucester Road	38	DIRECT	
South Kensington	40	DIRECT	
High Street Kensington	43	Change Earl's Court	
Knightsbridge	43	DIRECT	
Green Park	46	DIRECT	
Victoria ≠	46	Change Hammersmith	£1.50
Piccadilly Circus	47	DIRECT	(£1 Sunday)
Leicester Square	48	DIRECT	
Paddington ≠	49	Change Earl's Court	FARE TO ANY STATION IN CENTRAL ZONE
Charing Cross ≠	50	Change Green Park	
Holborn	52	DIRECT	
Russell Square	54	DIRECT	
Euston ≠	55	Change Green Park	
King's Cross, St. Pancras ≠	55	DIRECT	
Marble Arch	58	Change Earl's Court and Notting Hill Gate	
Liverpool Street ≠	61	Change Holborn	

≠ Principal British Rail Terminal Station.

Handwritten letter:

> You can either take the underground from Heathrow Airport to central London, and catch the train to Plymouth from Paddington Station, or you can get a coach from Heathrow to Reading, and catch the train there. It's usually both quicker and cheaper to go from Reading. I enclose the train timetables, and the timetable for the coach service between Reading and Heathrow.
>
> When you get to Plymouth, take a bus from the station and get off ... on the corner of the ... and Fisherman Way a...

Coach timetable

HEATHROW AIRPORT – READING

The easy way to catch your plane. Express luxury coaches go direct between all 3 Terminals at Heathrow and Reading Station. Frequent all year round service, extra trips during the busy Summer months. **Journey time 1 hour.** Passengers travelling to Heathrow should go to the Railair lounge on Platform 5 on Reading Station not later than 15 minutes before coach departure time. The times shown at Heathrow Airport apply to Terminal 3, departures from Terminals 1 & 2 are a few minutes later.

Mondays to Saturdays	Sundays
Heathrow depart	Heathrow depart
06 55	07 10
07 15	07 40
07 35	08 10
07 55	Then every 30 minutes until
Then every 20 minutes until	18 10
18 55	18 40
19 15	19 10
19 40	20 10
20 10	21 10
20 40	22 10
21 10	
21 40	
22 10	

Railair Link

Train timetable

London → Reading → Plymouth → Cornwall
Mondays to Fridays

Paddington* / Reading* / Totnes / Plymouth

departures

	Paddington	Reading	Totnes	Plymouth
× ⊕	F 15 30 F	16 00 F	18 58 F	19 33 F
× ⊕	16 25 E	16 48 E	→	19 58 E
× ⊕	F 16 25 F	16 48 F	→	19 58 F
× ⊕	17 25	→	21 40	20 46
× ⊕				21 48
× ⊕	18 25	18 47	22 05 F	22 38 F
	F 18 33 F		→	23 05
× ⊕	19 25	19 49		00 02
× ⊕	20 25	20 49	23 34	

Notes
E Mondays to Thursdays
F Fridays only
For whole or part of the journey
× Restaurant service according to time of day
⊕ Hot dishes to order also buffet service of drinks and snacks
⊖ Drinks and cold snacks

  Questions

Henrik arrives at Heathrow Airport on a Monday afternoon. He is through the customs by 4.45 p.m. Now he has to decide how to get to Plymouth.

1. If he goes to Reading on the coach, which is the first coach he can catch?
2. If he goes to Paddington on the underground
   (a) where will he have to change?
   (b) how long will the journey (Heathrow–Paddington) probably take?
   (c) how much will the journey (Heathrow–Paddington) cost?
3. Which is the earliest train he can get from
   (a) Reading?
   (b) Paddington?
4. Can Henrik get something to eat on the train to Plymouth?

Unit 8

 Role Play: Asking for travel information

A is a London Transport Information Officer. A uses the information on page 107 to answer questions.

B is a foreign visitor to Britain. B wants to travel from central London to Heathrow Airport, and telephones to enquire about underground trains. B has to check in at Heathrow at one o'clock, and his/her nearest underground station is Notting Hill Gate.

Example:

1. A: Can I help you?
2. B: Yes, I'd like some information about trains to Heathrow.
3. A: Which is your nearest underground station?
4. B: High Street, Kensington
5. A: And when do you want to be at the airport?
6. B: I have to check in at one o'clock.
7. A: Well, it takes about three-quarters of an hour from High Street, Kensington, so you should be at the station at about twelve o'clock.
8. B: Do I have to change?
9. A: Yes, you have to change at Earl's Court.
10. B: And how much is the fare, please?
11. A: One pound fifty.
12. B: Thank you very much.

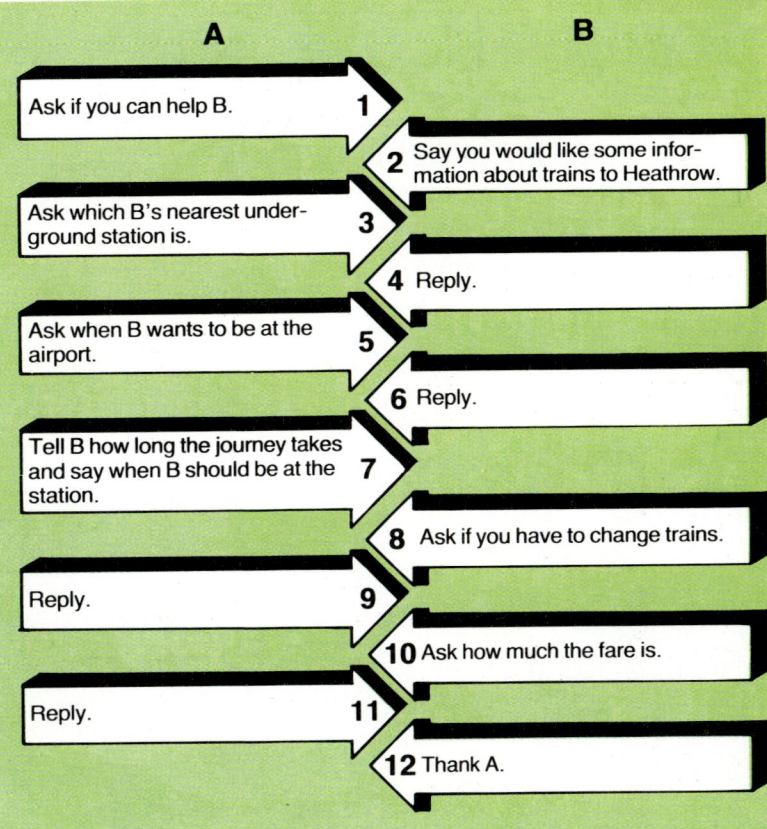

A
1. Ask if you can help B.
3. Ask which B's nearest underground station is.
5. Ask when B wants to be at the airport.
7. Tell B how long the journey takes and say when B should be at the station.
9. Reply.
11. Reply.

B
2. Say you would like some information about trains to Heathrow.
4. Reply.
6. Reply.
8. Ask if you have to change trains.
10. Ask how much the fare is.
12. Thank A.

Further situations:

	B's nearest underground station	B's check-in time
1.	Victoria	09.30
2.	King's Cross	14.15
3.	Knightsbridge	18.00
4.	Green Park	10.35
5.	Liverpool Street	15.30
6.	Euston	17.10

1. Many words have two or more completely different meanings. Think of at least two different meanings for each of the words below. Then check your definitions in the dictionary.

   book   left   match   right
   kind   letter   table   watch

2. Use the dictionary to check on the spelling and definitions in your vocabulary notebook. See if some of the words in your notebook have more than one meaning.

Language Study Exercises   8.13   8.15   8.17   8.18   8.19

LESSON 40

 COMMUNICATION ACTIVITY

Do this activity in pairs (A and B).
A's instructions are below and B's instructions are at the bottom of the page.

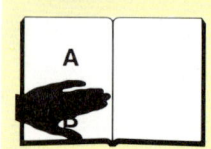 **Student A**
COVER THE BOTTOM HALF OF THE PAGE. YOU MUST NOT LOOK AT B'S INSTRUCTIONS.

How to use a skateboard

Skateboarding is a popular sport for young people. B wants to learn how to use a skateboard. Look at the pictures and notes. Then tell B what to do.

In order to..........you need................................
....

Put your front foot on..........and point it straight ahead.

Push off with your back..........so that the..........
moves.......... Put your back foot across..........
Then move your.......... into the same position.
Use your.......... to balance.

Getting off a.......... is very easy.
Put your back.......... on the.......... At the same time press down on the front of the board with your.......... foot. The..........will almost stop. Run a few steps forward as you get off so that you don't fall over.

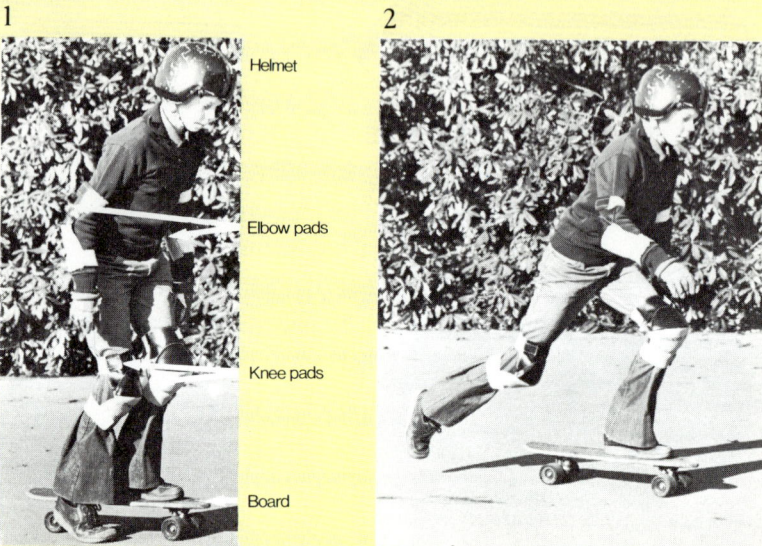

 **Student B**
COVER THE TOP HALF OF THE PAGE. YOU MUST NOT LOOK AT A'S INSTRUCTIONS.

How to use a skateboard

Skateboarding is a popular sport for young people. You want to learn how to use a skateboard. Look at the picture, and then listen as A tells you how to use one. Listen carefully and take notes.
Then use your notes to tell A how one works.

_____

_____

_____

_____

Unit 8

FOCUS ON READING

Exchanging homes

Reading purpose

Here is an extract from *Holiday Which*, a magazine which advises people on different kinds of holidays. Find the answers to these questions:
1. What are the advantages of a holiday home exchange?
2. What disadvantages can you think of?
3. Do you think a holiday home exchange would suit your family?

Case Histories

Gwen Davis, 28 yrs old from S Wales, wanted to stay near New York. She hadn't done an exchange before. She advertised her one-bedroom flat in a directory and wrote to 20 people she'd picked out as possibles. She prepared a typewritten page describing her home and things to do in the area, and sent this, together with tourist brochures, to those people who followed up her letters. A further 15 wrote to her about her advertisement, too. She decided that she was most interested to exchange with a retired couple who had a detached house in New Jersey. They were prepared to lend their car, which was very important to her, and they were flexible about the dates they could travel. Gwen wrote back to them with more details, and finally they wrote to her confirming the exchange.

They all decided not to charge for fuel and so on. Gwen had no phone, but the American couple said she could use theirs free, although in fact she left some money to cover the cost. She informed her insurance company about the car and was charged an extra £5. She put papers and valuables in a cupboard.

On arriving at J F Kennedy Airport, Gwen was met by the couple who took her to their home. It was larger than hers, having three bedrooms and two bathrooms, a swimming pool, and equipment – a washing machine, dryer, and dishwasher. She didn't stay in the house all the time – during her four-week stay she visited relatives in Boston.

The only thing that went wrong during Gwen's stay was the exhaust coming off the car. She took it into the local garage, where they said that they had been told beforehand that any repair charges would be paid for by the owners.

Gwen enjoyed her stay very much and said that 'living in a house rather than a hotel gives a much better idea of how people in other countries live'.

Mr and Mrs McCready and their three children (9, 11 and 13) live in a country house in Scotland. They decided they wanted to go to Canada, so they advertised in a directory and got five replies. They found a family in Ontario, with three children of similar ages, and after two letters, they had a phone call from Canada confirming the arrangement. They wrote several more letters and finally made a last minute telephone call themselves. They arranged to pay their fuel and phone bills as normal, checked their car insurance and had their car serviced. In Canada, they had the use of their exchange family's car.

In Scotland the Canadian family found a large garden with vegetables and fruit, and they were able to swim and fish in the river running through the property. The McCreadys had a pool in the Canadian home.

They went for three weeks in August and thought it a very cheap holiday. They saw quite a lot of the countryside and met a lot of people, as their exchange family had arranged for people to call on them. They enjoyed themselves very much and feel that their first exchange was a success; they intend to do one again.

Mr and Mrs Jenner have a young baby: they wanted to go to the Mediterranean, but felt that a hotel would not be suitable. After advertising in a directory, they got six replies and replied to all, making a couple of telephone calls. They found a family who wanted to exchange their seaside holiday flat near Venice and after exchanging letters and making a few more phone calls to Italy, everything was arranged.

The Jenners have a 3-bedroom terraced house in London, which they felt would be large enough to accommodate the Agnelli family with their three teenage children. The Jenners left a list of phone charges and asked the Agnellis to leave the money; the Italian flat had no phone. They left food for their cats, made a straight exchange of fuel charges and told their insurers.

The Jenners had a very enjoyable three weeks. The only mishap they had was that a fitting was pulled off the wall in the Italian flat, so Mr Jenner stuck it back up again and left a note saying what he had done. On their return they found money to cover a torn sheet. They felt that it was the best way to holiday with a young child, and quite economical.

Conclusions

There are, of course, snags, and exchanging homes can never be everyone's idea of a holiday. *'You must trust the people coming to your house, otherwise your holiday will be a misery wondering what is happening to your home'* was a feeling echoed by many, while others stressed that if you were extremely houseproud you would probably not be able to relax. However, it was pointed out that *'people who exchange tend to look after the exchange home as they hope others are looking after theirs'*.

A few people had found the pre-visit preparation hard work: *'we spent a lot of time tidying up cupboards, wardrobes, drawers, and in decorating, so that our home was indeed spotless. The time and effort needed to do all this should not be underestimated'*.

Holiday Which December 1978

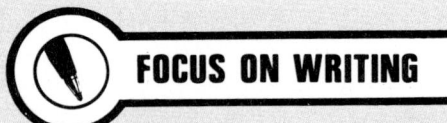
FOCUS ON WRITING

Writing purpose

To write notes for someone who is coming to stay in your home when you are away.

1. *Headings:* Use these headings for your notes.
   How to use household machines
   Local shopping information
   Deliveries and services
   How to get to my home
   Emergency telephone numbers

2. *Contents:* Before writing make sure that you have all the information you need.
   How to use household machines: See Sandra's note on hot water and central heating, fuse box, and water in Lesson 37, your notes on heating in the same lesson, and your notes giving instructions in Lesson 38.
   Local shopping information: See suggestions in 'Exchangers' Tips' on the right.
   Deliveries and services: See Sandra's notes on milk, papers, rubbish and post in Lesson 37, and your own notes on deliveries in the same lesson.
   How to get to my home: See Sandra's notes for Henrik in Lesson 39. Describe how to get to your home from the nearest big airport.
   Emergency telephone numbers: See suggestions in 'Exchangers' Tips' on the right and Sandra's list of useful telephone numbers in Lesson 37.

3. *Before writing:* Read this extract from *Holiday Which*. Do you need to prepare any extra sections for your notes?
   For example: watering plants

4. Write your notes and show them to another student.

Exchangers' tips:

● write down in simple terms how appliances work; one family who went to Italy and had bad weather was unable to turn on the central heating and had to buy a portable fire to keep warm
● make a list of emergency telephone numbers such as those of a doctor, dentist, insurance company, garage, vet, police station, and who should be called to mend things like washing machines, TVs, burst pipes, and so on
● make a list of local shopping information – early closing days, which shops are best for certain things and so on
● make lists of other information, such as good restaurants, pubs, sports facilities
● make notes about when the dustman, milkman and other deliveries call
● make notes about when plants should be watered and animals fed
● collect together local maps, timetables and tourist office brochures
● clear out plenty of drawer and hanging space
● make sure you've explained exactly how to get to your house
● tell people names (and phone numbers) of neighbours – and tell the neighbours
   Some of our exchangers had arranged to meet the other family – perhaps for lunch at a half-way point or for a short time at one of the homes. Those that did generally agreed that it was a good idea to do so.

Holiday Which December 1978

You can spend weeks getting your house clean before the exchange

... we agreed to water their houseplants (over 100) once a day

Make sure you exchange with a family who have children about the same age

Unit 8

LANGUAGE STUDY

Lesson 36–40

STRUCTURE

8.1 Study

> THE PASSIVE + 'BY' + AGENT
>
> *Example:* The boiler is controlled *by* a thermostat and time-switch.
>
> *Compare:* A thermostat and time-switch control the boiler.

8.2 Answer the questions

Example: Who delivers the papers? (the newspaper boy)
The papers are delivered by the newspaper boy.

1. Who delivers the milk? (the milkman)
2. Who collects the rubbish? (the dustmen)
3. What heats the water? (the boiler)
4. What turns on the heating? (a time-switch)
5. What controls the temperature? (a thermostat)

Now look at the front of the book, and answer these questions.

Example: Who published the book?
It was published by Heinemann Educational Books.

1. Who wrote the book?
2. Who wrote the songs?
3. Who designed the book?
4. Who printed the book?

8.3 Ask and answer

Find the answers in the list on the right.
Example: meat/sell
S1: *Who is meat sold by?*
S2: *A butcher*

meat/sell	a hairdresser
vegetables/sell	an architect
hair/cut	a butcher
bread/make	a baker
a house/design	a greengrocer

Example: the Pyramids/build
S1: *Who were the Pyramids built by?*
S2: *The Egyptians*

the Pyramids/build	Leo Tolstoy
the Mona Lisa/paint	Lennon and McCartney
'Yesterday'/compose	Thomas Edison
radium/discover	Leonardo da Vinci
'War and Peace'/write	Marie Curie
the electric light bulb/invent	The Egyptians

8.4 Study

> RELATIVE PRONOUNS IN DEFINING RELATIVE CLAUSES
>
> WHO/THAT to define people
>
> *Example:* He's the kind of person *who/that* never complains.
> The relative clause defines 'the kind of person': *who/that* is the subject of the clause.
>
> WHICH/THAT to define things
>
> *Example:* I contacted an agency *which/that* specialises in home exchanges.
> The relative clause defines 'agencies': *which/that* is the subject of the clause.
>
> WHERE to define places
>
> *Example:* That's the shop *where* you can buy fresh bread.
> The relative clause defines 'the shop'.

8.5 Join the sentences

Choose the correct sentences from the second list to define the famous people.

Example: Charles Dickens was an author. He wrote 'Oliver Twist'.
Charles Dickens was the author who wrote 'Oliver Twist'.

Charles Dickens was an author.
Alexander Bell was a man.
Marilyn Monroe was an actress.
Roald Amundsen was an explorer.
Yuri Gagarin was an astronaut.
Indira Gandhi was a politician.
Alexander Fleming was a man.

He first reached Antarctica.
He invented the telephone.
She became India's first woman prime minister.
He wrote 'Oliver Twist'.
He discovered penicillin.
He made the first space-flight.
She starred in 'Gentlemen Prefer Blondes'.

8.6 Give definitions

Match the words below with the definitions in the list on the right. Look the words up in the dictionary if necessary.
Example: thermostat
A thermostat is something that/which controls temperature.

thermostat	takes pictures
thermometer	heats rooms
microscope	shows where North is
telescope	measures temperature
speedometer	shows what the date is
radiator	controls temperature
compass	measures speed
camera	helps you see things a long way away
calendar	makes small things look big

8.7 Give definitions

Define the following words. Look up the words in a dictionary if necessary.
Example: laundrette
A laundrette is a place where you can wash clothes.

bank	station	post office
zoo	cafe	bus stop
newsagent's	restaurant	airport
pub	cinema	travel agency

112

8.8 Complete

Put in the correct relative pronoun.
Use: *who, which, where*

A library is a place (1) . . . has a large collection of books. Most towns in Britain have libraries (2) . . . are open to the public. Anyone (3) . . . lives or works in the area can join the local library. Most libraries have a lending section containing books (4) . . . you can borrow, and a reference section of books (5) . . . you cannot take out of the library. Borrowers (6) . . . return books late are fined, but otherwise the service is free. Many libraries have rooms (7) . . . you can study. The assistants (8) . . . work in libraries are called librarians, and they are ready to help people (9) . . . are looking for information. Libraries will deliver books to the homes of old people (10) . . . are unable to get to the library.

8.9 Study

'BY' and 'FOR' + GERUND ('-ing' form)

by + gerund expresses *means*, and answers the question: *How* . . . ?
Example: Open the camera back *by pressing* the catch.

for + gerund expresses *definition*.
Example: This is *for winding on* the film.

 ## 8.10 Ask and answer

Find the answers in the list on the right.
Example: S1: How do you call the fire brigade?
S2: *By dialling 999.*

How do you
- call the fire brigade?
- get a cheque book?
- get a driving licence?
- apply for a passport?
- find out how to get to a place?
- find out what a word means?
- borrow books?
- keep fit?

- use a dictionary
- join a library
- dial 999
- look at a map
- take exercise
- pass your test
- get a form from a post office
- open a bank account

 ## 8.11 Ask and answer

Example: washing machine
S1: *What's a washing-machine for?*
S2: *It's for washing clothes.*

- freezer
- vacuum cleaner
- kettle
- dishwasher
- toaster
- camera
- record player
- thermostat
- iron
- hairdryer
- tin-opener
- dictionary

EXPRESSING FREQUENCY

8.12 Complete

ACROSS
3. every 24 hours = _____ a day
5. hourly = once an _____
6. every six hours = four _____ a day
8. every six months = twice a _____
9. nightly = every _____
11. every Saturday = on _____
13. every two weeks = _____ a month

DOWN
1. every two weeks = once a _____
2. every Friday morning = on Friday _____
4. once each week = _____ week
7. each day of the week = _____
10. every four months = _____ times a year
12. every thirty minutes = twice _____ hour

VOCABULARY

When you are studying this vocabulary section, you will find a dictionary is very helpful.

WORD BUILDING

8.13 Make compounds

Join each of the words below with *three* words from the lists to make compounds.

Example: line   headline
HEAD + phones = headphones
ache   headache

1. TOOTH 2. BED 3. POST 4. SUN 5. HOUSE
- man
- sitter
- wife
- brush
- card
- hold
- paste
- room
- ache
- shine
- -box
- glasses
- time
- work
- tan

PHRASAL VERBS

8.14 Replace the words in italics

Substitute the words in italics with a suitable phrasal verb in the correct form.
Use: *carry on fill in find out give back
give up go down go up push down
put in take out turn down*

Example: Jenny *completed* the questionnaire.
Jenny *filled in* the questionnaire.

1. The policeman locked the door and *removed* the key.
2. Jenny's weight has been *increasing* recently.
3. 'This knob is for *lowering* the volume.'
4. Mr Langley has *stopped* smoking.
5. The assistant refused to *return* the deposit.
6. '*Depress* the handle to open the door.'
7. The bank *discovered* that it had been robbed.
8. The population of London is *decreasing*.
9. '*Insert* the film and close the camera.'
10. The game was over, but the teams *continued* playing.

Unit 8

WHAT DO YOU SAY?

 8.15 Listen and choose the most suitable response

1. (a) He shouldn't have done it.
   (b) Why? It's not very long.
   (c) No, he hasn't.
   (d) Yes, it looks much better now, doesn't it?
2. (a) It starts the machine.
   (b) By pushing it.
   (c) There are only three of them.
   (d) Because it turns on the light.
3. (a) Twice a week.
   (b) About fifty dollars a day.
   (c) For three months.
   (d) About a year.

INTONATION AND STRESS

 8.16 Answer the questions

Prepositions of one syllable are usually *unstressed*. (Phrasal verbs are an exception.)

Example: Whāt's he wāiting for? (a bus)
He's waiting for a būs.

1. What's she afraid of? (spiders)
2. What's he looking at? (the clock)
3. Where does he come from? (Canada)
4. Who was it written by? (a doctor)
5. What are they sitting on? (the floor)
6. Where's she going to? (Sweden)
7. What's he interested in? (motorbikes)
8. Who's she angry with? (her brother)
9. What's he asking for? (the bill)
10. Who's she talking to? (her boyfriend)

SENTENCE LINKING

8.17 Study

> **COORDINATING CLAUSES**
>
> 'either . . . or' to express *alternatives*.
> *Example:* You can *either* take the underground, *or* you can get a coach.
>
> 'both . . . and' to express *addition*.
> *Example:* It's *both* quicker *and* cheaper to go from Reading.
>
> ⚠ Here, *either* and *both* add emphasis.
> *Compare:* I like coffee and tea.
> I like *both* coffee and tea.

8.18 Join the sentences

Use: either . . . or,   both . . . and
Examples: Steve applied for a scholarship. So did Jenny.
Both Steve *and* Jenny applied for a scholarship.
I'd like spaghetti / pizza.
I'd like *either* spaghetti *or* a pizza.

1. Jenny speaks Spanish. Steve speaks Spanish.
2. Margaret wanted to stay in a hotel. So did Jane.
3. There's a train at 10.30/11.30.
4. Fred likes parties. So does Liz.
5. Sandra is going on holiday today/tomorrow.
6. You can catch a bus/go by train.

8.19 Write a paragraph

An English-speaking friend is visiting your country for the first time. Your friend wants to see as much of the country as possible, and has asked for information about different forms of transport. Write a short paragraph giving information and advice. Try to use coordinating clauses from LS 8.17.
Think about the following:
Which is the best way to travel long distances: by train, coach, plane, or car?
Which is the best way to travel in the city: by bus, underground, taxi, car, or bicycle?
Give details of economy fares, cheap return tickets, car-hire prices, etc.

Examples: The best way to travel long distance is either by train or plane.
Travelling long distance by coach is both tiring and uncomfortable.

DIY CHECK UP   Unit 3

When Sandra arrived at Henrik's flat in Stockholm, she found this note. Choose the most suitable word, or put the verbs in brackets into the correct form.

> Dear Sandra,
> Welcome to Stockholm. I hope you had a good journey, and are not too (1) *tired/tiring*.
>
> Just a note about the car. The keys (2) *(keep)* by the telephone in the hall. The engine (3) *(check)* last week, but the car is quite new so you (4) *shouldn't/oughtn't* drive it over 90 k.p.h. And please make sure you lock it properly. The car (5) *(steal)* twice since I bought it!
>
> Ulrika, my sister, is coming to visit you, and she'll tell you where (6) *(find)* everything. Ask her (7) *(tell)* you all about Stockholm. It is a very (8) *interested/interesting* city, so I hope you enjoy yourself here.
>
> Yours,
> Henrik

* Look up the answers in the DIY Check-up Key. Discuss any mistakes you have made.
* Look up your mistakes in the Structural Reference List. Then turn to the Language Study exercises suggested.

Unit 9
LESSON 41

Making and accepting suggestions

The people who make the television programme 'What Do You Think?' are having a meeting.

Bridget King — She is in charge of the 'What Do You Think?' series.

"I like the idea we talked about last week."

Ned Giles — His job is to decide where to put the cameras in the studio and what pictures to show.

```
What do you think?   Programme 9
Producer ......... Bridget King
Director ......... Ned Giles
Researcher ....... Bob Lambert
Presenter ........ Anita Lyons
```

Anita Lyons — She introduces the programme in the studio, and also helps with the planning.

Bob Lambert — Bob finds out the information needed for the programme. He also persuades experts to take part.

ANITA: Oh, you mean a programme about the silicon chip – the micro-chip.
BRIDGET: Yes. We could show how the chip is affecting our lives today, and how it's likely to affect us in the future.
ANITA: I don't know. Aren't people bored with hearing about silicon chips?
BOB: Do you really think so? Perhaps they just don't understand the technology. I think we should explain what the chip is and how it works.
BRIDGET: I agree. We could start with a short film about the history of computers. We could show their development from the first computers to the micro-chip technology of today, and then go on to explain . . .
NED: Can I make a suggestion? How about using cartoons instead of film?
BRIDGET: Sorry, Ned, what are you getting at?
NED: We want to make it as easy to understand as possible, so why don't we describe the history of the chip, and explain how it works, with a series of cartoons?
BRIDGET: What a good idea!
NED: And then we'll have a section showing how the chip affects us in everyday life. You find the micro-chip everywhere, not just in offices. Shops are using electronic cash registers, thousands of people have pocket calculators . . .
ANITA: Aren't we forgetting the interview? I suggest we get a couple of experts to talk about the future – robots and so on.
BRIDGET: Yes, that's a good idea. Can you arrange that, Bob?
BOB: Yes, I'll do that. There's another point to consider. Wouldn't it be a good idea to show how the silicon chip is creating problems – by causing unemployment?
BRIDGET: Of course. Actually, that would be an excellent subject for discussion with the studio audience. O.K., so we've got lots of ideas. Shall we have a cup of coffee before we work out the order of the programme?

A silicon chip in the eye of a needle

Unit 9

  Questions

1. *Disagreeing:* When Bridget suggests making a programme about the silicon chip, Anita does not agree with her. What does Anita say to show that she disagrees? Bob also expresses disagreement. What does he say? Make a list of five different ways of showing disagreement. (Look at Lessons 12 and 13.)
2. *Asking for explanation:* At one point, Bridget does not understand what Ned means. What does she say? Make a list of three different ways of asking for explanation. (Look at Lesson 11.)
3. *Introducing new ideas:* Anita introduces a new idea by saying, 'Aren't we forgetting . . . ?' Bob also introduces a new idea. How does he do this?
4. *Making suggestions:* Ned says, 'Can I make a suggestion?' He makes his suggestion in two different ways. What does he say? Bridget, Bob and Anita also make suggestions. Make a list of five different ways of making suggestions.
5. *Accepting suggestions:* Bridget accepts Bob's suggestion that the programme should explain what the chip is and how it works. What does she say? She accepts suggestions three more times during the discussion. Make a list of four different ways of accepting suggestions.

 Make a list

Make a list of the ideas for the programme. When you have finished, compare your list with Ned's on page 117.

Role Play: Making and accepting suggestions

The class is going to have a party. A and B are planning the party.
They discuss the following questions:
When and where are we going to have the party?
Who shall we invite?
What kind of food and drink shall we have?
What kind of music shall we have?

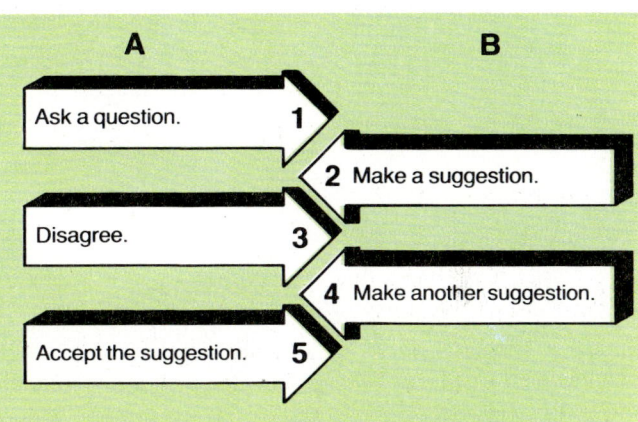

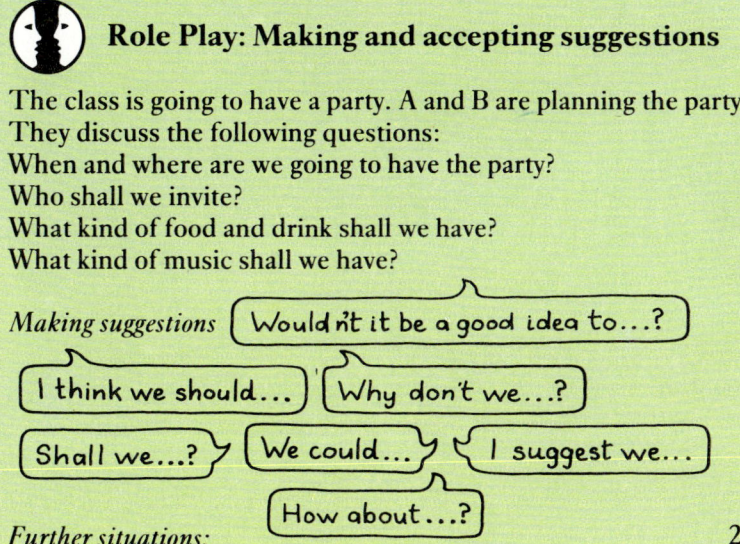

Further situations:

1. The class is going to put on a play. A and B are planning what to do. They discuss the following questions:
What kind of play shall we choose?
Which play shall we decide on?
When and where shall we put it on?

2. The class is going on a trip. A and B are planning the trip. They discuss the following questions:
Where shall we go?
How shall we get there?
What shall we do there?
How long shall we stay there?
How shall we pay for the trip?

 Project: **Your radio programme**

Planning
In this unit you are going to plan and make a radio programme about the future. The programme will be ten minutes long. Discuss the following topics:

1. *Subject: Life in the Future.*
What will your programme be about?
– Your town in ten year's time?
– Life in the year 2000?
– The future of the motor car?
– Space travel?

2. *Contents:* The parts of the programme. Make suggestions for the contents of the programme. Make a list of all the suggestions.

Example:
1. An introduction by the presenter.
2. An interview with an important person.
3. A report from outside the studio.
4. A discussion with experts.
5. A conclusion by the presenter.

3. *Roles:* Decide who is/are going to be:
The producer
The presenter
The people who appear on the programme

LANGUAGE STUDY Exercises: 9.10   9.11   9.15   9.21

LESSON 42

Discussing the best order

The different parts of a television programme are called sequences. The 'What Do You Think?' team are discussing the best order for the sequences.

ANITA: I'd like to start the programme with a film showing how the silicon chip affects our lives today. That would get the viewers interested.

BOB: What I think is that . . .

NED: Just a minute, Bob. Wouldn't it be better to start with the cartoon sequence – about what the chip is and how it works – so that the viewers know what we're talking about? Then we can go on to show how the chip affects us in everyday life.

BRIDGET: Yes, you're probably right. What were you going to say, Bob?

BOB: I was just going to say that Anita usually starts the programme by introducing her guests in the studio, doesn't she?

ANITA: So shall I introduce the experts, and ask them one quick question each, before we show the cartoon?

BRIDGET: I think so. I agree with what Bob said. The viewers are used to the programme starting in the same way each week. And then after we've shown the film about the chip in everyday life, there'll be a discussion with the experts about the future.

NED: Then we can end with a discussion with the studio audience about problems such as unemployment, can't we?

BRIDGET: Fine. Now how about timing? How long will each sequence . . .

BOB: Bridget, there's one more thing.

BRIDGET: What's that?

BOB: We haven't decided on a title.

ANITA: How about 'The World of the Silicon Chip'?

NED: Hmm. A bit dull, isn't it? What about 'Silicon Chips with Everything'?

BRIDGET: I know. Just 'Chips with Everything'. Why not?

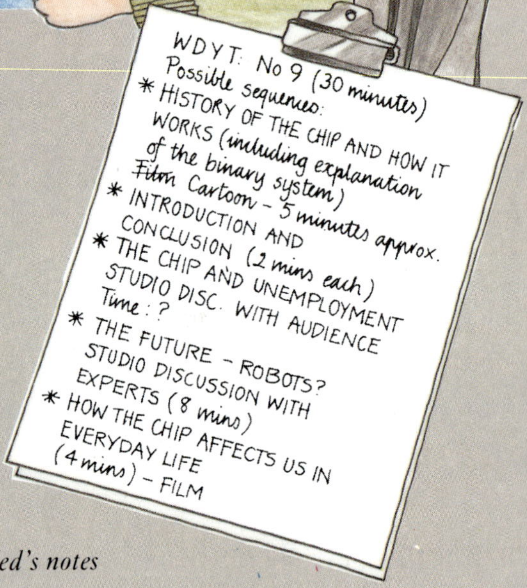

Ned's notes

WDYT: No 9 (30 minutes)
Possible sequences:
* HISTORY OF THE CHIP AND HOW IT WORKS (including explanation of the binary system) Film Cartoon – 5 minutes approx.
* INTRODUCTION AND CONCLUSION (2 mins each)
* THE CHIP AND UNEMPLOYMENT STUDIO DISC. WITH AUDIENCE Time: ?
* THE FUTURE – ROBOTS? STUDIO DISCUSSION WITH EXPERTS (8 mins)
* HOW THE CHIP AFFECTS US IN EVERYDAY LIFE (4 mins) – FILM

  Questions

1. *Expressing agreement:* Bridget says, 'I agree with what Bob said.' What did Bob say? Find three other examples of expressing agreement in the conversation. Make a list of seven different ways of expressing agreement. (Look at Lessons 12 and 13.)

2. *Interrupting:* Ned interupts Bob. What does he say? Make a list of three different ways of interrupting. (Look at Lesson 13.)

Unit 9

 Complete: Putting things in order

Complete the table with details of the order of the sequences in the programme. Read the conversation again and look at Ned's notes to help you. Notice that Ned's notes are not in the right order.

Programme Title :		
SEQUENCE	DESCRIPTION	PROBABLE LENGTH
1.	Introduction	2 mins
2.		
3.		
4.		
5.		
6.	Conclusion	2 mins

Public Meeting
- Describe the history of the school.
- Ask for money to keep the school open.
- Explain why the school is closing.
- Serve drinks and snacks.
- Ask for the parents' opinions.
- Ask for the pupils' opinions.
- Explain how the school can be saved.

 Role Play: Discussing the best order for doing things

It is planned to close your school/institute. You do not agree with this, so you have decided to have a public meeting to complain. Plan an agenda for the meeting by putting the items in this list in the right order. Discuss the agenda with other students.

Use expressions for:
making and accepting suggestions   interrupting
agreeing and disagreeing   introducing new ideas
asking for explanation

Example:

A: I think we should start by asking for money to keep the school open.
B: Yes, then we will know how much . . .
C: Just a minute, shouldn't we explain why the school is closing first?
D: I was just going to say that.

Evening BBC2
Starting March
(times to be announced)
The Silicon Factor
The implications of the micro-electronics revolution. The programmes look at:
1. What the chip is, how it works and what it can do. 2. Its likely impact on manufacturing industry; and 3. The future effects of micro-electronics on people's lives and jobs.
The programmes have been filmed in the USA, Germany, Holland, Sweden, Norway and Britain
Wednesday 7.45-8.25 pm BBC2
19 March – 2 April
The Skill of Lip-Reading

11.0 The Robots are Coming
The present generation of robots are still pretty stupid; but university research is investigating the possibilities of giving robots sight, touch and hearing. How many of our jobs will they then be able to do?
Narrator PAUL VAUGHAN
A *Horizon* production
Editor SIMON CAMPBELL-JONES
Written and produced by HILARY HENSON
(*First shown on BBC2*)
11.50-11.55 News Headlines Weatherman/Regional News

 Project: **Your radio programme**

Planning the order of your programme

1. *Title:* Decide on a title for your programme.
2. *Contents:* Look at the list of suggestions made for the contents of your programme. Choose the ones you are going to use in the programme.
3. *Order:* Work out a running order with timings. Remember you only have ten minutes.
4. *Roles:* Decide who is going to do what:
   Producer: Write out the order, as in the table above.
   Presenter: Prepare a list of questions. (Look at the kinds of question Anita asks in Unit 3.)
   Experts: Make notes on who you are.
   Prepare what you are going to say.
5. *Publicity:* Write a short description of your programme for a radio magazine. Look at two examples from the BBC on the left.

Your description
Title:
Parts of the programme:
1.
2.
3.
Presenter:
Producer:

Language Study Exercises: 9.1   9.2   9.9   9.18

LESSON 43

Discussing changes of plan

'What Do You Think' is being rehearsed in the TV studio.

NED:	Bad news, I'm afraid. We'll have to make some cuts, because the programme is too long.
ANITA:	Perhaps we could shorten the introduction.
BRIDGET:	No, we can't do that. It would be too short. I think we'll have to leave out the explanation of the binary system. It lasts for two minutes.
ANITA:	Oh, what a pity. I thought that bit was really interesting.
NED:	I know, but there isn't anything else we can do, is there?
ANITA:	I suppose you're right. But can't we make up our minds later?
BRIDGET:	Not really. We can't record until we've decided.
NED:	Dr Byrne, could you try to talk more briefly?
DR BYRNE:	I'm sorry, I was trying to explain things very clearly . . .
NED:	Yes, I realise that, but we've got to make the discussion shorter. Would you mind speaking a little faster, too?
DR BYRNE:	Not at all, I hadn't realised I was talking slowly.
NED:	Camera 3, would you come in closer on Anita, please?
CAMERAMAN:	Right.
BRIDGET:	Ned, I don't think we have any choice about the cut. We can't shorten the studio discussion any more, can we? So we'll have to cut the binary system.
NED:	All right. We'd better do that, I suppose. Let's have a break for lunch now.
DR BYRNE:	Do you mind if I make a phone call before lunch?
NED:	Not at all. There's a phone in the office.

  Questions

1. *Half-agreeing:* Bridget says, '. . . there isn't anything else we can do . . .' and Anita half agrees. What does Anita say? Ned also half agrees. What does he say? Make a list of four different ways of expressing half-agreement. (Look at Lesson 13).
2. *Rejecting suggestions:* Anita makes two suggestions which Bridget rejects. What does Bridget say in each case?
3. *Polite requests:* During the conversation Ned makes three polite requests and Dr Byrne makes one. What do they say?

Unit 9

Role Play: Changing plans

A and B are driving to a wedding. Their car breaks down 75 kilometres from the wedding. The nearest town is 10 kilometres away. They have a heavy wedding present in the car.

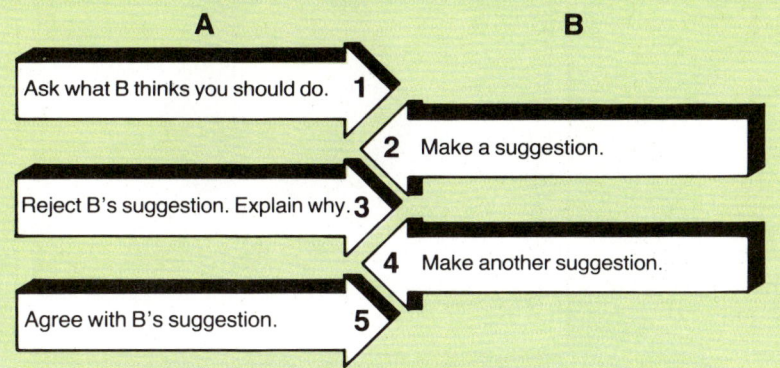

A
1. Ask what B thinks you should do.
3. Reject B's suggestion. Explain why.
5. Agree with B's suggestion.

B
2. Make a suggestion.
4. Make another suggestion.

Example:
1. A: What do you think we should do?
2. B: We could telephone a garage.
3. A: No, we can't do that. There isn't a telephone here.
4. B: Yes, you're right. I think we'll have to leave the car and walk to the next town.
5. A: I don't think we have any choice. All right then, let's go.

Further situations:
1. It is late Friday afternoon. The banks are closed for the weekend. Neither A nor B has more than a few pounds on them. They see a picture in an antique shop and want to buy it. But the shop will not take a cheque.
2. A has invited B to stay for the weekend. A meets B at the station and they go to a restaurant. But when they get back to A's flat, A cannot find the front door key. It is nearly midnight.

Tell each other: Polite requests

When a TV programme is being recorded, the director in the control room cannot speak to the people in front of the camera. A person called the floor manager passes on the director's instructions using special signals. Look at some of these signals on the right, and a list of instructions.

1. Match the signals and instructions.
2. Turn the instructions into polite requests.

Example: Move further apart. (A3)

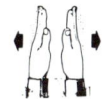
Please move further apart.
Would/could you move further apart?
Would you mind moving further apart?

TV studio signals

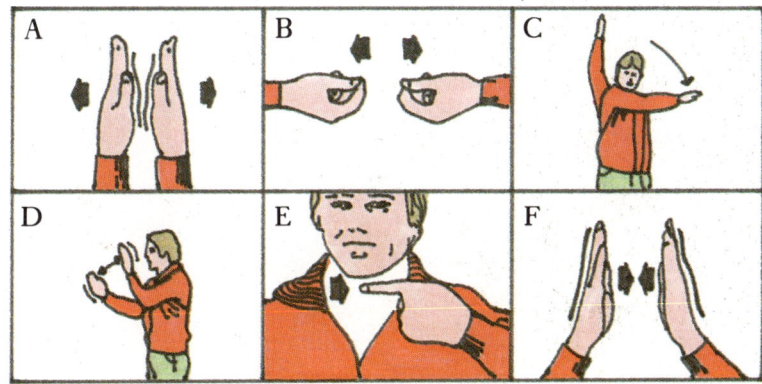

1. Get ready. Start
2. Stand closer together.
3. Move further apart.
4. Clap.
5. Slow down.
6. Stop now.

Puzzle: The binary system

Computers use the binary system of numbers. The binary system uses two digits only: 0 and L. Work with another student, and complete the table below.

Decimal system	Binary system
0	00000
1	0000L
2	000L0
3	000LL
4	00L00
5	00L0L
6	00LL0
7	00LLL
8	0L000
9	
10	
11	
12	0LL00
13	
14	
15	

If 1 is 0000L, and 8 is 0L000, then 9 must be . . . .

 Project: Your radio programme

Rehearsal

1. *First rehearsal:* Rehearse your radio programme. Check how long each part of the programme takes. If possible, record your rehearsal and listen to it. Make any changes you think are necessary.
2. *Final rehearsal:* Rehearse the programme again and check the time of each item. Make any further changes you think are necessary.

Language Study Exercises 9.6 9.7 9.8 9.13 9.14 9.17 9.19

LESSON 44

Commenting and criticising

> Will there be a place for us in a world where robots are running our lives? If the robots are able to design, build and repair themselves, will they need us?
>
> I'd like to leave you with that thought, and say thank you to our studio guests and audience for taking part in the programme. To you at home, thank you, for joining us. Good night.

Ned and Anita are chatting in the control room after recording the programme.

> How did it go? What did you think?

NED: It could have been worse! No, seriously, I thought it went very well. We can't go into much detail in a half-hour programme.

ANITA: It would have been better if George Byrne hadn't talked so much.

NED: Yes, he went on and on with his statistics, didn't he? But the audience came up with some great comments.

ANITA: Well, that's that. Time to go home. Shall I give you a lift?

NED: Yes, thanks! I just want to have a word with Bridget.

ANITA: O.K. You won't be long, will you?

NED: No. See you downstairs.

LAST NIGHT'S TV

19.30
WHAT DO YOU THINK?

I shall look at my digital watch with new eyes after seeing 'Chips with Everything' last night. Anita Lyons and her team showed us the development of the computer industry from 1946, when a computer filled a huge room, to the present day, when a 'chip' half the size of a finger nail can carry a quarter of a million components. In tomorrow's world robots will be running our factories, teaching us foreign languages, and even cooking our meals.

I think the guests on the programme may have been robots, judging by the quantity of facts and figures they produced. Dr Byrne of the Institute of Future Studies said, 'If the car industry had improved its technology at the same rate as the computer industry has, Rolls-Royce cars would now cost about £1.50 each.' The human point of view was summed up by a member of the studio audience. 'I don't want to be unemployed. Personally, I'd rather keep my job and my old black and white TV, and do without all these robots!'

The programme was too short for a full discussion of the subject. However, it certainly gave us a good idea of the effect of the silicon chip on the twentieth century. We must expect great changes in the shape of our lives — after all, we can't put the digital clock back!

 Questions

1. *Commenting favourably:* Ned makes two favourable comments on the TV programme. What does he say? What favourable comment does the TV critic make in the newspaper review?
2. *Criticising:* How does Anita criticise the programme? Which sentence in the newspaper review expresses criticism of the programme?
3. *Drawing conclusions:* What conclusions do Anita and the TV critic draw from the information in the programme?

Unit 9

 Listening: Advantages and disadvantages

Before the discussion with Dr Byrne and
Mr Murray there was a short film about life in the future.
Listen to the description of life in the future and make
notes about the changes mentioned.

 Discuss: Drawing conclusions

Look at the list of the ten top multinational corporations.
What does the list tell you about the world today?
What do you think will happen in the future to:

1. the car industry?
2. the oil industry?
3. the computer industry?

How has the world changed in the last 25 years?
How and why is it likely to change in the next 25 years?
How will we be living in the year 2000?

The 10 top multinationals (1982)

			Sales in millions of dollars
1	Exxon	oil	97,173
2	Royal Dutch/Shell	oil	83,759
3	General Motors	motor cars	60,026
4	Mobil	oil	59,946
5	British Petroleum	oil	51,322
6	Texaco	oil	46,986
7	Ford Motor	motor cars	37,067
8	IBM	computers	34,364
9	Socal	oil	34,362
10	Du Pont	chemicals	33,331

Listed by *Fortune* the American business magazine. Sales figures for 1982.

 Complete: Questionnaire

QUESTIONNAIRE: WHAT DO YOU THINK OF TELEVISION?

1. How often do you watch TV each week?
   - ☐ Less than 5 hours
   - ☐ 5-10 hours
   - ☐ 11-20 hours
   - ☐ More than 20 hours

2. Which kinds of programmes do you enjoy watching most?
   - ☐ Plays   ☐ The News
   - ☐ Drama series   ☐ Current affairs
   - ☐ Films   ☐ Documentaries
   - ☐ Sports   ☐ Comedy series
   - ☐ Music   ☐ Other

3. If you have more than one television channel, which do you watch most often?

4. Which is your favourite programme?

5. If you have advertisements on television, which is your favourite advertisement?

6. Is TV more important to you than

	more important	as important	less important
Radio?	☐	☐	☐
Records?	☐	☐	☐
Books?	☐	☐	☐
Holidays?	☐	☐	☐

7. Does watching TV mean that you spend less time
   - ☐ Talking to people?
   - ☐ Going out?
   - ☐ Reading?
   - ☐ Taking part in sports?

8. Do you think TV is bad for children?
   How much TV should children watch every week?

 Project: **Your radio programme**

1. *Publicity:* Show the rest of the class the description of your radio programme (Lesson 42).
2. *Recording:* If you can use a tape recorder, make a recording of your programme.
3. *Broadcast:* Put on your programme for the rest of the class, or play the recording if you have one.
4. *Comment:* Discuss the programmes produced by the other groups.
5. *Review:* Work with the other students in your group to write a review of one of the radio programmes.

Language Study Exercises 9.3 9.4 9.5 9.12 9.16 9.20 9.22

LESSON 45

COMMUNICATION ACTIVITY

Discussing the best order

Do this activity in pairs (A and B). A's instructions are below and B's instructions are at the bottom of the page.

Student A
COVER THE BOTTOM HALF OF THE PAGE. YOU MUST NOT LOOK AT STUDENT B'S INSTRUCTIONS.

This is an extract from a detective story. The detective is called Lenny Samuel. He is on his way to the Manson Building, and is being followed by a yellow car. But, before you can read the extract, you have to put the sections in the right order. You have some of the sections (a, b, c, d), and B has the others (e, f, g, h).

1. Read through the sections a, b, c, and d.
2. Work with B to put all eight sections in the right order. Section (a) is the first section. You may read your sections out to B, but do not show them to B.

(a)   As I was driving happily towards the Manson Building, I had a surprise. I looked in the mirror. The yellow car was coming up fast behind me.

(b)   The porter was sitting at his desk, asleep. His feet were on the desk and he was lying back in his chair. I walked quickly and quietly into the room and closed the door.

(c)   'You ought to be more careful,' I said to the driver. 'You were driving very dangerously. It's lucky for you that my car isn't badly damaged.'
'But ...but ...,' the driver began to say, but I didn't wait to listen. I ran back to the Chrysler, jumped in and drove off. The last I saw of the yellow car was the two men pushing it to the side of the road.

(d)   I braked hard and the tyres screamed as the Chrysler stopped suddenly to avoid the dog. Then there was the scream of more tyres as the driver of the yellow car tried to stop.

Student B
COVER THE TOP HALF OF THE PAGE. YOU MUST NOT LOOK AT STUDENT A'S INSTRUCTIONS.

This is an extract from a detective story. The detective is called Lenny Samuel. He is on his way to the Manson Building, and is being followed by a yellow car. But, before you can read the extract, you have to put the sections in the right order. You have some of the sections (e, f, g, h), and A has the others (a, b, c, d).

1. Read through sections e, f, g and h.
2. Work with A to put all eight sections in the right order. A has the first section. You may read your sections out to A, but you must not show them to A.

(e)   I was soon at the Manson Building and I went into the hall to look for the porter. I couldn't see him anywhere. Then I noticed a door with a sign on it, saying 'Porter'. I knocked quietly, but there was no answer. I opened the door slowly and looked into the room.

(f)   There was a loud crash and a bang as the small yellow car ran right into the back of my big, old grey Chrysler. The two men in the yellow car weren't hurt, but their car was badly damaged at the front. Oil and water were running out on to the road. The old Chrysler wasn't damaged at all. I got out and walked back to the yellow car.

(g)   I drove as fast as I could, but the yellow car got closer and closer. Just then, a dog ran across the road in front of the Chrysler.

(h)   I went up to the desk and noticed a piece of paper lying by the telephone. There was a telephone number written on the paper – 323.0313.
'Las Cabanas,' I said to myself. 'That's the telephone number of the night club.'

Unit 9

FOCUS ON READING

How fast can you read

Reading purpose

To practise reading fast. Do not read the passage word by word. Read the passage through quickly to find the answers to these questions:

1. When did the British television service start?
2. Something happened in 1953 which made people buy TVs. What was it?
3. When were the first colour TV broadcasts in France?

Note the time before you start reading, and after you have found the answers to the questions.

After reading

Look carefully back through the text and find the answers to these questions:
1. How many TV sets were there in the USA in 1959?
2. How many TV sets were sold each year in Britain in the 1950s?
3. When was 625-line TV developed?
4. When did Japan start colour broadcasts?
5. When will people be able to watch teletext on their televisions?

Turn back to the *Focus on Reading* sections at the end of **Unit 3** (p.38) and **Unit 5** (p.66). Read each story through quickly for pleasure. Time yourself and compare the timings with other students.

TELEVISION IN BRITAIN

The Growth of Television

After only three years, the British television service was closed down when war was declared in 1939. It did not re-open until 1946.

Meanwhile, Germany had had a regular 180-line service in operation since 1935, and experiments were being carried out by the Philips company in Holland. But most other countries were not ready to start transmissions until the 1950s.

The exception was America, where regular broadcasts began in 1941. By 1949 there were over a million television sets in the USA. Ten years later there were over 50 million. Today there are nearly 100 million.

By the early 1970s, the number of television sets in use throughout the world amounted to about 275 million.

Television did not become a mass medium overnight. In Britain, the pre-war audience was only 20,000 homes, and all these were in the London area. By 1952, with the service extended as far as Scotland, the audience was still only about 1½ million.

Then in 1953 came an event which was to speed up the growth of the audience: the Coronation of Queen Elizabeth II. About a million people bought TV sets to see the procession and the ceremony. And within a year a million more people, having seen the transmission in their friends' houses, bought sets of their own.

In 1955 a second channel was introduced. Called Independent Television (ITV), it was financed by advertising, while the BBC continued to be paid for by the licence fees collected from all set owners. The new channel proved so popular that the number of sets continued to increase by about a million every year.

In the early 1960s the BBC was given another channel (BBC 2) so that a greater variety of programmes could be produced. At the same time, a 625-line system was developed to improve picture quality. This system has since been adopted as the European standard and British TV is generally recognised as the best in the world.

Into Colour

By the 1950s the time was ripe for colour television to be developed. But because so many black-and-white sets had already been sold, it had to be a system which could be received by them as well as by the new colour sets.

Experiments with colour had been going on since the birth of television itself. But none proved satisfactory until in 1953 a system was developed by the National Television Systems Committee (NTSC) in America. This system successfully combined two signals, one for black-and-white and one for colour.

The NTSC system was adopted in the USA in 1954, and in Japan in 1960. But other countries adopted slightly different methods. One of these was a West German system known as PAL (Phase Alternation Line) and another was the French SECAM (Système Électronique Couleur avec Mémoire). Britain and Germany adopted the PAL system in 1967, and in the same year France and Russia began SECAM transmissions.

By the early 1970s there were more than 40 million colour sets in use around the world.

Tomorrow's Television – A Way of Life

There is no doubt that television will play an even bigger part in our lives in future years.

We already have television sets. It won't be long before we can have huge, flat screens that simply hang on the wall like pictures.

People are already buying television sets that can provide printed information as well as programmes. Called *teletext*, it's like a newspaper that never goes out of date, bringing viewers all the latest news at the touch of a button.

Eventually, *domestic computers* will be available. These will enable viewers to ask questions of the teletext system, and get the answers in seconds on their screens. With similar computers in all the shops, it will be possible for viewers to examine goods and make purchases without leaving their armchairs.

Telephone subscribers will be able to have a *videophone* installed. This combines the telephone with television, so callers can see as well as hear each other.

From *Television* by Michael Loftus

FOCUS ON WRITING

Narrative description

Writing purpose
To write a description of past events and a forecast of future events.

Language preparation
1. Read these facts:

1950-1960	Most countries started TV transmissions
1941	TV transmissions started in America
1949	Over a million TV sets in America
1959	Over 50 million TV sets in America
Today	About 125 million TV sets in America

2. Now look at this extract from 'Television in Britain'.

But most other countries were not ready to start transmissions until the 1950s. The exception was America where regular broadcasts began in 1941. By 1949 there were over a million television sets in the USA. Ten years later there were over 50 million. Today there are about 125 million.

3. Underline these words in the extract:

   until   in   by   later

   Find words in the extract which mean:

   transmissions   more than   almost   started

4. Write a similar passage about these facts:

1950-1960	Most countries started TV transmissions
1936	TV transmissions started in Britain
1939	20,000 TV sets in Britain
1952	1½ million TV sets in Britain
1953	2½ million TV sets in Britain
Today	Over 25 million TV sets in Britain

5. Read the first two paragraphs of 'Tomorrow's Television – A Way of Life' again and find phrases which mean:

   in the future   we will soon be able to have

Writing
Use these facts to help you write a description of the development of computers and a forecast of their future.

A valve   A transistor

A chip   An industrial robot

The Development of Computers

1945	First electronic computer built at the University of Pennsylvania. Weight 30 tonnes. Size: covered 160 square metres. Used 18,000 valves. Now a silicon chip 5 mm square can do the same amount of work
1947	Transistor invented by The Bell Telephone Co.
1950	Computers using valves available
1955	Transistor radios on sale
1960	Computers using transistors available
1960	Fairchild Semiconductors made first silicon chip
1960	A 5 mm square chip could have 16 components on it
1965	Chips with 30 components made
1975	Chips with 30,000 components made
1978	Chips with 135,000 components made
1980	Chips with more than 250,000 components made. Soon chips with more than a million components possible

The Future?

1990-2000	Computers which learn from their mistakes will be developed. Robots will be doing most skilled work in factories
2000-2050	Chips will be put in the human brain to help injured people
2050-2100	Computers will control the world
After 2100	Half-human, half-machine robots called CYBORGS will be developed. Computers will be more intelligent than humans

Unit 9

LANGUAGE STUDY

Lessons 41–45

STRUCTURE

9.1 Study

> FUTURE IN THE PAST
> 'was/were going to' + INFINITIVE
>
> *Example:* What *were you going to say*, Bob?
>
> 'going to' in the past tense indicates that something which was intended to happen, did not happen. In the example above, Bob was interrupted before he could say anything.

9.2 Drill

Why did the policeman make an arrest? What was going to happen? Find the answers in the list below and put them in the correct tense.

Example:

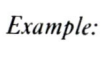 

He was going to rob the bank.

1.
2.
3.
4.
5.

steal the car
cut down the trees
leave without paying
break the window
blow up the plane

9.3 Study

> FUTURE CONTINUOUS TENSE
> 'will be' + PRESENT PARTICIPLE
>
> *Example:* In tomorrow's world, robots *will be running* our factories, *teaching* us foreign languages, and even *cooking* our meals.
>
> This tense describes continuous activity in the future. It often suggests that the activity is part of the normal course of events.

9.4 Ask and answer

Look at this page from the Minister of Education's diary. These are his appointments for tomorrow. The Minister of Transport wants to see him tomorrow, and telephones his secretary.

Example: S1: *Is he free at 9.30?*
S2: *No, he'll be opening a new school.*

```
9.30   Open a new school.
10.30  Meet the Minister of Health
11.45  Go to the dentist
1.00   Have lunch with Education Officers
2.30   Go to Parliament
4.45   Have tea at the Savoy Hotel.
6.00   Go to the T.V. studios.
7.30   Give a T.V. interview.
9.00   Have dinner with the Prime Minister
```

9.5 Answer the questions

Example: What will Jenny be doing next Monday? (fly to Mexico)
She'll be flying to Mexico.

1. What will Sandra be doing next month? (have a holiday)
2. What will Steve be doing tonight? (watch television)
3. What will Fred be doing tomorrow morning? (deliver milk)
4. What will Anita be doing tomorrow evening? (interview the Minister of Education)
5. What will Jenny be doing next year? (study in Mexico)
6. What will the Langleys be doing at 11 o'clock tonight? (go to bed)
7. What will Liz be doing this afternoon? (do the football pools)
8. What will Zed be doing on Saturday night? (sing at a rock concert)

9.6 Study

> PRESENT PERFECT TENSE IN ADVERBIAL CLAUSES OF TIME
> The present perfect tense refers to the *future* in adverbial clauses of time.
>
> *Examples:* *After we've shown* the film, there'll be a discussion.
> We can't record *until we've decided.*
>
> The following conjunctions are used to introduce time clauses:
> *after, before, as soon as, when, until, by the time (that)*

9.7 Complete

Look at the list of instructions, and tell someone how to use the washing-machine.

```
 How to use the washing-machine
  1.  Put washing into machine.
  2.  Close door.
  3.  Pour soap into soap compartment.
  4.  Choose correct temperature.
  5.  Press button (for cold, warm, or hot).
  6.  Insert money, and machine will start.
```

Begin: Put the washing into the machine.
1. When you've put the washing into the machine, close the door.
2. When you've closed the door, ...
3. When you've ....
4. When ....
5. ....
6. ....

Now repeat your instructions using *after* in place of *when*.

9.8 Answer the questions

Respond to the requests, saying you cannot do what is asked at once.
Example: Will you lend me £5? (go to the bank)
I can't until I've been to the bank.

1. Will you give me a lift to work? (mend the car)
2. Can you help me with the washing-up? (finish this letter)
3. Can you come to the cinema? (do my homework)
4. Would you help me paint this room? (change my clothes)
5. Would you like to come to a party? It's starting now. (wash my hair)
6. Will you phone the doctor? (find the telephone directory)

NOUN CLAUSES INTRODUCED BY 'WHAT'

 9.9 Answer the questions

Examples: What did you say? ('Be quiet!')
What I said was, 'Be quiet!'
What do you want? (a holiday)
What I want is a holiday.

1. What did you buy? (a raincoat)
2. What do you hate? (washing up)
3. What are you reading? (a book about computers)
4. What do you enjoy? (meeting people)
5. What did you do? (telephone the police)

9.10 Study

> MAKING SUGGESTIONS AND OFFERS WITH 'SHALL I/WE . . .?'
> 'shall' is mainly used in first person questions to make suggestions and offers.
>
> *Examples:* Shall I introduce the experts? (Suggestion)
> Shall we have a cup of coffee? (Suggestion)
> Shall I give you a lift? (Offer)

 9.11 Make suggestions

You and a friend have just rented a flat.
What do you say in the following situations?

Example: You would like to paint the walls.
Shall we paint the walls?

You would like to move the furniture.
    clean the windows.
    wash the curtains.
    put up some pictures.
    get a television.
    have a party.

 9.12 Make offers

You are staying with a friend, and want to help as much as you can.

Example: Offer to do the washing-up.
Shall I do the washing-up?

Offer to make some coffee.
    do the shopping.
    answer the phone.
    cook something for dinner.
    look after the children.
    post the letters.

9.13 Study

> 'MIND': POLITE REQUESTS
>
> *Examples:* *Would you mind speaking* a little faster?
> (Asking someone to do something)
> *Do you mind if* I make a phone call?
> (Asking for permission to do something)
>
> ⚠ The usual polite answers are:
>
> | | NO | YES |
> |---|---|---|
> | (Would you mind . . .ing . . .?) | Not at all. | I'm afraid I . . . |
> | (Do you mind if I . . . . . .?) | Not at all. | I'd rather you didn't. |

 9.14 Make polite requests

You are on a train. The train is full.
What do you say in the following situations?

Examples: You want *someone* to close the window.
Would you mind closing the window?
You want to close the window.
Do you mind if I close the window?

1. You want someone to open the window.
2. You want to sit by the door.
3. You want to smoke.
4. You want someone to move her suitcase.
5. You want to look at someone's paper.
6. You want someone to lend you their matches.
7. You want someone to tell you the time.

VOCABULARY

When you are studying this vocabulary section, you will find a dictionary is very helpful.

WORD BUILDING

9.15 Make nouns

Make nouns from the verbs below by adding the suffix '-er' or '-or'.
Check the spelling and the meaning in your dictionary.

Examples: sing *singer* write *writer*
         sail *sailor*

advise	employ	present	survive
dance	interpret	produce	teach
direct	interview	listen	view
drive	inspect	research	visit
edit	own	speak	work

PHRASAL VERBS

9.16 Complete

Put in the correct preposition: *down, on, out, up, to, without*

1. Steve made . . . his mind to stop teaching.
2. The police worked . . . how the robbers got into the bank.
3. Although Fred asked her to stop, Liz went . . . spending money.
4. The student left . . . the difficult questions.
5. The receptionist explained that the lift had broken . . . .
6. Anita summed . . . the discussion in the TV studio.
7. No one can do . . . sleep for long.
8. Sandra was looking forward . . . her holiday.

Unit 9

WHAT DO YOU SAY?

 9.17 Listen and choose the most suitable response

1. (a) I didn't see anything.
   (b) Yes, I did.
   (c) I went to see a play.
   (d) It wasn't important.
2. (a) I didn't notice.
   (b) I'm afraid I don't.
   (c) Not at all.
   (d) Is it on?
3. (a) I've got a bad cold.
   (b) I'm going to Manchester.
   (c) What I mean is this.
   (d) I'm getting a hat for the wedding.

INTONATION AND STRESS

 9.18 Ask for agreement

Make these statements into requests for agreement.

Examples: Jenny won a scholarship.
Jenny won a schōlarship, dĭdn't she?
Steve will find a job.
Steve will fĭnd a job, wōn't he?

1. Fred learnt to fly.
2. Jenny should stop smoking.
3. You've got a radio.
4. The robbers were clever.
5. Sandra can type.
6. Jenny will be travelling a lot.
7. The children would like it.
8. I must take my passport.
9. Jenny was learning Spanish.
10. We're late.

 9.19 Ask for agreement

Make these statements into requests for agreement.
Examples: Mr Langley isn't very well.
Mr Langley isn't very wĕll, ĭs he?
Liz didn't like living in the country.
Liz didn't like lĭving in the cŏuntry, dĭd she?

1. Steve doesn't like working.
2. The police couldn't catch the robbers.
3. You haven't been to Matona.
4. Zed wasn't polite.
5. Sandra can't speak Swedish.
6. We don't know.
7. People shouldn't fight.
8. Jenny isn't going to Brazil.
9. The Mills haven't got much money.
10. You aren't afraid.

 9.20 Ask for agreement

Examples: You'll help me.
You'll hĕlp me, wŏn't you?
You won't be long.
You won't be lŏng, wĭll you?

1. You won't drive fast.
2. You'll wake me up.
3. You'll write to me.
4. You won't forget.
5. You won't be late.
6. You'll look after her.
7. You'll try.
8. You won't hurt yourself.
9. You won't lose it.
10. You'll talk to him.

SENTENCE LINKING

 9.21 Join the sentences using relative clauses

Example: I like the idea. We talked about it.
I like the idea we talked about.

1. The police found the man. They were looking for him.
2. That's the place. I'm thinking of it.
3. Steve applied for the jobs. He was interested in them.
4. Fred explained the problem. He was worried about it.
5. Jenny got the information. She asked for it.

Example: The candidate won the election. I voted for him.
The candidate I voted for won the election.

1. The house was expensive. Liz looked at it.
2. The train is late. I'm waiting for it.
3. The film is on TV. We read about it.
4. The hotel wasn't built. They booked into it.
5. The person lived in Stockholm. Sandra wrote to him.

9.22 Write a paragraph

Write a brief description of your school/institute/college/university.
Describe: (1) its history (2) what it is like today (3) what it will be like in the future. Try to use relative clauses when possible.

Example: The college I go to is quite new. It was opened in 1968. The building the college is in used to be an office......

DIY CHECK UP Unit 4

This is part of a conversation between Ned Giles and Louis Murray, before the recording of 'What Do You Think?'
Choose the most suitable word, or put the verbs in brackets into the correct form.

LOUIS: How long have you been (1) *working/worked* in television?
NED: Oh, (2) *since/for* nearly ten years. And I (3) *am/have been* directing programmes for about six years.
LOUIS: Is it a difficult job? It looks very tiring.
NED: Well, of course, you (4) *must/need* to work very fast, because there's never enough studio time. And you (5) *must/need* be able to make decisions quickly. But I enjoy it – and I (6) *mustn't/don't have to* work every day.
LOUIS: Have you ever thought of (7) (*work*) in the film industry?
NED: No, I (8) (*not change*) my job for anything. (9) (*Make*) a good TV programme is very exciting.
LOUIS: Do you think this one will be good?
NED: I (10) (*do*) my best, I promise.

* Look up the answers in the DIY Check-up Key. Discuss any mistakes you have made.
* Look up your mistakes in the Structural Reference List. Then turn to the Language Study exercises suggested.

Unit 10
LESSON 46

Educational details and plans

Claudio Giuliani comes from Italy and wants to train as a professional pilot. He has applied for a course for a Commercial Pilot's Licence (CPL) at the Oxford Air Training School (OATS).

```
Oxford Air Training School
Oxford Airport
Kidlington
Oxford  OX5 1RA


Dear Sir

     I would like to apply for a place on the beginner's course for
a Commercial Pilot's Licence, starting in October this year.

     I am 22, and have just obtained a first degree ('diploma di
laurea') in physics at the University of Genoa.  Before I went
to university, I attended a Scientific Upper School in Genoa
until I was eighteen, when I received a 'diploma di maturita
scientifica'.  My subjects included English, mathematics, physics
and chemistry.  During my university vacations, I worked as a
waiter in London while studying for the Cambridge Certificate of
Proficiency in English examination, which I passed last year.

     I enclose copies of my educational certificates and diplomas,
together with a completed application form.

     I look forward to hearing from you soon,

     Yours faithfully
     Claudio Giuliani

     Claudio Giuliani
```

 Complete

Study Claudio's letter of application and the extract from the OATS brochure. Then complete this table.

Requirements for admission to the ATS	Claudio's qualifications.
1.	
2.	
3.	

  Questions

1. Does Claudio have the necessary qualifications for a place on the CPL course?
2. What examination must students pass before a place can be confirmed?

Qualifications for Admission

Students applying for an ab initio course must be over the age of 17½ and possess minimum educational qualifications of five GCE subjects at 'O' level including English, Mathematics and a science subject, preferably Physics. Equivalent qualifications may be accepted in lieu upon application to the Civil Aviation Authority, FCL 1, Third Floor, Aviation House, 129 Kingsway, London WC2B 6NN. Overseas students should have had a similar standard of education and must have a high standard in written and spoken English. In all cases educational certificates or diplomas must be submitted to the School with the initial application. Before confirmation of a place on a course students must have passed the initial professional pilots medical examination.

The Commercial Pilot's Licence is the professional licence taken by ab initio students and, together with an Instrument Rating is the minimum qualification for employment as a professional pilot with an airline.

Unit 10

 Writing: Telexes

Claudio received this telex from the Air Training School. It was sent to his father's office.

1. ACCEPTED FOR PLACE ON CPL COURSE STARTING OCTOBER 5 PLEASE INFORM ARRIVAL DETAILS

2. ORDER NO T 6734 NOT YET RECEIVED PLEASE CHECK DATE OF DESPATCH

3. CONGRATULATIONS NEW CONTRACT FLYING OUT SUNDAY BA 924 PLEASE MEET AIRPORT

4. PLEASE BOOK SINGLE ROOM BATH NIGHTS 23RD 24TH JANUARY IN NAME OF JOHNSON AND CONFIRM

5. MANAGING DIRECTOR ARRIVING LONDON FRIDAY AM PLEASE MAKE APPOINTMENT SALES MANAGER FRIDAY PM

In telexes and telegrams we leave out some words.

Example: You have been ACCEPTED FOR a PLACE ON the Commercial Pilot's Licence COURSE STARTING on OCTOBER 5th.

What kind of words are left out?

Rewrite the contents of these telexes in full sentences.

  Study and complete: Reasons for studying

When Claudio arrived at the school, he had an interview with one of the instructors. Look at his letter of application, and at the extract from the application form. Then complete Claudio's part of the interview.

MR HENDERSON: Come in, Mr Giuliani. My name's Henderson. How do you do?
CLAUDIO: ....
MR HENDERSON: Please sit down. I hope you had no problems getting here?
CLAUDIO: ....
MR HENDERSON: Good. Now I'd like to check a few details. You're twenty-one, aren't you?
CLAUDIO: ....
MR HENDERSON: And when did you leave school?
CLAUDIO: ....
MR HENDERSON: What have you been doing since then?
CLAUDIO: ....
MR HENDERSON: That's a useful subject for pilots! Tell me, what are your reasons for wanting to be a pilot?
CLAUDIO: ....
MR HENDERSON: Why did you decide to train in England?
CLAUDIO: ....
MR HENDERSON: I see. Well, I hope you enjoy the course. Your English is very good. Did you learn it at school?
CLAUDIO: ....
MR HENDERSON: Oh, that explains it. Do you have any questions?
CLAUDIO: ....
MR HENDERSON: Not immediately, I'm afraid. You have to start with training on the ground.

> Describe briefly in the space below why you want to be a pilot.
>
> I've always wanted to be a pilot because I love planes and I enjoy travelling. But my parents wanted me to go to university. While I was studying physics, I made up my mind to learn to fly after I had graduated. I decided to apply for a course at the Oxford Air Training School because it has an excellent reputation and English is the international language for pilots.

 **Learning together**

'You're very good at . . .'

Talk to the other students about their English. Tell each student something good about their English which you have noticed during your course.

Examples:

'I've noticed that you're very good at reading. You've read lots of books.'
'I think you're very good at learning new words. How do you do it?'
'You're very good at making up questions. You always ask for help when you don't understand.'

LANGUAGE STUDY Exercises 10.1 10.2 10.3 10.4

130

LESSON 47

Using libraries and books

Claudio went to a library to borrow a book about flying.

  Listen and complete

In the library, Claudio listened to a tape explaining how to find books. Listen to the explanation and look at the pictures. Then complete the diagram below.

 Tell each other

Use your completed diagram to tell each other:

(a) How to find a book if you know the author's name.
(b) How to find a book on a particular subject.

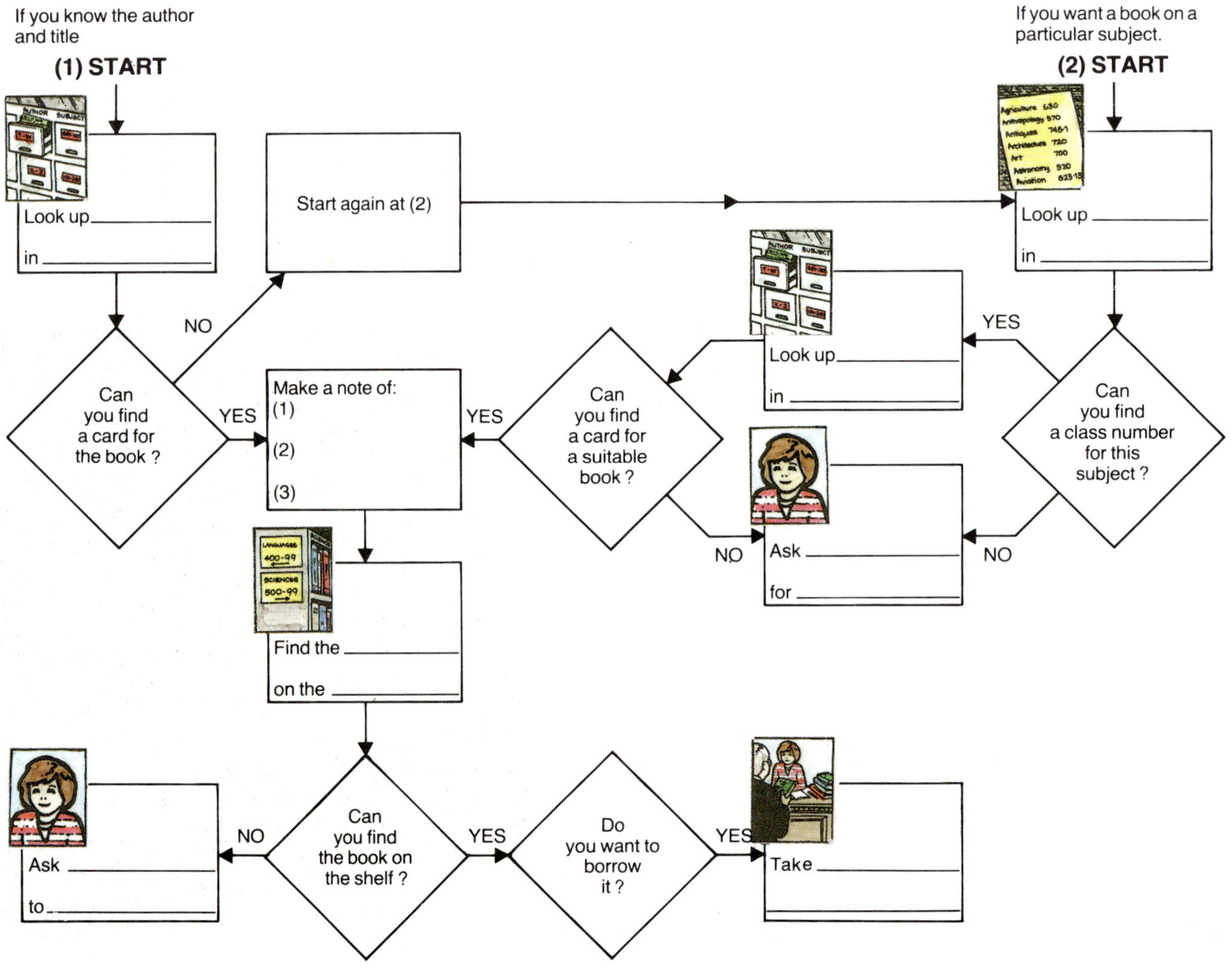

Unit 10

 Reading

Claudio borrowed a book about flying from the library. Find the answers to the questions in the following extracts from the book.

1. Which page should Claudio turn to to read about instruments?
2. What does the compass show the pilot?
3. What is air speed?
4. Which page refers to:
   (a) air speed?
   (b) flying speed?
   (c) ground speed?
5. What does altitude mean?
6. On which page is altitude mentioned?
7. Which chapters are about landing?
8. Which chapter is about different kinds of aircraft?

Index

aids 24	drive 4
ailerons 13	drift 20
aircraft 4	
air pressure 14	elevator 13
air speed (indicator) 17	equivalent volume 5
altimeter 17	fin 13
altitude 17	flap 7
angle of attack 5	flying speed 22
approach lights 24	fuselage 13
artificial horizon 17	
automatic 26	glide slope 25
autopilot 26	ground speed 20
barometer 18	heading 19
blade 10	heavier-than-air 4

Contents

1	Types of aircraft	4
2	What makes an aeroplane fly	6
3	Forces acting in flight	8
4	Thrust	10
5	Stability and control	12
6	The air around the aeroplane	14
7	Instruments on the aeroplane	17
8	Navigation	19
9	Taking off, turning and landing	21
10	Landing systems	24
11	Supersonic flight	27

7 Instruments on the aeroplane

During flight, the pilot is helped by a number of **instruments** in the cockpit (Fig. 21). He has a **magnetic compass**. This shows the direction of his flight. He has an **air speed indicator**. This tells him the speed of the aeroplane in relation to the air around it. Other instruments indicate (or show) movements of the aeroplane. In Figure 21, for example, you can see the **rate of climb indicator** and the **turn and bank indicator**. The **artificial horizon** indicates whether the wings are level with the horizon. It also shows whether the nose is pointing up or down.

Another important instrument is the **altimeter**. The altimeter is used in two ways (Fig. 22). It can measure altitude (i.e. vertical distance above sea-level). It can also measure height (i.e. vertical distance above the ground).

  Learning together

'We've made progress...'
Talk to the other students about their progress in English. Tell them how much better their English is now, than when they started their course.

Examples:
'You talk a lot more than you used to. You're able to say what you want.'
'I understand a lot more now when I listen to songs or recordings.'

Language Study Exercises 10.9 10.10

LESSON 48

Making notes

At the Air Training School Students' Club.

MR HENDERSON: We'll start as usual with short talks by some of the new trainees. They'll be telling us about airlines in the countries they come from. After that we've got music from South America and India, songs from all over the world, and snacks and drinks from seven different countries. So, let's start. The first speaker is Tony Palmer, from Australia.

TONY PALMER: Hello, I'm Tony and, as Mr Henderson said, I'm from Australia. I'm on the CPL course, and I want to tell you about TAA – that's Trans-Australia Airlines. In fact, it's TAA who are paying for my course here. What I'd like to do is to start with TAA's history, then go on to the airline as it is today, and finally say something about TAA in the future.

Tony Palmer's notes

> Then: 1st flight 9/9/46 DC3
> Laverton–Sydney
> Only 21 pass.
> 1961: 1,000,000 pass
>
> Now: 5× as many pass.
> 38 aircraft. 51 places
> 65,000 tonnes cargo
>
> Future: 10% pass growth.
> 4 airbuses on order
> first internal airline
> in Australia with
> wide-bodied aircraft

 **Questions**

1. *Signposting a talk:* Tony says his talk is divided into three parts. What are they?
2. *Reading notes:* Look at Tony's notes. What do the abbreviations stand for?

Listening: Recognising the structure of a talk

Listen to Tony's talk and note down:
1. How many of each kind of aircraft does TAA have.
2. The ways in which Tony starts and finishes the parts of his talk.

   Example:
   He introduces the first part by saying, 'So, to start with, let's do a little history.'
3. How Tony ends his talk.

TAA's first flight

The TAA fleet

The Aircraft speeds (over the ground) are dependent on wind velocity, height, and temperature. These figures are therefore approximate.

		Length	Wingspan	Cruising Speed	Normal Cruising Altitude	Max seating *Cargo capacity, with typical passenger load.
	A300B4 Airbus Maker: Airbus Industrie Europe	53.6m	44.8m	880 km/h	9500m	270 passengers *14000 kg
	727-200 Advanced Series T-Jet Maker: Boeing U.S.A.	48m	32.9m	880km/h	10,000m	158 passengers *6900 kg
	DC9-30 T-Jet Maker: McDonnell-Douglas Corporation U.S.A.	36.4m	28.5m	845km/h	9500m	100 passengers *5100 kg
	F27 Friendship Maker: Fokker Holland	24m	29m	420km/h	5000m	40 passengers *1200 kg
	DHC-6 Twin Otter Maker: De Havilland Canada	15.8m	19.8m	320km/h	2000m	20 passengers *200 kg

Unit 10

 Tell each other: Giving a talk

1. Use Tony's notes to give a short talk about TAA.
   Notice that Tony:
   (a) Introduces himself
   (b) Introduces the subject
   (c) Signposts the talk
   (d) Shows the audience clearly the beginning and end of each part of the talk.
   (e) Finishes by summing up and asking for questions
2. Practise starting talks in the situations on the right.
   (a) Introduce yourself
   (b) Introduce the subject
   (c) Signpost the talk

(a) WHO YOU ARE	(b) THE SUBJECT OF THE TALK	(c) SIGNPOSTS
Roger Shepherd, Lecturer in Education, Thames University.	Education in Britain	1. Schools a hundred years ago 2. A typical school today 3. Education in fifty years' time
Anne Page, Careers Advisor.	Getting a job	1. Deciding what you are good at 2. Finding out what jobs are available 3. Filling in an application form 4. Going to an interview
Peter Westbrook, Export Salesman, English Transport.	English Transport	1. How the company started 2. The cars we make now 3. Our plans for the future

 Make notes and tell each other: Preparing and giving a talk

1. Make notes for two short talks (three minutes each). Divide your notes into sections as Tony does. Decide on your own topic or choose from these suggestions: The town I live in/A famous person/Education in my country/A book I have read.
2. Use your notes to give talks to the other students, who should take notes and ask questions.

 Study and write

1. Read these extracts from the ATS brochure and look back at the extract on 'Qualifications for admission' on page 129.
2. Write a short description of your English course (or another course which you are following) giving information on:

   Qualifications for admission
   Course content
   Timetable

The Course
The CPL/IR course lasts for 52 weeks plus two separate weeks vacation. Of this the first nine months leads to the C.P.L. stage with the technical examinations taken in the 41st week of training. The remainder of the course comprises advanced flying for the Instrument Rating.

The C.P.L. stage comprises daily alternating ground and flying training after an initial period of full time ground school, thus maintaining the essential close integration between both aspects of the course. The syllabus of ground training is in preparation for the following technical examinations set by the Civil Aviation Authority.

Aviation Law   Radio Aids
Flight Planning   Navigation Plotting
Meteorology   Navigation General
Aircraft Technical   Signals
Aircraft Performance
Group 'A'

Other subjects in the syllabus include lectures on air transport operations, economics, and on various non-aviation subjects of a general interest. Much use is made of films, slides and other modern visual and audio aids. Progress tests in all subjects are held at regular intervals throughout the course.

During the course ab initio students fly a minimum of 230 hours. This includes both day and night flying and covers general handling, navigation by map reading and by the use of radio aids and instrument flying.

The normal working day is from 0900 to 1730 hours Monday to Friday with students on flying reporting at 0830. Flying training may be necessary at weekends or evenings in the event of bad weather delaying courses or additional flying being necessary for a particular student.

 Learning together

'You helped me . . .'
Talk to the other students about how you have helped each other.

Examples:
'You always read through my homework and helped me correct my mistakes.'
'You explained what the teacher meant when I didn't understand.'

LANGUAGE STUDY Exercises 10.5 10.6 10.7 10.8

LESSON 49

Taking part in a discussion

Mr Henderson is teaching a group of new students at the Air Training School.

[Mr Henderson:] Let's start by talking about how a plane moves in the air. If you look at this diagram, you will see that four principal forces act upon an aeroplane in flight – Thrust, Lift, Drag and Weight.

TONY:	Excuse me, but could you explain in more detail?
MR HENDERSON:	Yes, I was coming to that. You see, *Thrust* pushes the plane forwards, *Lift* pushes the plane upwards, *Drag* pushes it backwards and *Weight* pushes it downwards.
TONY:	I'm sorry, I didn't quite catch that . . . Did you say that thrust pushes the plane forwards?
MR HENDERSON:	That's right. And of course, thrust is produced by the plane's engines. Yes?
CLAUDIO:	I was wondering about lift. What exactly do you mean by lift?
MR HENDERSON:	Lift is produced by the shape and angle of the wing when the plane moves forwards . . .
CLAUDIO:	So, in other words, the wing produces lift.
MR HENDERSON:	Or, more exactly, the forward movement of the wing. The weight of the plane and its load is the opposite force . . .
TONY:	I'm sorry. I don't quite understand. What about drag?
MR HENDERSON:	Drag is mainly produced by the air pushing against the plane. So, to sum up, for the plane to move forwards, thrust must be greater than drag. And for the plane to move upwards, lift must be greater than weight. Is that clear?
TONY:	I'm sorry, but I still don't see the connection between thrust and drag . . .
MR HENDERSON:	Can someone try to explain?

Questions

1. Find expressions in the discussion for each of the functions below.

   Starting talking *Example:* 'Let's start by . . .'

   Asking for explanation
   Asking for repetition
   Introducing a new idea
   Summarising

2. Mr Henderson says, 'Can someone try to explain?' Explain the connection between thrust and drag.

Unit 10

 Role Play: The new airport

1. The situation
It is planned to build a very big airport near your town. Aircraft will fly from the airport to countries all over the world. The town council has called a public meeting to discuss the airport. The council wants to know what people living in your town think about the airport.

2. Groups at the meeting
There are six groups at the meeting:

- Members of the town council
- Directors of the Airport Authority
- People who live near where the airport will be built
- Trade Unionists
- Members of the Anti-Airport Action Group
- Local businessmen

3. Agenda for the meeting
- The members of the town council explain why they have called the meeting.
- Each group speaks for three minutes and then answers questions.
- The members of the town council ask each group to give a one-minute summary of its views.
- Finally there is a vote to see if the meeting wants a new airport or not.

(*Note:* People who cannot make up their minds can say 'I abstain' instead of voting.)

Decide on your group and read your group's instructions. Discuss the airport with the other members of your group and decide what you are going to say at the meeting. When everyone is ready the meeting begins.

4. Group instructions
Members of the town council: Draw a map on the blackboard showing your town and marking where the new airport will be. The airport will need a space 5 km by 5 km and people will hear noise from the aircraft up to 18 km from the airport. The town council do not agree about the airport: some members want it and some do not. Choose one member of the group who will be the chairman of the meeting.

Directors of the Airport Authority: You want to build the airport because (a) air traffic is going to increase very quickly (b) other airports in the country are already overcrowded (c) the best place in the country for a new airport is near the town. You will promise to pay for sound-proofing houses near the airport – but only if the other groups complain about the noise.

People who live near where the airport will be built: You are worried about noise and air pollution. You are afraid that houses near the airport will be worth less money. You are sure that the airport will destroy the peace of the countryside around the town.

Trade Unionists: There are a large number of unemployed people in your town. The Trade Unions want a new airport because it will bring a lot of new jobs to the town. A new airport will make everyone in the town richer. Young people will be able to train for good jobs at the airport.

Members of the Anti-Airport Action Group: The AAAG does not think that a new airport is needed anywhere in the country. They do not think that air travel will increase much more. Anyway, say the AAAG, in fifty years there will be no oil left and therefore no planes.

Local businessmen: You want more information about the effects. On the one hand you are worried that noise from the airport will keep tourists away, but on the other hand you hope that the airport will bring money into the town. You would like the Airport Authority to use local companies to build the airport.

  Learning together

'I've enjoyed learning English because . . .'
Talk to the other students about why you enjoy learning English.

Examples:
'Because I like the other people in the class.'
'Because we always have to do things in the lessons. We don't just sit and listen.'

LANGUAGE STUDY Exercises 10.11 10.12

LESSON 50

Questionnaire

YOUR ENGLISH COURSE
What can you do now?

☑ = YES
☒ = NO
? = NOT SURE

Talking	Lesson Number	
Can you talk and enquire about:		
interests?	1	
education?	2	
wishes for the future?	3	
future intentions?	3	
skills?	4	
accommodation?	6, 8	
budgets?	7	
differences between life in the past and now?	9	
different customs in different countries?	11	
people's behaviour?	13	
opinions on important topics?	14	
present or future jobs?	16, 18	
qualifications and salaries?	17, 18, 46	
how something is made?	1, 7, 20	
learning and using foreign languages?	19, 50	
the news?	21	
a sequence of events?	22	
reasons for past events?	23	
future events?	24	
the weather?	24	
health?	26	
feelings?	27	
family?	28	
daily routine?	18, 28	
people's character?	29	
holidays?	31	
prices?	32, 35	
complaints?	33, 34	
how to get something done?	34	
how to do something?	36, 39, 47	
how things work?	37, 38	
how to plan something?	41, 42	
changes in plans?	43	
how good something was?	44	

Reading	Lesson Number	
Can you read:		
guided readers?	5	
quickly for information?	5, 45	
newspaper articles?	6, 24, 43, 44	
tables of figures?	7, 16, 18, 33, 35	
questionnaires?	10, 16, 19, 44	
tables of facts?	11	
a narrative carefully?	15, 23, 25, 45	
extracts from magazines?	11, 18	
personal descriptions?	30	
tourist brochures?	32	
town guides?	35	
instructions?	36, 39, 40	
descriptions of how things work?	37	
telegrams?	46	
indexes and reference lists?	47	

Writing	Lesson Number	
Can you:		
complete a form?	18, 20	
draw and label a diagram?	2, 36	
make notes?	2, 4, 46, 48	
write a simple letter of enquiry?	5, 10, 15	
write a cheque?	6	
complete a table?	8, 17, 31	
write a personal letter?	5, 15	
complete a questionnaire?	16, 19, 44	
write a letter of application?	20	
write a narrative?	25, 45	
write about the future?	25	
write a paragraph about holidays?	31	
write a description of your town?	35	
write a description of how something works?	37, 40	
write simple instructions?	36, 38, 40	

Listening	Lesson Number	
Can you understand:		
telephone conversations?	4, 13	
songs?	end of Parts A and B	
descriptions?	8, 10, 17	
arguments and discussions?	12, 31	
the radio news?	21, 24	
a radio or TV inteview?	19, 33, 44	
advice from a doctor?	26	
instructions?	36, 47	
a short talk?	48	

What else?		

Unit 10

 Discuss: Attitudes to foreign languages

Do you agree with these statements?
Remember that there are no right answers –
many people have different opinions.

Why people learn foreign languages
Everyone should learn at least one foreign language.
I am learning English in order to understand British culture and society better.
I am learning English in order to be able to read English literature.

Learning languages
Some languages are much easier to learn than others.
It is impossible to know two languages equally well.
You can never learn to speak a foreign language perfectly.
It does not matter if I make some mistakes, and speak with an accent, as long as people can understand me.
Only intelligent people can learn foreign languages.
Old people cannot learn foreign languages.
Children learn foreign languages very easily.

Methods of learning languages
The only way to learn a foreign language is to memorise grammar rules.
It is possible to learn a language without going to classes or studying.
The best way to learn a foreign language is to live in a country where it is spoken.
The only way to understand anything properly is to translate it into my own language.

 Discuss: Learning English

1. What things have you enjoyed most or least about your English lessons?
2. Do you think you had enough practice in: Talking? Listening? Reading? Writing?
3. How did you find working with other students in pairs and groups?
4. How have you been able to practise your English outside the classroom?
5. How about the future? This may be the end of your English course or you may have a long holiday before starting English lessons again. How can you continue learning by yourself? Think about:

Reading: How about newspapers and magazines? Guided readers? Reading through *Exchanges* again?

Writing: Have you got a pen friend? How about doing some of the *Language Study* exercises in writing?

Listening: Can you listen to the *Exchanges* tapes and songs? Are there programmes in English on your radio or TV? How about films or pop music in English?

Talking: How about making an English club with some of the other students? Then you can meet regularly and practise talking English. A very good way to start might be to do the *Exchanges* role plays again. If you have got a tape recorder, you can try recording yourself talking English.

Vocabulary: Can you continue with your vocabulary notebook? You can look up new words in your dictionary. Try to continue learning a few words every day.

Language Study: You can use the DIY Check-up sections in *Language Study* to test your own English and see where you need more practice.

What else can you do to continue learning by yourself?

138

LANGUAGE STUDY

Lessons 46–50

STRUCTURE

10.1 Study

PREPOSITIONS OF PLACE		
above	in	on
against	in front of	opposite
at	next to	under
between		

10.2 Complete

Look at the illustration and complete the paragraph with the most suitable preposition of place from the list above. Use each preposition or phrase once only.

Two people were standing (1) ... the pavement (2) ... the bus stop. A young man was leaning (3) ... the bus stop. A woman was standing (4) ... him, and there was a large suitcase (5) ... them. They were (6) ... a large modern building and the sign (7) ... their heads said General Bank. A large blue van was parked (8) ... the bank (9) ... a tree. There was a man (10) ... the telephone box.

10.3 Study

PREPOSITIONS OF MOVEMENT		
across	on	round
between	out of	through
into	past	to
off		

10.4 Complete

Put in the most suitable preposition of movement from the list above. Use each preposition or phrase once only.

Suddenly a man with a gun came (1) ... the bank. The robber ran (2) ... the road, jumped (3) ... the van, and started the engine. He drove (4) ... the telephone box, and (5) ... the corner. The man in the telephone box immediately jumped (6) ... a motorbike and followed the van (7) ... the city streets. He was obviously a policeman. Finally, the van got stuck in a traffic jam on the way (8) ... the airport. The policeman rode up (9) ... the lines of cars, climbed (10) ... his motorbike, and arrested the robber.

PREPOSITIONS AFTER ADJECTIVES

10.5 Ask and answer

Use these prepositions: *about, at, for, in, of*

Example: Claudio's excited. (flying)
S1: *What's Claudio excited about?*
S2: *He's excited about flying.*

1. Jenny's worried. (her father)
2. Margaret's interested. (art)
3. Sandra's afraid. (flying)
4. Jenny's surprised. (the news)
5. Liverpool's famous. (its football team)
6. Anita's pleased. (the programme)
7. The Wilkinsons are angry. (Matona)

10.6 Study

ORDER OF ADJECTIVES AND ADJECTIVAL PHRASES

Examples:
1. It's a long, black nylon umbrella, with a wooden handle.
2. It's a small round blue paper thing.
3. It's a useful old Swiss knife, with a tin-opener.

	1	2	3
YOUR OPINION	—	—	useful
SIZE/SHAPE	long	small round	–
AGE	—	—	old
COLOUR	black	blue	—
ORIGIN	—	—	Swiss
MATERIAL	nylon	paper	—
NOUN	*umbrella*	*thing*	*knife*
OTHER DETAILS	with a wooden handle	—	with a tin-opener

10.7 Make sentences

You have lost the following things. Describe each one in a sentence.

Your pen   A shopping bag
This book   A coat
Your purse/wallet

10.8 Complete

You have lost something on a number 24 bus while travelling from Camden Town to Tottenham Court Road in London. Fill in the enquiry form below.

ENQUIRY FOR LOST PROPERTY

Date lost	Bus/Coach	Route
	Train	Line

Got on at _____ Time _____

Got off at _____ Time _____

Full description of property (size, shape, colour and material) including contents of cases, parcels and bags.

_____

_____

Continue over if necessary

Enquirer's name
and full address
(BLOCK LETTERS) _____

_____

Unit 10

VOCABULARY

When you are studying this vocabulary section, you will find a dictionary is very helpful.

WORD GROUPS

10.9 Ask each other

Look at the guide to the library, and ask each other where you can find the following:

1. a book about jazz
2. a map of Europe
3. information about universities in Britain
4. a book about different kinds of jobs
5. a technical dictionary
6. a book about golf
7. information about cameras
8. a telephone number
9. a book about Picasso
10. information about Birmingham
11. a book about the life of George Washington
12. information about computers

Example: a book about jazz
  S1: *Where can I find a book about jazz?*
  S2: *In the music section on the first floor.*

GUIDE TO THE LIBRARY			
The main subjects are listed below with locations indicated.			
G = Ground Floor F = First Floor S = Second Floor			
Agriculture	G	History	F
Anthropology	F		
Antiques	S	Industry	G
Architecture	S		
Art	S	Languages, Literature	F
Astronomy	G	Law	G
Aviation	G		
		Magazines	G
Ballet	F	Maps and Atlases	G
Biography	F	Mathematics	G
Biology	F	Medicine	G
Botany	F	Music	F
Building	G		
Business	G	Painting	S
		Philosophy	F
		Photography	G
Careers	F	Physics	G
Chemistry	G	Political Science	G
Cinema	F	Psychology	G
Commerce	G		
		Religion	F
Dance	F		
Dictionaries:		Sculpture	S
Fine Art	S	Sport	F
General	F	Stamp Collecting	G
Technical	G	Statistics	G
Economics	G	Technology	G
Education	F	Telephone Directories	G
Encyclopaedias	F	Theatre	F
Engineering	G	Time Tables	G
Evening Class		Town Guides	G
brochures	F	Travel	F
Furniture	S	United Nations Publications	G
Geography	F		
Government Publications	G	Zoology	F

10.10 Make groups of words

Arrange the nouns below in groups of five according to topic. There are six different topics: clothes, the telephone, the weather, school subjects, kinds of illness, occupations.

blouse	fog	raincoat
call	geography	receiver
chemistry	headache	scientist
cloud	history	secretary
cold	biology	snow
cough	number	suit
dial	physics	teacher
directory	pilot	thunder
doctor	pneumonia	tights
flu	rain	vest

WHAT DO YOU SAY ?

10.11 Listen and choose the most suitable response

1. (a) Congratulations!
   (b) I'm sure I will.
   (c) Yes, I enjoyed it very much.
   (d) I make it ten past four.
2. (a) Never mind, there's another train in five minutes.
   (b) Nonsense. You did very well.
   (c) Do you want some more?
   (d) Spencer. S-P-E-N-C-E-R.
3. (a) It's just round the corner.
   (b) That's quite all right.
   (c) Do you know where it is?
   (d) Do you work there?

INTONATION AND STRESS

10.12 Listen and choose the most suitable question for each response

1. (a) Where have you been?
   (b) Who's been to Italy?
   (c) Have you been to Italy?
2. (a) Can we meet tomorrow?
   (b) What shall we do tomorrow?
   (c) When shall I call you?
3. (a) What do you want to drink?
   (b) Would you like some tea?
   (c) How about a cup of coffee?
4. (a) What's he like?
   (b) What are they like?
   (c) Is he interesting?
5. (a) How do you feel about flying?
   (b) Do you enjoy travelling?
   (c) Are you afraid of flying?

DIY CHECK UP

* When you have completed each section, look up the answers in the DIY Check-up Key. Discuss any mistakes you have made.
* Look up your mistakes in the Structural Reference List. Then turn to the Language Study exercises suggested.

Unit 5

Claudio and Tony are chatting in the Students' Club. Put their conversation into indirect speech (using *said* and *asked* only).

1. TONY: Are you enjoying the course, Claudio?
2. CLAUDIO: I want to start flying!
3. TONY: We'll start flying soon.
4. CLAUDIO: Have you ever flown a plane before?
5. TONY: No, I haven't.

Put into direct speech.

(6) Tony said that Claudio's English was very good, and (7) asked Claudio if he had been to England before. (8) Claudio said that he had been to London several times when he was a university student. (9) Tony said he didn't speak any other languages. (10) Claudio said he would teach Tony Italian if he wanted.

Fill in the correct form of the verbs in brackets, or choose the most suitable word.

After Claudio had left school, he (11) (*go*) to university in Genoa. While he (12) (*study*), he (13) (*decide*) to learn to fly. As soon as he had graduated, he (14) (*apply*) to the Air Training School. He'll (15) *likely/ probably* be a very good pilot.

Unit 6

Jenny wrote a letter to her parents from Mexico. Choose the most suitable word, or put the verbs in brackets into the correct form.

Mexico City
19th February

Dear Mum and Dad,

How are you both? I'm sorry I haven't written (1) *since/until* now, but I (2) (*look*) for somewhere to live. I (3) (*see*) several flats, and I (4) (*think*) I've found somewhere at last - a lovely modern flat in the centre.

Mexico City is very exciting and I'm doing quite (5) *good/well* at the university. But speaking Spanish all the time makes me (6) (*feel*) very tired, and when I'm tired, I (7) ..... mistakes. (8) .....'s the only problem!

Unit 7

The Wilkinsons decided to have a holiday in Ireland. When they returned to London, they found that they had been burgled.
Choose the most suitable word, or put the verbs in brackets into the correct form.

TREVOR: If we hadn't been on holiday, it (1) (*not happen*). I wish we (2) (*stay*) at home.
MARGARET: It's your fault, Trevor. You (3) *may/ should* have put the ladder in the garage. I (4) *told/said* you to hide it.
JANE: Oh, come on, Mum. It's (5) *useless/ useful* to argue about it now. We'd (6) ...... phone the police. And we must have the window (7) (*mend*), (8) *although/because* the rain's coming in.
MARGARET: I wish it (9) (*not rain*) now. I feel like another holiday. Let's go (10) ...... sunny, like Italy!

Unit 8

Choose the most suitable word, or put the verbs in brackets into the correct form.

The first telephone call was made (1) ... Alexander Bell in 1876. He was a Scottish doctor (2) *which/who* went to America (3) *where/that* he tried to design a machine for (4) (*talk*) to deaf people. When someone speaks they make vibrations in the air. Bell found (5) ... that he could carry these vibrations from a mouthpiece to a receiver through an electric wire. His invention was developed into the telephone.

Telephone calls are often (6) *either/both* cheaper and quicker than writing letters, and now millions of calls are made (7) *all/every* minute. You can call almost anywhere in the world just by (8) (*dial*) a number, thanks to the telephone!

Unit 9

Anita is giving Ned a lift home in her car.
Choose the most suitable word, or put the verbs in brackets into the correct form.

NED: Would you mind (1) (*stop*) at a newsagent's? I want an evening paper.
ANITA: O.K. It's a bit cold, (2) ... it? (3) ... I turn the heating on?
NED: Good idea. It's a great little car.
ANITA: It's all right when it doesn't break (4) ...!
NED: I wonder what we (5) (*do*) in the year 2000.
ANITA: Living on another planet, probably. (6) ... I'd like is a robot to do the housework!
(*Later*)
NED: We're nearly there. It's the fourth turning on the right after you (7) (*cross*) the bridge.
ANITA: You don't mind (8) ... I drop you on the corner, (9) ... you? I'm in a bit of a hurry.
NED: Not at all - I (10) (*be going*) to suggest it. Thanks very much.

Songs

Unit 6   **Don't Ask The Family**

My uncle George has been eating a lot
He's become incredibly fat
He rolled through the hall
Like a giant beach ball
When he bent down to stroke the cat.

My cousin Jane is extremely boring
She talks and talks all day
She talks while she's eating
She talks while she's sleeping
She talks – and she won't go away.

Chorus   I don't mind talking about my relatives
They're all very odd, you see
But please, please
Don't ask the family
What they think of me.

My younger brothers are always in trouble
They're known as 'the terrible twins'
Their favourite trick
Is to make themselves sick
Eating cream and banana skins.

Unit 8   **Find The Door**

Sit on the floor, relax and cross your legs
Straighten your back to help yourself breathe freely
Prepare yourself, free your mind
Think about what you want to find
Forget what you know about space and time.

Chorus   Yoga, yoga, it's so easy to do
Yoga yoga yoga, good for me, good for you.

Soon you'll learn that yoga can be a door
Which you can only open by practising daily
Every week try something new
Every month do a full review
By the end of the year the door will open for you.

Fold your arms and then stand on your head
Now cross your legs, behind your back, together
If you hear a crack, don't be alarmed
Call a doctor to look at your arm
In the meantime use your yoga to stay calm.

Unit 9   **It's A Good Idea**

Every day you get to work, you're waiting
Waiting for discussion to begin
Meeting follows meeting, but the words still sound the same
Arguments that no one really wins
'What do you think of this?'
Or 'What do you think of that?'
People trying to make their meaning clear
As soon as someone tells you the things you want to hear
You're quick to say 'It's a good idea'.

Chorus   It's a good idea
It's a good idea
I really wish I'd thought of it first
It's such a good idea.

I'd be happy to give it a try
Good! So would I!
I'm glad that we've decided what to do.
As soon as someone tells you the things you want to hear
You're quick to say 'It's a good idea'.

Unit 7   **Wild Country Dream**

Sometimes I'd like to be far from here
And leave this city of hate and fear
Grab my coat, then just disappear
That's my wild country dream.

Soon I'll be gone, leave my worries behind
I'll get on a train to the end of the line
I know the way because I've seen the sign
In my wild country dream.

Yes, I was told about all the gold
I would find in the streets of this town
But the glitter has gone
Buildings block out the sun
And trouble is all I've found.

I'll head for the green fields to pause for a while
Live where real people find time to smile
Where there's no cheating, no fighting, or lying
That's my wild country dream.

But here I stay, still dreaming away
I wish I could make up my mind
Why I don't go
I really don't know
'Cause I'm just wasting my time

I said I would leave in a day or so
It could be tomorrow, well I just don't know
You can tell me I'm a fool or say I'll never go
But I need my wild country dream
Yes, I need my wild country dream.

Unit 10   **I Got The News Today**

Chorus   I got the news today (you've been accepted)
I got the news today (congratulations)
I've worked so hard
I've worked so long (you got the news today)
I've been accepted
Got the news today.

I'd always known that I could do it
If I had the chance, I knew I could prove it
I realised it was up to me to try
By working hard till I qualified to fly.

Taking the controls for the first time
I knew I had to learn to do it by myself
I've never wanted anything so much in my life
Clear the runway, I'm ready to fly!

Applications and taking exams
Qualifications to show how good I am
Making the effort – it's all been worthwhile
............learning to fly.

Listening Passages

UNIT 6 Lesson 26

DOCTOR: Now, Miss Langley, I see that you're quite a heavy smoker...

JENNY: ...about thirty a day...

DOCTOR: ...yes. Well, my advice is quite simple: stop smoking. You know that cigarettes cause cancer and heart disease. Have you tried to give up?

JENNY: Yes, lots of times. But I just find it impossible to stop.

DOCTOR: Well, in that case, let me suggest five things which you can do. First of all, if you smoke strong cigarettes, you should change to milder ones.

JENNY: Yes, doctor.

DOCTOR: But that won't help if you smoke more. So, secondly, don't smoke as many cigarettes. Try to cut down by one or two every day. O.K.? The next three points are to do with how you smoke. The most important is this: don't breathe the smoke in. It's when you breathe in the smoke that you do most damage to your health. Next, don't keep the cigarette in your mouth all the time. Put it in an ashtray when you're not smoking it. And finally, don't smoke all the cigarette. The end of a cigarette is very dangerous to your health. So put the cigarette out after you've smoked half of it. All right?

JENNY: Yes, I'll try, doctor...

UNIT 7 Lesson 31

TREVOR: What I'd really like is a cottage by the sea. We could do what we liked, when we liked. And we could do our own cooking. It would be much cheaper, too – especially if I caught lots of fish.

JANE: Oh no! I'm sure you wouldn't catch any at all! And anyway, who wants to eat fish every day? I want to stay in a great big hotel, with a disco and a swimming pool, where there are lots of people of my age.

MARGARET: Jane's right. If we have a holiday, we ought to have a proper holiday. I don't want to spend all day cooking. But why do we have to stay in a big hotel? I think a small family hotel would be much nicer. And I'm sure the food would be better.

JANE: Not hotel food! We ought to eat in restaurants, not in the hotel. All you get in hotels is international food. You get the real food of the country in little restaurants.

TREVOR: But you've just said that you wanted to stay in a big hotel! I don't mind staying in a hotel, but I don't know about Italy: What about David and Alan? They're only eight and they don't speak Italian. Nor do I for that matter. Can't we go somewhere English-speaking?

MARGARET: I don't mind, but you know Jane wants to practise her Italian.

JANE: How about Switzerland? They speak Italian there.

TREVOR: But it's a long way from the sea!

MARGARET: Come on, let's have another look at the brochures.

UNIT 7 Lesson 33

ANITA: Good evening, ladies and gentlemen, and welcome to 'What Do You Think?' Our first guest is the Director of Tourism for the island of Matona. Recently there've been a number of letters in the newspapers complaining about holidays in Matona. I'd like to ask about three topics. The first is the tourist brochure produced by a company called 'Holidays in Matona'. In the brochure it says that there are miles and miles of beaches, but in fact the beaches are covered in oil. The brochure speaks of marvellous museums, but actually there's only one small museum on the island, and that's been closed for years. But perhaps most important of all, the Matona Holiday Village which is featured in the brochure hasn't even been built yet!

DIRECTOR: To start with, I should explain that the brochure is produced by an independent company, and not by our tourist department. However, there certainly are one or two small mistakes in the brochure, and my office will be writing to the 'Holidays in Matona' company about this. I'm sure that next year everything will be all right.

ANITA: How do you mean? Everything will be all right on the island, or in the brochure?

DIRECTOR: Both. Yes, next year Matona will be a wonderful place for a holiday.

ANITA: The second subject I wanted to discuss is the airport. There've been a number of accidents at Matona Airport. Are tourists safe when they fly to Matona?

DIRECTOR: Certainly they are. But just to make sure, we are building a new airport. It'll be the most moden airport in the Mediterranean.

ANITA: When will the new airport be ready?

DIRECTOR: Not for a little while, I'm afraid.

ANITA: Has work actually started on the new airport?

DIRECTOR: Not yet. We hope to start next year.

ANITA: Finally, perhaps I could ask a question about the weather in Matona. I have here the official figures issued by your government and they're not the same as the ones in the 'Holidays in Matona' brochure.

DIRECTOR: What exactly do you mean?

ANITA: Let me give you an example. The official figures show that in July and August the temperature is only 28°, not 30° and 32°. In May and June, there are only eight hours of sunshine a day, not ten and eleven hours. Finally, the brochure shows only five rainy days in December and January, but in fact there are twelve rainy days in each month.

DIRECTOR: I'm afraid there's been a mistake. We'll make sure that the company changes the brochure.

ANITA: Well, thank you very much for coming to the studio to talk to us.

UNIT 8 Lesson 36

WOMAN: Passport Office, good morning.
SANDRA: Good morning. I'm going to Sweden on holiday this summer and I need a passport. Could you tell me what I have to do?
WOMAN: Yes, of course. Are you over sixteen?
SANDRA: Yes.
WOMAN: And were you born in this country?
SANDRA: Yes, I was born in London.
WOMAN: Right. You can obtain an application form at any post office. Just ask for Form 'A'. Fill it in and post it to your regional passport office with two recent photos of yourself, countersigned by a professional person . . .
SANDRA: I'm sorry, can you say that again?
WOMAN: Two photos of yourself which someone like a lawyer, or a doctor, has signed on the back – it's all explained in the notes you get with the application form.
SANDRA: What else do I have to send?
WOMAN: Your birth certificate, your marriage certificate if you're married, and the fee of £11.
SANDRA: I see, thank you.
WOMAN: When are you going abroad?
SANDRA: In six weeks' time.
WOMAN: That's fine. It usually takes about three weeks for the passport to be issued. But you should apply immediately, in case there are any problems.
SANDRA: O.K., I'll do that. Thanks very much. Goodbye.

UNIT 9 Lesson 44

Hello, and welcome to the twenty-first century! I've got lots to tell you. You want to buy a newspaper? I'm afraid that's impossible – they don't sell newspapers any more. If you want to read the news, you just switch on the TV screen, any time of the day or night.

Would you like to sit down and watch a film? We don't go to the cinema any more, they all closed down years ago. Now you just choose any film you like, and you can watch it on the screeen at home. So much cheaper and more convenient than going out. I don't go out much at all these days.

You see, most people work or study from home. As you know, petrol became so expensive that people couldn't afford to travel to work. I'm a student, and I follow a study programme on the screen. I also use this small computer, which is linked to the central computer at the university. No, I don't have any books. They're terribly expensive now, so people use the electronic library. You can request any book you want, and read it on the screen. That's my videophone. You can see the person you're talking to. If you don't want to be seen, it's quite simple, you just switch off the picture.

Yes, I suppose I do get lonely, but at least I'm not bored. I mean, I enjoy studying, but a lot of people are very unhappy because they're not working, and they don't know what to do with themselves. They don't even have to do the housework or the gardening because the robots can do all that. These people are lonely because they've got no one to talk to. And they're bored because they've got nothing to do. That's a real problem. (*Phone rings*) Oh, excuse me, that'll be my doctor. Can you wait in the next room for a few minutes while I have a medical examination? Over the phone? Naturally!

UNIT 10 Lesson 47

How to find a book in the library
You'll probably be looking for a book in one of two ways: either you'll know the author and title of the book, or else you'll want a book on a particular subject.

Let's start with what to do if you know the author's name and the title of the book. The first thing to do is to look up the author's name in the Author Catalogue. If you can find a card for the book you want, you should then make a note on a piece of paper of three things: the author, the title and the class number. Now find the class number on the library shelves. There are notices on the bookcases called shelf guides, which show you what class numbers are on each shelf. If you find the book you want on the shelf, and you want to borrow it, take it to the Issue Desk. If you can't find the book on the shelf, it means that someone else has borrowed it, so you should ask the librarian to reserve it for you.

Now let's deal with what to do if you want a book on a particular subject (for example, if you find that the book you were looking for is not in stock). First of all, look up the subject in the Subject Index. This will tell you the class number of the subject. If you can't find the subject you want in the Index, ask the librarian for help. But usually you'll find a class number, and the next thing to do is to look this class number up in the Subject Catalogue. Look through the cards for the class number and see if there's a suitable book there. If there is a suitable book, make a note of the author, title and class number and find it on the shelves. If there isn't a suitable book on the cards, it's a good idea to ask the librarian for help.

Remember that the librarian is always happy to give advice and help with any problems you may have, so don't hesitate to ask if you are in any difficulty.

UNIT 10 Lesson 48

So to start with, let's do a little history. I'd like to take you back to Laverton Airport near Melbourne just after the Second World War, on September 9th 1946, to be exact. Early that morning a DC3 took off. On board there were twenty-one passengers on their way to Sydney. It was TAA's first flight. From this small start the airline grew rapidly, and by 1961 TAA became the first internal airline in Australia to carry a million passengers in one year.

So much for the past. What about the present? Today we carry about five times that number of passengers and have a fleet of 38 aircraft – 10 Boeing 727-200s, 12 DC9-30s, 12 F27s and 4 Twin Otters. We fly to 51 destinations in Australia and carry 65,000 tonnes of cargo annually. That's how big we are now.

Finally, let's have a look at the future. Well, we expect the number of passengers we carry to grow by about ten per cent a year. We've therefore ordered four 270-seater Airbuses. When we receive these we will be the first Australian airline to use wide-bodied aircraft on internal flights. So the future looks good for us.

Now, I've tried to tell you something about TAA – as it was, as it is, and as it will be. I think that's all, thank you very much. Oh yes, I'd be very happy to answer any questions.

Irregular Verbs

This is a list of irregular verbs introduced in *Exchanges*. The past simple and the past participle are the same in many verbs.
Those which are different are marked * below.

VERB	PAST SIMPLE	PAST PARTICIPLE
be	was, were	been*
become	became	become*
begin	began	begun*
blow	blew	blown*
break	broke	broken*
bring	brought	brought
broadcast	broadcast	broadcast
build	built	built
burn	burnt	burnt
buy	bought	bought
catch	caught	caught
choose	chose	chosen*
come	came	come*
cost	cost	cost
cut	cut	cut
dig	dug	dug
do	did	done*
draw	drew	drawn*
drink	drank	drunk*
drive	drove	driven*
eat	ate	eaten*
fall	fell	fallen*
feel	felt	felt
fight	fought	fought
find	found	found
fly	flew	flown*
forget	forgot	forgotten*
freeze	froze	frozen*
get	got	got
give	gave	given*
go	went	been, gone*
grow	grew	grown*
hang	hung	hung
have	had	had
hear	heard	heard
hide	hid	hidden*
hit	hit	hit
hold	held	held
hurt	hurt	hurt
keep	kept	kept
know	knew	known*
lean	leant	leant
learn	learnt	learnt
leave	left	left
lend	lent	lent
let	let	let
lose	lost	lost
make	made	made
mean	meant	meant
meet	met	met
pay	paid	paid
put	put	put
read /ri:d/	read /red/	read /red/
ride	rode	ridden*
ring	rang	rung*
run	ran	run*
say	said	said
see	saw	seen*
sell	sold	sold
send	sent	sent
set	set	set
show	showed	shown*
shut	shut	shut
sing	sang	sung*
sit	sat	sat
sleep	slept	slept
smell	smelt	smelt
speak	spoke	spoken*
spell	spelt	spelt
spend	spent	spent
split	split	split
stand	stood	stood
steal	stole	stolen*
swim	swam	swum*
take	took	taken*
teach	taught	taught
tell	told	told
think	thought	thought
throw	threw	thrown*
understand	understood	understood
wake	woke	woken*
wear	wore	worn*
win	won	won
wind	wound	wound
write	wrote	written*

Structural Reference List and Summary

This is a summary of the structures covered in the **Language Study** sections. After each item, the numbers of the **Language Study** exercises are listed. The numbered items on the right are for use with the **DIY Check-up: Key to Answers** on page 149.

	Language Study	DIY Check-up
Adjectives		
Comparison of adjectives: regular and irregular	2.14 – 2.16	1
Adjectives formed from participles	3.12 3.13	2
Adjectives with prefix *'un-'*	6.13 6.14	
Adjectives formed with suffixes *'-ful'* and *'-less'*	7.13 7.14	3
Compound adjectives	2.18	
Order of adjectives	10.6 – 10.8	
too + adjective	2.17	
Adjective + *enough*	2.17	
Adjectives followed by prepositions	10.5	
Adverbs		
Adverbs of time: *just*	1.1 1.3	
yet	3.6	
any more	2.10	
Adverbs of manner: regular (formed with *'-ly'*) and irregular	6.10 – 6.12	4
Adverbs and adverbial phrases of frequency	8.12	5
Adverbs for listing: *first of all, secondly, thirdly*	3.19 3.20	
Adverbs for a sequence of actions or events: *first, next, then, after that, finally*	4.22 5.14	6
Causative verb: *have*	7.10	
Clauses		
Clauses joined by: *and/but*	1.21 5.21	7
although	7.18	8
either . . . or/both . . . and	8.17 8.18	9
Adverbial clauses introduced by : *because* to express reason	1.13 3.19 4.2 5.21 7.18	10
in order to to express purpose	1.14	11
so to express result	1.15 1.21 5.21	12
if to express condition	2.1 – 2.9 7.2 7.5	
as if to express comparison	5.15	
Adverbial clauses of time introduced by: *since*	1.4 1.5	
until	2.11 6.9 9.6 9.8	
when	5.11 – 5.14 5.21 9.6 9.7	
while	5.11 5.12 5.21	
after	5.13 5.14 5.21 6.9 9.6 9.7	
before	5.13 6.9 9.6	
by + time phrase	5.13 5.14 6.9 9.6	
as soon as	5.13 5.21 9.6	
Defining relative clauses (contact)	4.20 4.21 9.21	
Defining relative clauses with relative pronouns	8.4 – 8.8	
Noun clauses introduced by: *I think that . . .*	3.19 3.20	
It's likely that . . .	5.16	
What . . .	9.9	13
so/not: replacing noun clauses after *I suppose . . .*	3.11	
Conditional sentences		
Cause and effect	2.1 – 2.3	14
Type 1	2.4 – 2.6	15
Type 2	2.7 – 2.9	16
Type 2 without *'if'* clause	4.11 4.12 7.1	17
Type 3	7.2 7.5	18
Type 3 without *'if'* clause	7.3 7.4	
wish to express regret	7.6 – 7.8	19
do/make	6.15 6.16	20
Gerunds ('-ing' forms)		
like + gerund contrasted with *would like to*	1.9 1.10	21
like, enjoy, hate, prefer, love + gerund	1.11 1.12	
mind + gerund contrasted with *Do you mind if . . .?*	9.13 9.14	22
Gerund after prepositions and phrasal verbs	1.11 1.12 4.15	23
by + gerund to express means	8.9 8.10	24
for + gerund to express definition	8.9 8.11	25
Gerund as subject	4.13 4.14	26

Indefinite pronouns
   anyone, anything, someone, something,
   everyone, everything, no one, nothing   2.12 2.13
   Indefinite pronouns followed by adjectives   7.12   28
Infinitives
   would like to contrasted with *like* + gerund   1.9 1.10
   want to, would like to, hope to, intend to, be going to   1.13   29
   make + infinitive without *to*   6.8   30
   it as introducer   5.4 5.15 5.16
Modal auxiliaries
   used to to express state or habit in the past   2.10   31
   should and *ought to* to express criticism and obligation   3.9 3.10   32
   should have/shouldn't have to express criticism   7.9   33
   had better to express advice   7.11   34
   must, have to, have got to   4.7 – 4.9   35
   need to   4.7 4.10   36
   may (and *may have*)   5.17 5.20   37
   can to express ability and permission   6.6 6.7
   shall to express suggestions and offers   9.10 – 9.12   38
Nouns
   Compound nouns   8.13
   Nouns formed from verbs   9.15
Passive
   Present simple tense   3.1 – 3.3 4.22   39
   Past simple tense   3.1 3.4   40
   Present perfect tense   3.1 3.5 3.6   41
   Passive with *by* + agent   8.1 – 8.3   42
Phrasal verbs   5.18 8.14 9.16   43
Pointing words: *this, that, these, those, here, there, now, then*   6.19 6.20   44
Possessive pronouns   2.23 2.24
Prepositions
   Prepositions in adverbial phrases of time   6.9   45
   Prepositions of place   10.1 10.2
   Prepositions of movement   10.3 10.4
   Prepositions after adjectives   10.5
probably/likely   5.15 5.16   46
Question tags   9.18 – 9.20   47
Relative pronouns: *who, that, which, where*   8.4 – 8.8   48
Reported Speech
   Reported statements after *say*   3.17 5.1 – 5.4 5.8 – 5.10 7.17   49
   Reported requests and commands: with *ask/tell* + direct object + infinitive   3.7 3.8   50
   Indirect questions   1.16 1.17 5.5 – 5.7   51
say/tell   7.15   52
Tenses
   Present simple tense   1.8
   Present simple tense contrasted with present continuous   6.4 6.5   53
   Future tense: *will*: to express offers, promises and decisions   4.5 4.6   54
                   to forecast the future   5.8 – 5.10
   Future continuous tense   9.3 – 9.5   55
   Past simple tense with *until*   2.11
   Past simple tense in relation to past continuous   5.11 5.12   56
   Past simple tense contrasted with present perfect   1.6 1.7   57
   Past simple tense in relation to past perfect   5.13 5.14   58
   Past continuous tense   4.18 5.11 5.12   59
   Future in the past: *was/were going to* + infinitive   9.1 9.2   60
   Present perfect tense: recent past   1.1 1.2   61
   Present perfect tense with *just*   1.1 1.3   62
   Present perfect tense: unfinished past with *since/for*   1.4 1.5   63
   Present perfect tense: indefinite past (contrasted with past simple)   1.6 1.7
   Present perfect tense contrasted with present perfect continuous   6.1 – 6.3   64
   Present perfect tense in adverbial clauses of time   9.6 – 9.8   65
   Present perfect continuous tense   4.1 4.2
   Present perfect continuous tense with *since/for*   4.1 4.3 4.4 6.1 6.3   66
   Present perfect continuous tense contrasted with present perfect simple   6.1 – 6.3   67

DIY Check-up: Key to Answers

Look up your mistakes in the **Structural Reference List** on page 146. Then turn to the **Language Study** exercises shown.

Example:
DIY Check-up Unit 1 Question 1
If you have made a mistake look at number 61 in the **Structural Reference List** (Present perfect tense: recent past) and turn to **Language Study** exercises 1.1 and 1.2.

Structural Reference List Number

Unit 1
1. has had — 61
2. has just booked — 62
3. going — 23
4. went — 57
5. but — 7, 12
6. in order — 10, 11
7. has been — 63
8. for — 63
9. working — 21
10. but — 7
11. to do — 21
12. to travel — 29

Unit 2
1. stay — 14
2. goes — 15
3. would be able — 16
4. could — 16
5. used — 31
6. anything — 27
7. most expensive — 1
8. more — 1

Unit 3
1. tired — 2
2. are kept* — 39
3. was checked — 40
4. shouldn't — 32
5. has been stolen* — 41
6. to find — 50
7. to tell — 50
8. interesting — 2

* See list of Irregular Verbs in *Exchanges: Part A, Part B* and *Complete Edition*.

Unit 4
1. working — 66
2. for — 66
3. have been — 66
4. need — 36
5. must — 35
6. don't have to — 35
7. working — 23
8. wouldn't change — 17
9. Making — 26
10. will do — 54

Unit 5
1. Tony asked Claudio if he was enjoying the course.
2. Claudio said (that) he wanted to start flying.
3. Tony said (that) they would start flying soon.
4. Claudio asked Tony if he had ever flown a plane before.
5. Tony said (that) he hadn't.
6. Tony: Your English is very good.
7. Have you been to England before?
8. Claudio: I went to London several times when I was a university student.
9. Tony: I don't speak any other languages.
10. Claudio: I'll teach you Italian if you want.

} 49, 51

11. went — 58
12. was studying — 59
13. decided — 56
14. applied — 58
15. probably — 46

Unit 6
1. until — 45
2. have been looking — 67
3. have seen — 64
4. think — 53
5. well — 4
6. feel — 30
7. make — 20
8. That — 44

Unit 7
1. wouldn't have happened — 18
2. had stayed — 19
3. should — 33, 37
4. told — 52
5. useless — 3
6. better — 34
7. mended — 6
8. because — 8, 10
9. wasn't raining — 19
10. somewhere — 28

Unit 8
1. by — 42
2. who — 48
3. where — 48
4. talking — 25
5. out — 43
6. both — 9
7. every — 5
8. dialling — 24

Unit 9
1. stopping — 22
2. isn't — 47
3. Shall — 38
4. down — 43
5. will be doing — 55
6. What — 13
7. have crossed — 65
8. if — 22
9. do — 47
10. was going — 60

148

Heinemann Educational Books Ltd
22 Bedford Square, London WC1B 3HH

LONDON   EDINBURGH   MELBOURNE   AUCKLAND
SINGAPORE   KUALA LUMPUR
NEW DELHI   IBADAN   NAIROBI   JOHANNESBURG
PORTSMOUTH (NH)   KINGSTON

© Philip Prowse, Judy Garton-Sprenger and T. C. Jupp 1980
First published 1980
Exchanges A reprinted 3 times, *Exchanges B* reprinted twice,
Exchanges Complete reprinted 3 times,
New colour edition first published 1985.
Reprinted 1986, 1987

Exchanges A	Students Book A	0 435 28435 5
Units 1–5	Workbook A	0 435 28441 X
	Test Book A*	0 435 28443 6
	Teachers' Book A	0 435 28437 1
	Cassettes (3)	0 435 28465 7
Exchanges B	Students' Book B	0 435 28436 3
Units 6–10	Workbook B	0 435 28442 8
	Test Book B*	0 435 28444 4
	Teachers' Book B	0 435 28438 X
	Cassettes (3)	0 435 28463 0
Exchanges Complete Edition	Students' Book	0 435 28434 7
Units 1–10	Songs and Dialogues Cassette	0 435 28459 2
* *Main Course Tests: Teachers' Guide* 0 435 28454 1 covers these titles		

In the lesson material we have created characters in order to contextualise the language being taught. Where we have done this we have not intended to depict any person living or dead.

Acknowledgements
The authors would like to thank the students at Bell College, Saffron Walden (part of the Bell Educational Trust) for helping to try out *Exchanges* materials, and for acting as photographic models for the role play situations in this new colour edition of Main Course English.
   While every effort has been made to trace the owners of copyright material in this book, there have been some cases where the publishers have been unable to find the sources. We should be grateful to hear from anyone who recognises their copyright material and who is unacknowledged. We shall be pleased to make make the necessary corrections in future editions of the book.
Illustrated by Chris Evans throughout. Other illustrations by The New Book Factory, John Whittaker and Baseline Creative. Photographs by – Malvin Van Gelderen (pp. 88, 93, 94, 95, 129); Tony Payne (pp. 90, 95, 103, 106, 108, 124); Les Sullivan (pp. 81, 120, 122, 138).
   The authors and publishers would like to thank the following for permission to reproduce their material and for providing illustrations: p. 73 The Department of Health and Social Security; p. 75 Fernand Hazan – Paris, for permission to reproduce Vasarely's *Koska, 1972*; Centre National d'Art et de Culture George Pompidou – Paris, for permission to reproduce Matisse's *Tête blanche et rose, 1914*; p. 77 Extract from *The Traffic Light Guide to Staying Slim* reproduced by kind permission of the Health Education Council; p. 80 Zefa Picture Library, bar graph from survey conducted by MORI for the *Sunday Times* (March 1980); p. 81 Mary Evans Picture Library, Syndication International; p. 82 Exley Publications Ltd for the cover of *Happy Families*; p. 90 Carole Sumption; p. 92 Office of Fair Trading for extract from 'How to put things right' leaflet (1981); p. 96 Tony Stone Photolibrary – London, extracts from 'SAS City Portraits' (1973), courtesy of Scandinavian Airlines; p. 97 Travel Photo International; p. 101 Passport Office; p. 102 Cartoons from *The Green Cross Code* reproduced with the permission of the Controller of Her Majesty's Stationery Office, extract from *The Oxford Student's Dictionary* by AS Hornby © Oxford University Press, 1978, by permission of Oxford University Press; p. 104 Extracts from *Understanding Science* (Vol. 1) Purnell and Sons © Samson Law, Marston and Co. Ltd. 1962; pp. 105–6 Kodak Limited; p. 107 British Railways Board, London Regional Transport Executive; p. 109 Illustrations and photographs from *Safe Skateboarding* by Christopher Pick by permission of Evans Brothers Limited 1978; pp. 110–111 Consumers' Association for extracts from *Holiday Which?* (1978); p. 115 Ferranti plc, Electronics Division; p. 118 *Radio Times*; p. 119 Tony Stone Photolibrary – London; p. 123 James Watson; p. 124 Extract from *Television* by Michael Loftus reproduced by permission of the Hamlyn Publishing Group Limited 1979, photo of 1949 TV by courtesy of Trustees of the Victoria and Albert Museum, photo of 1984 TV by kind permission of Philips Electronics, Video Division; p. 125 Paul Brierley, Science Photo Library; pp. 129, 134 The Oxford Air Training School; p. 132 Extract from text and cover photograph from *Flight* by John Atkinson and Maliha Azar, Heinemann Educational Books, 1980; pp. 133, 144 Trans-Australia Airlines; p. 136 Zefa Photo Library.

Note for teachers using this book in Spain:
Aprobado por el Ministerio de Educación y Ciencia, para su utilización en B.U.P., por orden ministerial del 1-12-83. B.O.E. 17-1-84.

Original design by Brian Lee
Cover design by Indent
Songs written and arranged by Russ Shipton and Kieran Fogarty
Set in Monophoto Ehrhardt by BAS Printers Limited,
Over Wallop, Hampshire
Printed and bound in Hong Kong
by Mandarin Offset